DC/AC ELECTRONICS

LAB MANUAL

CUSTOM EDITION

Taken from:

*Experiments in Electronics Fundamentals
and Electric Circuits Fundamentals*, Seventh Edition
by David M. Buchla

The Science of Electronics: DC/AC Lab Manual
by David M. Buchla

Custom Publishing

New York   Boston   San Francisco
London   Toronto   Sydney   Tokyo   Singapore   Madrid
Mexico City   Munich   Paris   Cape Town   Hong Kong   Montreal

Cover Art: Photodisc/Getty Images

Taken from:

Experiments in Electronics Fundamentals and Electric Circuits Fundamentals, Seventh Edition
by David M. Buchla
Copyright © 2007, 2004, 2001, 1998, 1995, 1991, 1987 by Pearson Education, Inc.
Published by Prentice Hall
Upper Saddle River, New Jersey 07458

The Science of Electronics: DC/AC Lab Manual
by David M. Buchla
Copyright © 2005, 1987 by Pearson Education, Inc.
Published by Prentice Hall

This special edition published in cooperation with Pearson Custom Publishing.

All trademarks, service marks, registered trademarks, and registered service marks are the property of their respective owners and are used herein for identification purposes only.

Printed in the United States of America

6 7 8 9 10 V092 16 15 14 13 12 11

2009520066

KW

**Pearson
Custom Publishing**
is a division of

www.pearsonhighered.com

ISBN 10: 0-558-41283-1
ISBN 13: 978-0-558-41283-8

This textbook, *DC/AC Electronics Lab Manual, Custom Edition*, combines selected content from two original textbooks specifically chosen for use in this course. Every attempt has been made to reflow content and renumber internal references to provide consistent pedagogy and ease of use.

Contents

Part II   AC Electronics Experiments

PART I

DC Electronics Experiments

1 Metric Prefixes, Scientific Notation, and Graphing

Name _____
Date _____
Class _____

OBJECTIVES
After performing this experiment, you will be able to:
1.   Convert standard form numbers to scientific and engineering notation.
2.   Measure quantities using a metric prefix.
3.   Prepare a linear graph and plot a family of curves on the graph.

MATERIALS NEEDED
Scientific calculator
Metric ruler

SUMMARY OF THEORY
The basic electrical quantities encompass a very large range of numbers—from the very large to the very small. For example, the frequency of an FM radio station can be over 100 million hertz (Hz), and a capacitor can have a value of 10 billionths of a farad (F). To express very large and very small numbers, scientific (powers of ten) notation and metric prefixes are used. Metric prefixes are based on the decimal system and stand for powers of ten. They are widely used to indicate a multiple or submultiple of a measuring unit.

   Scientific notation is a means of writing any quantity as a number between 1 and 10 times a power of 10. The power of 10 is called the exponent. It simply shows how many places the decimal point must be shifted to express the number in its standard form. If the exponent is positive, the decimal point must be shifted to the right to write the number in standard form. If the exponent is negative, the decimal point must be shifted to the left. Note that $10^0 = 1$, so an exponent of zero does not change the original number.

   Exponents that are a multiple of 3 are much more widely used in electronics work than exponents which are not multiples of 3. Numbers expressed with an exponent that is a multiple of 3 are said to be expressed in **engineering notation.** Engineering notation is particularly useful in electronics work because of its relationship to the most widely used metric prefixes. Some examples of numbers written in standard form, scientific notation, and engineering notation are shown in Table 1–1.

Table 1–1

Standard Form	Scientific Notation	Engineering Notation
12,300	1.23×10^4	12.3×10^3
506	5.06×10^2	0.506×10^3
8.81	8.81×10^0	8.81×10^0
0.0326	3.26×10^{-2}	32.6×10^{-3}
0.000 155	1.55×10^{-4}	155×10^{-6}

Numbers expressed in engineering notation can be simplified by using metric prefixes to indicate the appropriate power of ten. In addition, prefixes can simplify calculations. You can perform arithmetic operations on the significant figures of a problem and determine the answer's prefix from those used in the problem. For example, 4.7 kΩ + 1.5 kΩ = 6.2 kΩ. The common metric prefixes used in electronics and their abbreviations are shown in Table 1–2. The metric prefixes representing engineering notation are shown. Any number can be converted from one prefix to another (or no prefix) using the table. Write the number to be converted on the line with the decimal under the metric prefix that appears with the number. The decimal point is then moved directly under any other line, and the metric prefix immediately above the line is used. The number can also be read in engineering notation by using the power of ten shown immediately above the line.

Table 1–2

Power of 10:	10^9	10^6	10^3	10^0	10^{-3}	10^{-6}	10^{-9}	10^{-12}
Metric symbol:	G	M	k		m	μ	n	p
Metric prefix:	giga	mega	kilo		milli	micro	nano	pico

0   0 0 0   0 0 0   0 0 0 . 0 0 0   0 0 0   0 0 0   0 0 0   0

Example 1:

Convert 12,300,000 Ω to a number with an M prefix:

Metric prefix:	giga	mega	kilo		milli	micro	nano	pico

0   0 0 0   0 0 0   0 0 0 . 0 0 0   0 0 0   0 0 0   0 0 0   0
    1 2   3 0 0   0 0 0 . Ω

= 1 2 . 3 MΩ

Example 2:

Change 10,000 pF to a number with a μ prefix:

Metric prefix:	giga	mega	kilo		milli	micro	nano	pico

0   0 0 0   0 0 0   0 0 0 . 0 0 0   0 0 0   0 0 0   0 0 0   0
                            1 0   0 0 0   . pF

=. 0 1 0 μF

CALCULATORS

Scientific calculators have the ability to process numbers that are written in exponential form. In addition, scientific calculators can perform trig functions, logarithms, roots, and other math functions. To enter numbers in scientific notation on most calculators, the base number (called the *mantissa*) is first entered. If the number is negative, the +/− key is pressed. Next the exponent is entered by pressing the EE (or

EXP) key, followed by the power of ten.[1] If the exponent is negative, the $+/-$ key is pressed. Arithmetic can be done on the calculator with numbers in scientific notation mixed with numbers in standard form. On many calculators, such as the TI-86, there is an engineering mode. (The TI-86 is placed in engineering mode by pressing $\boxed{2^{nd}}$ $\boxed{MODE}$ and selecting $\boxed{Eng}$). Engineering mode is particularly useful for electronics calculations because of the direct correlation to the metric prefixes in Table 1–2.

SIGNIFICANT DIGITS

When a measurement contains approximate data, those digits known to be correct are called *significant digits*. Zeros that are used only for locating the decimal place are *not* significant, but those that are part of the measured quantity are significant. When reporting a measured value, the least significant uncertain digit may be retained, but all other uncertain digits should be discarded. It is *not* correct to show either too many or too few digits. For example, it is not valid to retain more than three digits when using a meter that has three digit resolution, nor is it proper to discard valid digits, even if they are zeros. For example, if you set a power supply to the nearest hundredth of a volt, then the recorded voltage should be reported to the hundredth place (3.00 V is correct, but 3 V is incorrect). For laboratory work in this course, you should normally be able to measure and retain three significant digits.

To find the number of significant digits in a given number, ignore the decimal point and count the number of digits from left to right, starting with the first nonzero digit and ending with the last digit to the right. All digits counted are significant except zeros at the right end of the number. A zero on the right end of a number is significant *only* if it is to the right of the decimal point; otherwise it is uncertain. For example, 43.00 contains four significant digits. The whole number 4300 may contain two, three, or four significant digits. In the absence of other information, the significance of the right-hand zeros is uncertain, and these digits cannot be assumed to be significant. To avoid confusion, numbers such as these should be reported using scientific notation. For example, the number 2.60×10^3 contains three significant figures and the number 2.600×10^3 contains four significant figures.

Rules for determining if a reported digit is significant are as follows.
1. Nonzero digits are always considered to be significant.
2. Zeros to the left of the first nonzero digit are never significant.
3. Zeros between nonzero digits are always significant.
4. Zeros at the right end of a decimal number and to the right of the decimal are significant.
5. Zeros at the right end of a whole number are uncertain. Whole numbers should be reported in scientific or engineering notation to clarify the significant figures.

GRAPHS

A graph is a visual tool that can quickly convey to the reader the relationship between variables. The eye can discern trends in magnitude or slope more easily on a graph than from tabular data. Graphs are widely used in experimental work to present information because they enable the reader to discern variations in magnitude, slope, and direction between two quantities. In this manual, you will graph data in many experiments.

---

[1]Note that when you are entering numbers in scientific notation on the calculator, it is not necessary to enter the base ten, only the exponent.

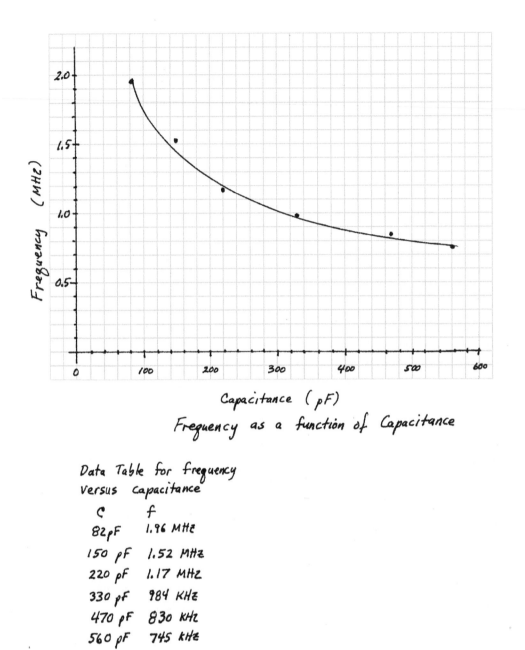

Capacitance (pF)

Frequency as a function of Capacitance

Data Table for frequency
versus capacitance

C	f
82 pF	1.96 MHz
150 pF	1.52 MHz
220 pF	1.17 MHz
330 pF	984 KHz
470 pF	830 KHz
560 pF	745 kHz

Figure 1–1

Figure 1–1 illustrates a set of data and a linear graph of the data. Notice that the six steps are followed in preparing this graph. For this particular example, the steps are:

Step 1: Select a linear scale. The independent variable (capacitance) is on the *x*-axis. Choose 20 pF/div on the *x*-axis and 0.1 MHz/div on the *y*-axis to fit all of the data on the plot.

Step 2: Number the major divisions. For the *x*-axis, select 100 pF increments; for the *y*-axis, select 0.5 MHz.

Step 3: Add labels and units to each axis. Place capacitance (pF) and Frequency (MHz) along their respective axis.

Step 4: Transfer data points from the Data table to the plot.

Step 5: Draw a smooth curve. Notice that it is not necessary to touch every data point.

Step 6: Add a title. In this case, the title describes the plot "Frequency as a function of capacitance."

PROCEDURE

1. Many of the dials and controls of laboratory instruments are labeled with metric prefixes. Check the controls on instruments at your lab station for metric prefixes. For example, check the SEC/DIV control on your oscilloscope. This control usually has more than one metric prefix associated with the switch positions. Meters are also frequently marked with metric prefixes. Look for others and list the instrument, control, metric unit and its meaning in Table 1–3. There are many possible answers. The first line of Table 1–3 has been completed as an example.

Table 1–3

Instrument	Control	Metric Unit	Meaning
Oscilloscope	SEC/DIV	ms	10^{-3} s

Table 1–4

Dimension	Length in Millimeters	Length in Meters
A	7.2 mm	7.2×10^{-3} m
B		
C		
D		
E		
F		
G		

2. The actual sizes of several electronic components are shown in Figure 1–2. Measure the quantities shown with a bold letter using a metric ruler. Report in Table 1–4 the length in millimeters of each lettered quantity. Then rewrite the measured length as the equivalent length in meters and record your results in Table 1–4. The first line of the table has been completed as an example. (Lengths are approximate.)

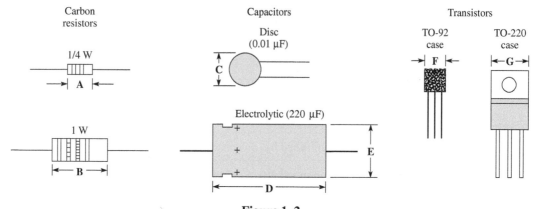

Figure 1–2

Table 1–5   Table 1–6

Number	Scientific Notation	Engineering Notation	Metric Value
0.0829 V	8.29×10^{-2} V	82.9×10^{-3} V	82.9 mV
48,000 Hz			
2,200,000 Ω			
0.000 015 A			
7,500 W			
0.000 000 033 F			
270,000 Ω			
0.000 010 H			

Metric Value	Engineering Notation
100 pF	100×10^{-12} F
12 kV	
85.0 μA	
50 GHz	
33 kΩ	
250 mV	
7.8 ns	
2.0 MΩ	

3.   Rewrite the numbers in Table 1–5 in scientific notation, engineering notation, and using one of the engineering metric prefixes. The first line has been completed as an example.

4.   Convert the metric values listed in Table 1–6 to engineering notation. The first line has been completed as an example.

5.   Metric prefixes are useful for solving problems without having to key in the exponent on your calculator. For example, when a milli prefix (10^{-3}) is multiplied by a kilo prefix (10^{+3}), the metric prefixes cancel and the result has only the measuring unit. As you become proficient with these prefixes, math operations are simplified and fewer keystrokes are required in solving the problem with a calculator. To practice this, determine the metric prefix for the answer when each operation indicated in Table 1–7 is performed. The first line is shown as an example.

Table 1–7

Metric Unit in Operand	Mathematical Operation	Metric Unit in Operand		Metric Unit in Result
milli	multiplied by	milli	=	micro
kilo	multiplied by	micro	=	
nano	multiplied by	kilo	=	
milli	multiplied by	mega	=	
micro	divided by	nano	=	
micro	divided by	pico	=	
pico	divided by	pico	=	
milli	divided by	mega	=	

6.   This step is to provide you with practice in graphing and in presenting data. Table 1–8 lists inductance data for 16 different coils wound on identical iron cores. There are three variables in this problem: the length of the coil (l) given in centimeters (cm), the number of turns, N, and the inductance, L, given in millihenries (mH). Since there are three variables, we will hold one constant and plot the data using the remaining two variables. This procedure shows how one variable relates to the other. Start by plotting the length (first column) as a function of inductance (last column) for coils that have 400 turns. Use Plot 1–1. The steps in preparing a graph are given in the *Introduction to the Student* and reviewed with an example in the Summary of Theory, page 3.

Table 1–8   Inductance, L, of coils wound on identical iron cores (mH).

Length, l (cm)	Number of Turns, N (t)			
	100	200	300	400
2.5	3.9	16.1	35.8	64.0
5.5	1.7	7.5	16.1	29.3
8.0	1.2	5.1	11.4	19.8
12.0	0.8	3.3	7.5	13.1

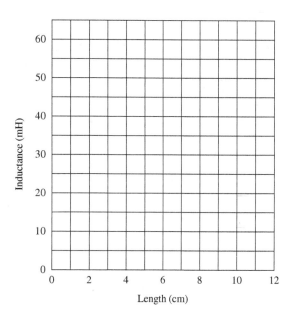

Plot 1–1

7.   On the same plot, graph the data for the 300 turn coils, then the 200 turn and 100 turn coils. Use a different symbol for each set of data. The resulting graph is a family of curves that give a quick visual indication of the relationship among the three variables.

CONCLUSION
Example
This experiment included exercises in measuring and plotting. The data in steps 6 and 7 show that, for a given number of turns, the inductance is smaller for a longer coil. The four lines indicate that inductance increases as the number of turns is larger.

EVALUATION AND REVIEW QUESTIONS

1.   For each metric prefix and unit shown, write the abbreviation of the metric prefix with the unit symbol:

        (a) kilowatt   (b) milliampere

        (c) picofarad   (d) nanosecond

        (e) megohm   (f) microhenry

2.   Write the metric prefix and unit name for each of the abbreviations shown:

        (a) MW   (b) nA

        (c) μJ   (d) mV

        (e) kΩ (f) GHz

3.   Using your calculator, perform the following operations:

        (a) $(3.6 \times 10^4)(8.8 \times 10^{-4})$

        (b) $(-4.0 \times 10^{-6})(2.7 \times 10^{-1})$

        (c) $(-7.5 \times 10^2)(-2.5 \times 10^{-5})$

        (d) $(56 \times 10^3)(9.0 \times 10^{-7})$

4.   Using your calculator, perform the following operations:

        (a) $\dfrac{(4.4 \times 10^9)}{(-7.0 \times 10^3)}$ (b) $\dfrac{(3.1 \times 10^2)}{(41 \times 10^{-6})}$

        (c) $\dfrac{(-2.0 \times 10^4)}{(-6.5 \times 10^{-6})}$ (d) $\dfrac{(0.0033 \times 10^{-3})}{(-15 \times 10^{-2})}$

5.   For each result in Question 4, write the answer as one with a metric prefix:

        (a)   (b)

        (c)   (d)

6.   Summarize the six steps in preparing a linear graph:

FOR FURTHER INVESTIGATION

In steps 6 and 7, it is apparent that the data for the 100 turn coils is close to the *x*-coordinate, making it difficult to read on the same graph as the 400 turn data. A solution to this problem is to plot the data on a log-log plot. A logarithmic scale increases the resolution when data encompasses a large range of values. To help you get started, the axes have already been labeled and values assigned. Plot the data from Table 1–8 onto Plot 1–2. You should observe that each data set will plot a straight line. This result indicates the form of the equation which relates the variables is a power function.

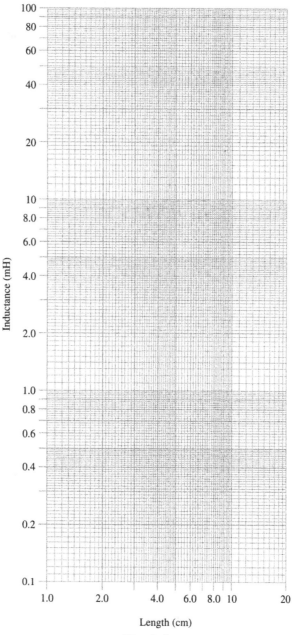

Plot 1–2

2 Laboratory Meters and Power Supply

Name _____

Date _____

Class _____

OBJECTIVES

After performing this experiment, you will be able to:
1.   Read analog meter scales including multiple and complex scales.
2.   Operate the power supply at your lab station.
3.   Explain the functions of the controls for the multimeter at your lab station. Use it to make a voltage reading.

MATERIALS NEEDED

None

For Further Investigation:
   Meter calibrator

SUMMARY OF THEORY

Work in electronic laboratories requires you to be familiar with basic instruments that you will use throughout your study of electronics. In this experiment, you will set up and measure voltage. You should review safety procedures for laboratory work before attempting to use the power supply and meters that are introduced in this experiment. You will only use low voltages, but you should still be aware of hazards when using any electrical equipment. You should never touch a "live" circuit, even if it is low voltage.

You can think of voltage as the "driving force" for a circuit. Technically speaking, it is not a force, but it does cause current. Electrical circuits contain a source of voltage and components connected in a manner to provide a path for current. Many components require a very stable source of constant voltage. This voltage is called dc (for direct current) and is usually supplied by a regulated dc power supply. Regulated power supplies are circuits that convert the alternating current (ac) line power into a constant output voltage in spite of changes to the input ac, the load current, or temperature.

The amount of voltage required varies widely for different circuits, depending on the type of circuit and the power levels. It is important that the power supply be set up *prior* to connecting it to the circuit to avoid damaging sensitive components. Most of the time the power supply voltage is checked with a meter called a *voltmeter*. The measurement of voltage is also important for determining circuit performance in many cases. Another important electrical parameter is resistance, which is the opposition to current, measured in ohms. The meter that measures resistance is called the *ohmmeter*. Voltage and resistance measurements will be the main focus of this experiment because they are often measured with the same meter. Other measurements will be described in later experiments.

Many electrical quantities are measured with meters. The schematic symbol for a basic meter is shown in Figure 2–1. The meter function is shown on the schematic with a letter or symbol. One popular

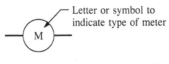

Figure 2–1 Meter symbol.

type of meter is the *multimeter*, an instrument which combines three basic meters into one. The multimeter can measure resistance, voltage, or current and sometimes includes other types of measurements. Multimeters may be either analog or digital. An analog multimeter (VOM or <u>V</u>olt-<u>O</u>hm-Milliammeter) uses a pointer to indicate on a numbered scale the value of the measured quantity. A digital multimeter (or DMM) shows the measured quantity as a number. Digital multimeters are more widely used than analog multimeters because of superior performance and ease of use. Examples of a portable VOM and DMM are shown in Figure 2–2.

For voltage measurements, the multimeter needs to be set up for either ac or dc. Depending on the meter, you may need to select a *range* for the reading. Electrical quantities extend from the very small to the very large. Resistance, for example, can vary from less than 1 Ω to over 1,000,000 Ω. Meters must have some means of accommodating this large range of numbers. The position of the decimal point is determined by the range switch on the meter. The user selects an appropriate range to display the measured number. Some meters have autoranging, which means they can change ranges automatically. An autoranging meter may also have an AUTO/HOLD switch that allows the meter to either operate in the autoranging mode or to hold the last range setting.

When you use an autoranging multimeter, the multimeter will normally be in the AUTO mode. The function to be measured is selected, and the multimeter is connected to the circuit under test. The user must be careful to connect the meter correctly for the measurement to be made. Examples of how to connect an autoranging DMM for measurement of voltage and resistance are shown in Figure 2–3. There are often limitations to the ability of a meter to measure accurately, so you should be familiar with these limitations before using it.

Current measurements require special care to avoid damage to the multimeter. An ammeter must never be connected across a voltage source. When a multimeter is used to measure current, the function-

(a) VOM

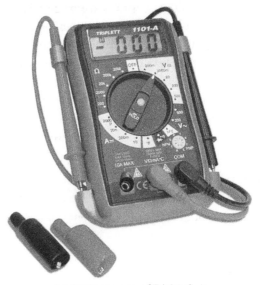

(b) DMM (courtesy of Triplett Co.)

Figure 2–2

14

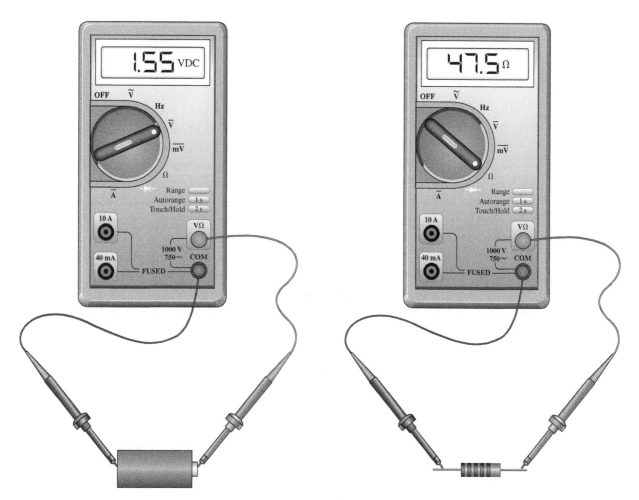

Figure 2–3

select switch is moved to the current position; the probe must be moved to a current-measuring socket before connecting the meter in the circuit. In this experiment, current will not be measured.

Many electronic measurements are made with analog meters. Analog meters can be calibrated to read almost any physical quantity, including voltage, current, power, or even nonelectrical quantities such as weight, speed, or light. The scales on analog meters may be either linear or nonlinear. They may have several scales on the same meter face. Various types of meters will be described in the Procedure section of this experiment.

PROCEDURE

1. A linear meter scale is marked in equally spaced divisions across the face of the meter. Figure 2–4 shows a linear meter scale. The major divisions, called *primary* divisions, are usually numbered. Between the primary divisions are smaller divisions called *secondary* divisions. To read this scale, note the number of secondary divisions between the numbered primary divisions and determine the value of each secondary division. The scale shown has 10 subdivisions.

    What is the value of each secondary division in Figure 2–4? _____ What is the meter reading? _____

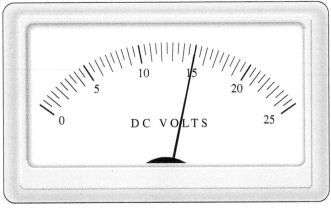

Figure 2–4

2. Frequently a meter is used for several ranges. The meter shown in Figure 2–4 could, for example, have a 2.5 V full-scale range, a 25 V full-scale range, and a 250 V full-scale range. It is up to the user to then set the decimal place, depending on which range has been selected. If the user selects the 250 V full-scale range, then there are 50 V between each primary division.

If the meter shown in Figure 2–4 is on the 250 V range, what is the value of each secondary division? _____ What is the meter reading? _____

3. Usually, meters with more than one range have several scales called *multiple* scales. A meter with multiple scales is illustrated in Figure 2–5. Each scale can represent one or more ranges. In this case, the user must choose the appropriate scale *and* set the decimal place.

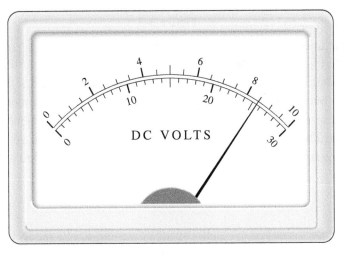

Figure 2–5

The top scale has a full-scale value of 10 V. This scale should be read if the 10 V range is selected. It is also used for any range which is a multiple of 10. For example, assume the meter shown has a 1.0 V range that has been selected. The user inserts a decimal and reads the top scale as 1.0 V full scale. The primary divisions are 0.2 V, and the secondary divisions are equal to 0.05 V. The reading on the meter is then interpreted as 0.85 V.

What is the meter reading if the range selected is the 30 V range? _____

16

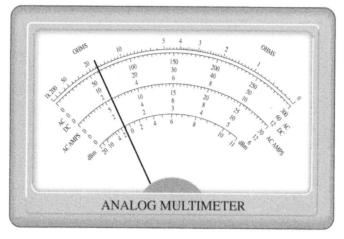

Figure 2–6

4. VOMs and some instruments contain meters that can be used for more than one function. These scales are called *complex* scales. To read a complex scale the user chooses the appropriate scale based on the function *and* the range selected. Figure 2–6 shows a complex scale from a VOM.

If the function selected is resistance, then the top scale is selected. Before using a VOM on the resistance scale, the meter is adjusted for a zero reading with no resistance. This scale is nonlinear. Notice that the secondary divisions change values across the scale. To determine the reading, the primary divisions on each side of the pointer are noted. The secondary divisions can then be assigned values by counting the number of secondary divisions between the primary marks.

For the meter in Figure 2–6, assume the OHMS function is selected, and the range selected is ×10 ohms. What does the meter indicate for a resistance? _____

Assume the meter is on the DC VOLTS function and the range selected is 12 V. What does the meter indicate for voltage? _____

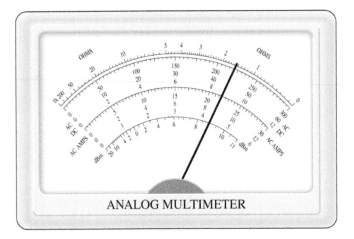

Figure 2–7

5. For the meter in Figure 2–7, assume the OHMS function is selected and the range selected is ×100. What does the meter read for resistance? _____

   Assume the meter in Figure 2–7 is on the AC VOLTS function and the range selected is 30 V. What does the meter indicate for voltage? _____

   The decibel scale (the lowest scale) is used in 600 Ω systems (such as many audio systems). It is a logarithmic scale in which the 0 dBm reference represents a power dissipation of 1 mW in a 600 Ω system (0.775 V across 600 Ω). For the meter in Figure 2–7, what is the reading in dBm? _____

6. Look at the meter on the power supply at your lab station. Some power supplies have meters that monitor either voltage or current. There may be more than one range or several supplies built into the same chassis, so the meter may have multiple or complex scales.

   Is the meter used for more than one function? _____ If so, what determines which function is monitored? _____

   Does the meter have multiple scales? _____ complex scales? _____

   What is the smallest primary voltage division? _____ The smallest secondary voltage division? _____

7. Review the controls for the power supply at your lab station. The operator's manual is a good resource if you are not sure of the purpose of a control. Describe the features of your supply: (multiple outputs, current limiting, tracking, etc.)

8. In this step, you will set the power supply for a specific voltage and measure that voltage with your laboratory meter. Review the operator's manual for the DMM (or VOM) at your lab station. Review each control on the meter. Then select +DC and VOLTS on the DMM. If your DMM is not autoranging, select a range that will measure +5.0 V dc. The best choice is a range which is the *smallest* range that is larger than +5.0 V. Connect the test leads together and verify that the reading is zero. (Note: A digital meter may have a small digit in the least significant place.)

9. Turn on the power supply at your station and use the meter on the supply to set the output to +5.0 V. Then use the DMM to confirm that the setting is correct.

   Reading on the power supply meter = _____ Reading on the DMM = _____

10. Set the output to +12.0 V and measure the output.

    Reading on the power supply meter = _____ Reading on the DMM = _____

11. Set the power supply to the minimum setting and measure the output.

    Reading on the power supply meter = _____ Reading on the DMM = _____

CONCLUSION

EVALUATION AND REVIEW QUESTIONS

1. Compare the precision of the power supply voltmeter with the DMM or VOM at your lab station. Does one meter have an advantage for measuring 5.0 V? Explain your answer.

2.   What is meant by an autoranging meter? What type is at your lab station?

3.   What is the difference between a multiple scale and a complex scale?

4.   What is the difference between a linear scale and a nonlinear scale?

5.   Assume a scale has four secondary marks between the primary marks numbered 3.0 and 4.0. If the pointer is on the first secondary mark, what is the reading on the meter?

6.   List the three basic measurements that can be made with a VOM or a DMM.

FOR FURTHER INVESTIGATION
The **sensitivity** of a panel meter is a number that describes how much current is required to obtain full-scale deflection from the meter. Meter sensitivity is easily determined with a meter calibrator. If you have a meter calibrator available, go over the operator's manual and learn how to measure the full-scale current in an inexpensive panel meter. Then obtain a small panel meter and measure its sensitivity. Summarize your results.

Checkup 1

Name _____

Date _____

Class _____

REFERENCE
Floyd, Chap. 1, and Buchla, Experiments 1 and 2

1. The metric prefix tera means:
   (a) 10^3 (b) 10^6 (c) 10^9 (d) 10^{12}

2. A nonzero digit in a reported number is:
   (a) never significant   (b) always significant   (c) sometimes significant

3. A meter that can be used to measure resistance is called:
   (a) an ohmmeter   (b) a wattmeter   (c) an ammeter   (d) an oscilloscope

4. An ohmmeter can be damaged if:
   (a) it is used in an energized circuit   (b) it is used on the wrong range
   (c) leads are reversed   (d) it is used to measure a diode

5. When using a multimeter to read an unknown voltage, you should start on the:
   (a) lowest range   (b) middle range   (c) highest range

6. The quantity 0.01 μF is the same as:
   (a) 10,000 mF   (b) 10,000 nF   (c) 10,000 pF   (d) none of these

7. The number 505,000 can be expressed as:
   (a) 0.505 M   (b) 505 k   (c) 505×10^3 (d) all of these

8. The metric prefix milli multiplied by the prefix mega produces:
   (a) kilo   (b) milli   (c) giga   (d) micro

9. One-fourth watt is the same as:
   (a) 0.025 W   (b) 250 mW   (c) 250 μW   (d) 2.50 W

10. Engineering notation uses exponents that are multiples of:
    (a) one   (b) two   (c) three   (d) four

11. What measurements can be made with a VOM?

12. Explain the difference between a primary division and a secondary division on an analog meter.

13. List the unit of measurement for each:
    (a) resistance   (b) capacitance
    (c) frequency   (d) inductance
    (e) voltage   (f) energy

14. Show the symbol for each of the following measurement units:
    (a) ohm   (b) farad
    (c) watt   (d) hertz
    (e) coulomb   (f) ampere

15. Express the following numbers in scientific notation as a number between 1 and 10 times 10 to the appropriate power:
    (a) 1050   (b) 0.0575
    (c) 251×10^2 (d) 89.0×10^{-5}
    (e) 0.000 004 91   (f) 0.0135×10^{-2}

16. Express the following numbers in engineering notation:
    (a) 0.00520   (b) 59 200
    (c) 760×10^5 (d) 19.0×10^{-4}
    (e) 1.22×10^2 (f) 0.0509×10^{-10}

17. Change each quantity from scientific notation to a number with a metric prefix:
    (a) 1.24×10^{-6} A   (b) 7.5×10^3 Ω
    (c) 4.7×10^4 Hz   (d) 3.3×10^{-8} F
    (e) 2.2×10^{-12} s   (f) 9.5×10^{-2} H

18. Change each quantity as indicated:
    (a) 70 μA to amps   (b) 50 MHz to hertz
    (c) 0.010 μF to farads   (d) 5.0 W to milliwatts
    (e) 22 mV to volts   (f) 3300 pF to microfarads

19. Perform the following additions. Express answers with three significant digits:
    (a) $5.25 \times 10^3 + 4.97 \times 10^3$ (b) $9.02 \times 10^4 + 1.66 \times 10^3$
    (c) $1.00 \times 10^{-2} + 2.25 \times 10^{-2}$ (d) $4.15 \times 10^{-6} + 6.8 \times 10^{-7}$
    (e) $9.60 \times 10^{-5} + 1.95 \times 10^{-4}$ (f) $8.79 \times 10^6 + 4.85 \times 10^7$

20. What type of variable is plotted on the x-axis of a graph?

21. If you are plotting data on a linear graph, what is true about each division assigned to an axis?

22

Application
Assignment 2

Name _____
Date _____
Class _____

REFERENCE

Floyd, Chapter 2, Application Assignment: Putting Your Knowledge to Work. The Application Assignment worksheet correlates to the Application Assignments in Floyd's text.

Step 1   Circuit choice and reason rejected circuits will not meet requirements:

_____

_____

Step 2   Wire list. (First item is given as an example.)

From	To
All lamps (pin #2)	Battery (− side)

Step 3   Fuse size selected is _____ A

Reason:

_____

Step 4   Required battery capacity is _____ Ah

Step 5   Test procedure for troubleshooting:

_____

_____

31

Possible faults:

Fault 1: All but one lamp can be turned on:

_____

_____

Fault 2: None of the lamps can be turned on:

_____

_____

Fault 3: Each lamp is too dim and cannot be brightened by adjusting the rheostat:

_____

_____

Fault 4: Each lamp is too dim; however, the amount of light can be varied with the rheostat but not to full brightness:

_____

_____

RELATED EXPERIMENT

MATERIALS NEEDED
Six 330 Ω resistors
Six small light-emitting diodes (LEDs)
One 1 kΩ potentiometer
One 5 V power supply

DISCUSSION
The lamps required for Application Assignment 2 use 110 V. *It is unsafe to experiment with this voltage level,* so a low-voltage simulation can be used to verify your solution using a 5 V dc power supply. The lights you will use are called light-emitted diodes (LEDs), which use a small current to emit light. LEDs emit light only when there is current in one direction. To limit the current to a level that is safe for the LEDs, a 330 Ω resistor is placed in series with each LED, as shown in Figure AA–2–1. The dimmer will consist of a 1 kΩ potentiometer. Be sure to check the polarity of the diodes—if they are installed backward, they will not light. A short jumper wire on your protoboard can serve as an open or closed switch to complete the circuit.

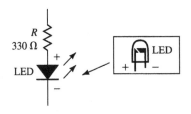

Figure AA–2–1

Checkup 2

Name _____
Date _____
Class _____

REFERENCE

Floyd, Chapter 2, and Buchla, Experiments 3 and 4

1. A material that is characterized by four valence electrons in its atomic structure is called:
   (a) a conductor   (b) an insulator   (c) a semiconductor

2. The basic particle of matter that carries a negative electrical charge is the:
   (a) atom   (b) electron   (c) proton   (d) neutron

3. The unit of electrical charge is the:
   (a) ampere   (b) coulomb   (c) joule   (d) volt

4. One coulomb passing a point in one second is defined as one:
   (a) ampere   (b) watt   (c) joule   (d) volt

5. A joule per coulomb is a measure of:
   (a) resistance   (b) power   (c) voltage   (d) current

6. The unit of resistance is named in honor of:
   (a) Joule   (b) Watt   (c) Ampere   (d) Ohm

7. A resistor used to control current in a circuit is called a:
   (a) circuit breaker   (b) rheostat   (c) potentiometer   (d) choke

8. The purpose of the third band of a four-band resistor is:
   (a) multiplier   (b) tolerance   (c) reliability   (d) temperature

9. An instrument used for measuring resistance is:
   (a) an ohmmeter   (b) a voltmeter   (c) an oscilloscope   (d) an ammeter

10. In a circuit, a reference ground is always:
    (a) the point with the lowest potential   (b) a common point
    (c) the same as earth ground   (d) the negative side of the source

11. If you are constructing a circuit for testing, why is it a good idea to measure and record the values of resistors used?

12. A 5.6 kΩ resistor has a fourth band that is gold. What are the largest and smallest values of resistance that are within the tolerance rating for this resistor?

13. In Experiment 4, V_{AB} was positive despite the location of ground. Explain why this was true.

14. Determine the color-code value of resistance and the tolerance for each resistor:
    (a)   white-brown-red-silver: _____
    (b)   green-blue-green-gold: _____
    (c)   brown-black-black-gold: _____
    (d)   yellow-violet-orange-silver: _____
    (e)   green-brown-gold-gold: _____

15. Determine the color code for each of the following resistors:
    (a)   470 kΩ ± 10% _____
    (b)   180 Ω ± 5% _____
    (c)   4.3 kΩ ± 5% _____
    (d)   1.0 Ω ± 10% _____
    (e)   2.7 MΩ ± 5% _____

16. Explain how both positive and negative voltages can exist at the same time in a circuit but with only one voltage source.

17. Assume that a circuit contains three points labeled **A, B,** and **C.** Point **A** has a potential with respect to ground of 10.2 V; point **B** has a potential of −12.4 V, and point **C** has a potential of −8.7 V. What is the potential difference between:
    (a)   point **A** with respect to point **B?**   _____
    (b)   point **B** with respect to point **A?**   _____
    (c)   point **A** with respect to point **C?**   _____
    (d)   point **C** with respect to point **A?**   _____
    (e)   point **B** with respect to point **C?**   _____
    (f)   point **C** with respect to point **B?**   _____

18. What is another word for potential difference?

5 Ohm's Law

Name _____

Date _____

Class _____

OBJECTIVES

After performing this experiment, you will be able to:

1. Measure the current-voltage curve for a resistor.
2. Construct a graph of the data from objective 1.
3. Given a graph of current-voltage for a resistor, determine the resistance.

MATERIALS NEEDED

Resistors:

       One 1.0 kΩ, one 1.5 kΩ, one 2.2 kΩ

One dc ammeter, 0–10 mA

For Further Investigation:

  One Cds photocell (Jameco 120299 or equivalent)

SUMMARY OF THEORY

The flow of electrical charge in a circuit is called *current.* Current is measured in units of *amperes,* or amps for short. The ampere is defined as one coulomb of charge moving past a point in one second. Current is symbolized by the letter I (for *Intensity*) and is frequently shown with an arrow to indicate the direction of flow. Conventional current is defined as the direction a positive charge would move under the influence of an electric field. When electrons move, the direction is opposite to the direction defined for conventional current. To clarify the difference, the term *electron flow* is frequently applied to current in the opposite direction of conventional current. The experiments in this lab book work equally well with either definition.

      The relationship between current and voltage is an important characteristic that defines various electronic devices. The relationship is frequently shown with a graph. Usually, the voltage is controlled (the independent variable), and the current is observed (the dependent variable). This is the basic method for this experiment, for which a series of resistors will be tested. As discussed in the Introduction to the Student, the independent variable is plotted along the x-axis and the dependent variable is plotted along the y-axis.

      Fixed resistors have a straight-line or *linear* current-voltage curve. This linear relationship illustrates the basic relationship of Ohm's law—namely, that the current is proportional to the voltage for constant resistance. Ohm's law is the most important law of electronics. It is written in equation form as:

$$I = \frac{V}{R}$$

where I represents current, V represents voltage, and R represents resistance.

PROCEDURE

1. Measure three resistors with listed values of 1.0 kΩ, 1.5 kΩ, and 2.2 kΩ. Record the measured values in Table 5–1.

Table 5–1

Component	Listed Value	Measured Value
R_1	1.0 kΩ	
R_2	1.5 kΩ	
R_3	2.2 kΩ	

2. Connect the circuit shown in Figure 5–1(a). Notice that the ammeter is in series with the resistor and forms a single "loop" as shown in the protoboard wiring diagram in Figure 5–1(b). The voltmeter is then connected directly across the resistor.

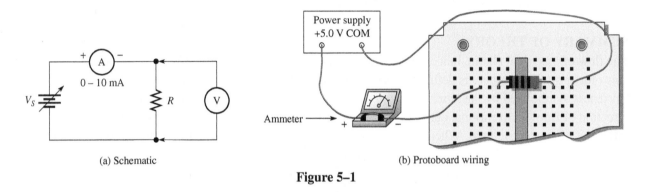

(a) Schematic   (b) Protoboard wiring

Figure 5–1

Caution! Ammeters can be easily damaged if they are incorrectly connected. Have your instructor check your connections before applying power.

---

3. Adjust the power supply for a voltage of 2.0 V. Read the current that is through the resistor and record it in Table 5–2.

4. Adjust the power supply for 4.0 V and measure the current. Record the current in Table 5–2. Continue taking current readings for each of the voltages listed in Table 5–2.

Table 5–2 (R_1)

$V_S =$	2.0 V	4.0 V	6.0 V	8.0 V	10.0 V
$I =$					

5.   Replace R_1 with R_2 and repeat steps 3 and 4. Record the data in Table 5–3.

Table 5–3 (R_2)

$V_S =$	2.0 V	4.0 V	6.0 V	8.0 V	10.0 V
$I =$					

6.   Replace R_2 with R_3 and repeat steps 3 and 4. Record the data in Table 5–4.

Table 5–4 (R_3)

$V_S =$	2.0 V	4.0 V	6.0 V	8.0 V	10.0 V
$I =$					

7.   On Plot 5–1, graph all three I-V curves using the data from Tables 5–2, 5–3, and 5–4. Plot the dependent variable (current) on the y-axis and the independent variable (voltage) on the x-axis. Choose a scale for the graph that spreads the data over the entire grid.

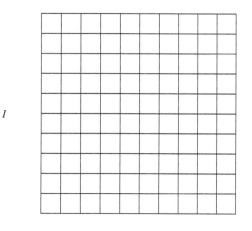

V

Plot 5–1

CONCLUSION

EVALUATION AND REVIEW QUESTIONS

1. The slope of a line is the change in the y direction divided by the change in the x direction. The definition for slope is illustrated in Figure 5–2. Find the slope for each resistor on Plot 5–1. Notice that the slope has units. If the change in y is measured in mA and the change in x is measured in V, the slope is mA/V = mS.

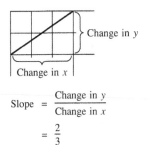

$$\text{Slope} = \frac{\text{Change in } y}{\text{Change in } x}$$

$$= \frac{2}{3}$$

Figure 5–2

2. What happens to the slope of the I-V curve for larger resistors?

3. (a) If the resistance is halved and the voltage is not changed, what will happen to the current in a resistive circuit?

   (b) If the voltage is doubled and the resistance is not changed, what will happen to the current in a resistive circuit?

4. If the current in a resistive circuit is 24 mA and the applied voltage is 48 V, what is the resistance?

5. What current is through a 10 Ω resistor with a 5.0 V applied?

FOR FURTHER INVESTIGATION

One interesting type of resistor is called a CdS cell (for Cadmium Sulfide). CdS cells are widely used as light-sensing elements in electronics. The resistance of the CdS cell decreases as the incident light increases.

In this investigation, find out if a CdS cell has an I-V curve like other resistors (a straight line) if the light is constant. Set up the experiment as in Figure 5–1, but use a CdS cell instead of a normal resistor. You will need to have a constant amount of light on the CdS cell as much as possible. Try adjusting the CdS cell to look at a light source such as a room light. You will notice that pointing it in different ways will change the current. A good starting point is to adjust it so that you have about 2 mA when the source voltage is 2.0 V. Then increase the voltage by increments of 2.0 V and record the current in Table 5–5 for each voltage setting. Plot the data in Plot 5–2 and summarize your findings.

Table 5–5 (CdS cell)

$V_S =$	2.0 V	4.0 V	6.0 V	8.0 V	10.0 V
$I =$					

I

V

Plot 5–2

6 Power in DC Circuits

Name _____
Date _____
Class _____

OBJECTIVES
After performing this experiment, you will be able to:
1.   Determine the power in a variable resistor at various settings of resistance.
2.   Plot data for power as a function of resistance. From the plot, determine when maximum power is delivered to the variable resistor.

MATERIALS NEEDED
One 2.7 kΩ resistor
One 10 kΩ potentiometer

SUMMARY OF THEORY
When there is current through a resistor, electrical energy is converted into heat. Heat is then radiated from the resistor. The *rate* that heat is dissipated is called *power*. Power is measured in units of joules per second (J/s), which defines the unit called the watt (W). The power dissipated by a resistor is given by the power law equation:

$$P = IV$$

By applying Ohm's law to the power law equation, two more useful equations for power can be found. These are:

$$P_2 = I_T R_2$$

and

$$P = \frac{V^2}{R}$$

The three power equations given above are also known as Watt's law. In this experiment, you will determine power using the last equation. Notice that if you measure the voltage in volts (V) and the resistance in kilohms (kΩ), the power will have units of milliwatts (mW).

The physical size of a resistor is related to the amount of heat it can dissipate. Therefore, larger resistors are rated for more power than smaller ones. Carbon composition resistors are available with standard power ratings ranging from 1/8 W to 2 W. For most typical low voltage applications (15 V or less and at least 1 kΩ of resistance), a 1/4 W resistor is satisfactory.

PROCEDURE

1. Measure the resistance of R_1. The color-code value is 2.7 kΩ. R_1 = _____

2. Construct the circuit shown in Figure 6–1(a). Figure 6–1(b) shows an example of the circuit constructed on a protoboard. R_2 is a 10 kΩ potentiometer. Connect the center (variable) terminal to one of the outside terminals. Use this and the remaining terminal as a variable resistor. Adjust the potentiometer for 0.5 kΩ. (Always remove power when measuring resistance and make certain you are measuring only the potentiometer's resistance.)

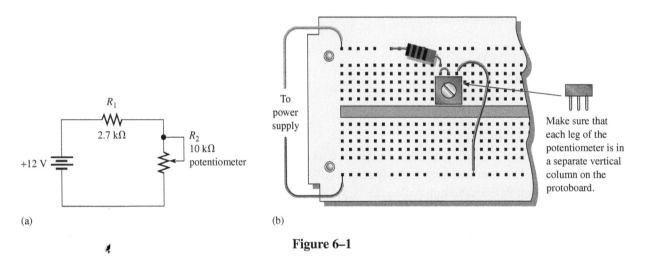

(a)   (b)

Figure 6–1

3. Use Ohm's law to compute the total current in the circuit. The total voltage is +12.0 V. The total resistance is $R_1 + R_2$. Enter the total current in Table 6–1. The first entry has been completed as an example.

Table 6–1

Variable Resistance Setting (R_2)	$I_T = \dfrac{V_T}{R_T}$	V_1 (measured)	V_2 (measured)	Power in R_2: P_2
0.5 kΩ	3.75 mA			
1.0 kΩ				
2.0 kΩ				
3.0 kΩ				
4.0 kΩ				
5.0 kΩ				
7.5 kΩ				
10.0 kΩ				

4. Measure the voltage across R_1 and the voltage across R_2. Enter the measured voltages in Table 6–1. As a check, make sure that the sum of V_1 and V_2 is equal to 12.0 V. Then compute the power in R_2 using either of the following equations:

$$P_2 = I_T R_2 \qquad \text{or} \qquad P_2 = \frac{V_2^2}{R_2}$$

Enter the computed power, in milliwatts, in Table 6–1.

5. Disconnect the power supply and set R_2 to the next value shown in Table 6–1. Reconnect the power supply and repeat the measurements made in steps 3 and 4. Continue in this manner for each of the resistance settings shown in Table 6–1.

6. Using the data in Table 6–1, graph the relationship of the power, P_2, as a function of resistance R_2 on Plot 6–1. Since resistance is the independent variable, plot it along the *x*-axis and plot power along the *y*-axis. An *implied* data point can be plotted at the origin because there can be no power dissipated in R_2 without resistance. A smooth curve can then be drawn to the origin.

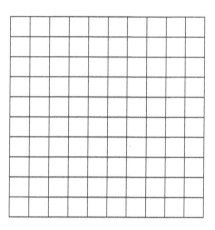

Plot 6–1

CONCLUSION

EVALUATION AND REVIEW QUESTIONS

1. Observe the graph of resistance versus power for your experiment. Compare the resistance of R_1 and R_2 when power in R_2 is a maximum.

2. What was happening to the total current in the circuit as R_2 was increasing?

3.   What was happening to the power in R_1 as the resistance of R_2 was increasing? Explain your answer.

4.   A 1.5 kΩ resistor is found to have 22.5 V across it.
        (a)   What is the current in the resistor? _____

        (b)   What is the power dissipated in the resistor? _____

        (c)   Could a 1/4 W resistor be used in this application? Explain your answer.

5.   What physical characteristic determines the power rating of a resistor?

6.   What happens to electrical energy in a resistor?

FOR FURTHER INVESTIGATION

Because it is a series circuit, the current was the same throughout for each setting of R_2. Find the current for each row in Table 6–1 by dividing the measured value of V_1 by the measured value of R_1. Plot this current as a function of R_2. On the same graph, plot V_2 as a function of R_2. What is the shape of the product of these two lines?

Application Assignment 3

Name _____
Date _____
Class _____

REFERENCE

Floyd, Chapter 3, Application Assignment: Putting Your Knowledge to Work

Step 1   Inspection

Step 2   Draw the schematic of the existing resistor box. Label the resistors (R_1 through R_6).

Step 3   Modify the schematic for the resistor box to meet the new requirements. Label the resistors (R_1 through R_8) and give their power rating.

Step 4   Modify the circuit. State the modifications that must be made.

Step 5   Test procedure:

Step 6   Troubleshooting:
                Fault 1 (infinite resistance in switch position 3): _____
                Fault 2 (infinite resistance in all switch positions): _____
                Fault 3 (incorrect resistance in switch position 6): _____

RELATED EXPERIMENT

MATERIALS NEEDED
One LED
One resistor to be determined

DISCUSSION
As in the application problem, it is frequently necessary to compute the value of a current-limiting resistor. An LED must have a certain current to properly light but can be destroyed if the current is too high. Assume a current of 8 mA is required in an LED. The LED drops approximately 2 V, leaving 3 V across the dropping resistor. Determine resistance and power rating of the dropping resistor needed. Construct the circuit and verify with measurements that you have correctly calculated the dropping resistor.

EXPERIMENTAL RESULTS

Checkup 3

REFERENCE

Floyd, Chap. 3, and Buchla, Experiments 5 and 6

1. Ohm's law states the relationship between voltage, current, and:
    (a) power (b) energy (c) resistance (d) time

2. In a given dc circuit, if the voltage were doubled and the resistance halved, the new current would be:
    (a) one-fourth (b) one-half (c) unchanged (d) doubled (e) quadrupled

3. A fixed resistance is connected across a 10 V source. The current in the resistance is found to be 21.3 μA. The value of the resistance is:
    (a) 213 $\mu\Omega$ (b) 213 Ω (c) 470 Ω (d) 0.470 MΩ

4. A blue-gray-orange-gold resistor is connected across a 25 V source. The expected current in the resistor is:
    (a) 368 μA (b) 368 mA (c) 1.7 μA (d) 1.7 mA

5. A 20 mV source is connected to a 100 kΩ load. The current in the load is:
    (a) 200 nA (b) 200 μA (c) 5.0 μA (d) 5.0 mA

6. The rate at which energy is used is called:
    (a) voltage (b) frequency (c) conductance (d) power

7. A megawatt is the same as:
    (a) 10^{-6} W (b) 10^{-3} W (c) 10^{3} W (d) 10^{6} W

8. Electric utility companies charge customers for:
    (a) voltage (b) current (c) power (d) energy

9. The SI unit of energy is the:
    (a) joule (b) watt (c) ampere (d) kilowatt-hour

10. A 1500 W resistance heater is connected to a 115 V source. The current in the heater is:
    (a) 77 mA (b) 8.8 A (c) 13 A (d) 19.6 A

11. An ammeter with an internal resistance of 0.5 Ω measures a current of 10 A. What is the voltage dropped across the ammeter?

12. In Experiment 6, a fixed resistor was in series with a variable resistor. You plotted the resistance of the variable resistor as a function of the power dissipated in it.
    (a)   What would you expect the graph to look like if the fixed resistor were a lower value?

    (b)   What would you expect to see if the resistance of the fixed resistor were zero?

13. A 100 Ω resistor is across a 20 V source.
    (a)   Determine the current in the resistor.

    (b)   Compute the power dissipated in the resistor.

14. In Experiment 5, a special caution is given regarding the connection of an ammeter in a circuit. What is the proper way to connect an ammeter?

15. A 10 W bulb is designed for use in a 12 V circuit.
    (a)   What current is in the bulb when it is connected to a 12 V source?

    (b)   If the bulb were placed across a 6 V source, what power would it dissipate?

7 Series Circuits

OBJECTIVES
After performing this experiment, you will be able to:
1. Use Ohm's law to find the current and voltages in a series circuit.
2. Apply Kirchhoff's voltage law to a series circuit.

MATERIALS NEEDED
Resistors:
One 330 Ω, one 1.0 kΩ, one 1.5 kΩ, one 2.2 kΩ
One dc ammeter, 0–10 mA

SUMMARY OF THEORY
Consider the simple circuit illustrated in Figure 7–1. The source voltage is the total current multiplied by the total resistance as given by Ohm's law. This can be stated in equation form as

$$V_S = I_T R_T$$

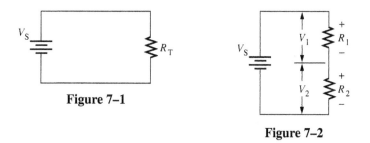

Figure 7–1

Figure 7–2

In a series circuit, the circuit elements are connected with only one path for current. For this reason, *the current is the same throughout a series circuit.*

Whenever we connect resistors in series, the total resistance increases. The total resistance of a series circuit is the sum of the individual resistors. Figure 7–2 illustrates a series circuit with two resistors. The total resistance is

$$R_T = R_1 + R_2$$

Substituting this equation into Ohm's law for the total circuit gives:

$$V_S = I_T(R_1 + R_2)$$

Multiplying both terms by I_T results in:

$$V_S = I_T R_1 + I_T R_2$$

Since the identical current, I_T, must be through each resistor, the voltage drops across the resistors can be found:

$$V_S = V_1 + V_2$$

This result illustrates that the source voltage is equal to the sum of the voltage drops across the resistors. This relationship is called Kirchhoff's voltage law, which is more precisely stated:

> The algebraic sum of all voltage rises and drops around any single closed loop in a circuit is equal to zero.

It is important to pay attention to the polarity of the voltages. Current from the source creates a voltage drop across the resistors. The voltage drop across the resistors will have an opposite polarity to the source voltage as illustrated in Figure 7–2. We may apply Kirchhoff's voltage law by using the following rules:

1. Choose an arbitrary starting point. Go either clockwise or counterclockwise from the starting point.
2. For each voltage source or load, write down the first sign you see and the magnitude of the voltage.
3. When you arrive at the starting point, equate the algebraic sum of the voltages to zero.

PROCEDURE

1. Obtain the resistors listed in Table 7–1. Measure each resistor and record the measured value in Table 7–1. Compute the total resistance for a series connection by adding the measured values. Enter the computed total resistance in Table 7–1 in the column for the listed value.

2. Connect the resistors in series as illustrated in Figure 7–3. Test various combinations of series resistors. Can you conclude that the total resistance of series resistors is the sum of the individual resistors? Then measure the total resistance of the series connection and verify that it agrees with your computed value. Enter your measured value in Table 7–1.

Table 7–1

Component	Listed Value	Measured Value
R_1	1.0 kΩ	
R_2	1.5 kΩ	
R_3	2.2 kΩ	
R_4	330 Ω	
$R_T =$		

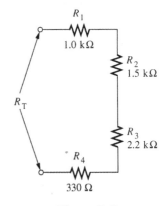

Figure 7–3

50

3. Complete the circuit shown in Figure 7–4. Be certain the ammeter is connected in *series*, otherwise damage to the meter may result. Before applying power, have your instructor check your circuit. Compute the current in the circuit by substituting the source voltage and the total resistance into Ohm's law. That is:

$$I_T = \frac{V_S}{R_T}$$

Record the computed current in Table 7–2. Apply power, and confirm that your computed current is within experimental uncertainty of the measured current.

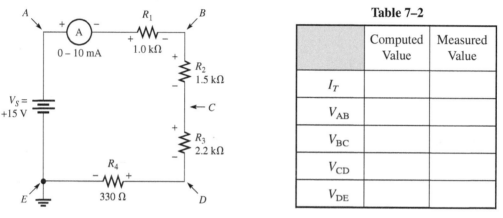

Figure 7–4

Table 7–2

	Computed Value	Measured Value
I_T		
V_{AB}		
V_{BC}		
V_{CD}		
V_{DE}		

4. In a series circuit, the same current is through all components. (Can you think of a simple proof of this?) You can use the total current measured in step 3 and Ohm's law to compute the voltage drop across each resistor. Compute V_{AB} by multiplying the total current in the circuit by the resistance between **A** and **B**. Record the results as the computed voltage in Table 7–2.

5. Repeat step 4 for the other voltages listed in Table 7–2.

6. Measure and record each of the voltages listed in Table 7–2.

7. Using the source voltage (+15 V) and the *measured voltage drops* listed in Table 7–2, prove that the algebraic sum of the voltages is zero. Do this by applying the rules listed in the Summary of Theory. The polarities of voltages are shown in Figure 7–4.

_____

8. Repeat step 7 by starting at a different point in the circuit and traversing the circuit in the opposite direction.

_____

9. Open the circuit at point **B**. Measure the voltage across the open circuit. Call this voltage V_{open}. Prove that Kirchhoff's voltage law is still valid for the open circuit.

_____

CONCLUSION

EVALUATION AND REVIEW QUESTIONS

1. Why doesn't the starting point for summing the voltages around a closed loop make any difference?

2. Kirchhoff's voltage law applies to any closed path, even one without current. How did the result of step 9 show that this is true?

3. Based on the result you observed in step 9, what voltage would you expect in a 110 V circuit across an open (blown) fuse?

4. Use Kirchhoff's voltage law to find V_X in Figure 7–5:

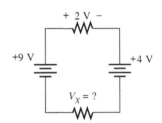

Figure 7–5

5. A 10 Ω resistor is in series with a bulb and a 12 V source.
    (a) If 8.0 V is across the bulb, what voltage is across the resistor? _____

    (b) What is the current in the circuit? _____

    (c) What is the resistance of the bulb? _____

52

FOR FURTHER INVESTIGATION

Resistors R_1, R_2, and R_3 used in this experiment have the same listed values as R_1, R_2, and R_3 from Experiment 5. Refer to your results of the current-voltage curve on Plot 1 of Experiment 5. Using the measured voltage in Table 7–2, find the current in the resistor based on Plot 5–1 of Experiment 5.

$I_1 = \underline{\hspace{2cm}}$

$I_2 = \underline{\hspace{2cm}}$

$I_3 = \underline{\hspace{2cm}}$

What observation did you make from this about the current in a series circuit?

MULTISIM TROUBLESHOOTING

This experiment has four Multisim files on the website (www.prenhall.com/floyd). Three of the four files contain a simulated "fault"; one has "no fault." The file with no fault is named EXP7-4-nf. You may want to open this file to compare your results with the computer simulation. Then open each of the files with faults. Use the simulated instruments to investigate the circuit and determine the problem. The following are the filenames for circuits with troubleshooting problems for this experiment.

EXP7-4-f1

Fault: _____

EXP7-4-f2

Fault: _____

EXP7-4-f3

Fault: _____

8 The Voltage Divider

Name _____
Date _____
Class _____

OBJECTIVES

After performing this experiment, you will be able to:
1.   Apply the voltage divider rule to series resistive circuits.
2.   Design a voltage divider to meet a specific voltage output.
3.   Confirm experimentally the circuit designed in step 2.
4.   Determine the range of voltages available when a variable resistor is used in a voltage divider.

MATERIALS NEEDED

Resistors:
        One 330 Ω, one 470 Ω, one 680 Ω, one 1.0 kΩ
One 1.0 kΩ potentiometer

SUMMARY OF THEORY

A voltage divider consists of two or more resistors connected in series with a voltage source. Voltage dividers are used to obtain a smaller voltage from a larger source voltage. As you saw in Experiment 7, the voltage drops in a series circuit equal the source voltage. If you have two equal resistors in series, the voltage across each will be one-half of the source voltage. The voltage has thus been divided between the two resistors. The idea can be extended to circuits with more than two resistors and with different values.

        Consider the series circuit illustrated in Figure 8–1. If the resistors are equal, the voltage across R_2 will be one-half the source voltage. But what happens if one of the resistors is larger than the other? Since both resistors must have the *same* current, Ohm's law tells us that the larger resistor must drop a larger voltage. In fact, the voltage across any resistor in a series circuit can be found by finding the *fraction* of the total resistance represented by the resistor in question. For example, if a series resistor represents one-third of the total resistance, the voltage across it will be one-third of the source voltage.

        To find the voltage across R_2, the ratio of R_2 to R_T is multiplied by the source voltage. That is:

$$V_2 = V_S \left(\frac{R_2}{R_T} \right)$$

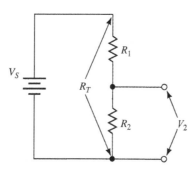

Figure 8–1

55

The voltage divider formula can be extended to find the voltage in a series circuit between any number of resistors. Call the resistance that is between the output terminals R_X. Then the voltage across this resistance can be written:

$$V_X = V_S \left(\frac{R_X}{R_T} \right)$$

where R_X represents the resistance between the output terminals.

This equation is a general form of the voltage divider equation. It can be stated as: "The output voltage from a voltage divider is equal to the input voltage multiplied by the ratio of the resistance between the output terminals to the total resistance." When several resistors are used, the output is generally taken with respect to the ground reference for the divider, as shown in Figure 8–2. In this case the output voltage can be found by substituting the value of R_2 and R_3 for R_X as shown.

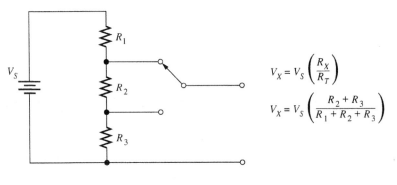

Figure 8–2

Voltage dividers can be made to obtain variable voltages by using a potentiometer. The full range of the input voltage is available at the output, as illustrated in Figure 8–3(a). If one desires to limit the output voltage, this can be done by using fixed resistors in series as illustrated in the example shown in Figure 8–3(b).

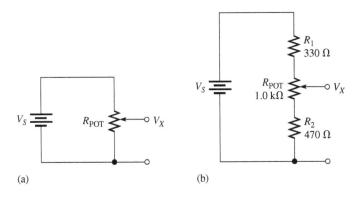

(a)   (b)

Figure 8–3

PROCEDURE

1. Obtain the resistors listed in Table 8–1. Measure each resistor and record the measured value in Table 8–1, column 3. Compute the total resistance for a series connection by adding the measured values. Enter the computed total resistance in Table 8–1.

Table 8–1

Resistor	Listed Value	Measured Value	$V_X = V_S\left(\dfrac{R_X}{R_T}\right)$	V_X (measured)
R_1	330 Ω			
R_2	470 Ω			
R_3	680 Ω			
R_4	1000 Ω			
Total			10.0 V	

2. Connect the resistors in the series circuit illustrated in Figure 8–4. With the source disconnected, measure the total resistance of the series connection and verify that it agrees with your computed value.

3. Apply the voltage divider rule to each resistor, one at a time, to compute the expected voltage across that resistor. Use the measured values of resistance and a source voltage of +10 V. Record the computed voltages (V_X) in Table 8–1, column 4.

4. Turn on the power and measure the voltage across each resistor. Record the measured voltage drops in Table 8–1, column 5. Your measured voltages should agree with your computed values.

5. Observe the voltages measured in step 4. In the space provided, draw the voltage divider, showing how you could obtain an output of +6.8 V.

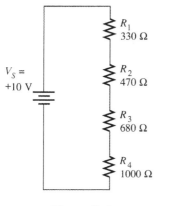

Figure 8–4

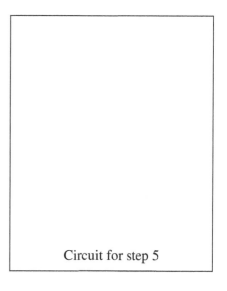

Circuit for step 5

6. Using the 330 Ω, 680 Ω, and 1.0 kΩ resistors, design a voltage divider with a +5.0 V output from a source voltage of +10 V. Draw your design in the space provided below.

7. Construct the circuit you designed and measure the actual output voltage. Indicate the measured value on your drawing.

8. Use two of the resistors from this experiment to design a divider with a +10 V input and a +7.5 V output. Draw your design in the space provided.

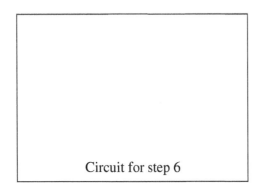

Circuit for step 6

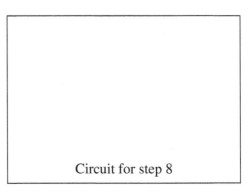

Circuit for step 8

9. The circuit shown in Figure 8–3(b) uses a 1.0 kΩ potentiometer and R_1 and R_2 to limit the range of voltages. Assume V_S is +10 V. Use the voltage divider formula to compute the minimum and maximum voltages available from this circuit:

$V_{MIN} =$ —————— $V_{MAX} =$ ——————

10. Construct the circuit computed in step 9. Measure the minimum and maximum output voltages:

$V_{MIN} =$ —————— $V_{MAX} =$ ——————

CONCLUSION

EVALUATION AND REVIEW QUESTIONS

1. (a) If all the resistors in Figure 8–4 were 10 times larger than the specified values, what would happen to the output voltage?

   (b) What would happen to the power dissipated in the voltage divider?

2. Refer to Figure 8–3(b). Assume V_S is 10.0 V.
   (a) If R_1 is open, what is the output voltage? _____

   (b) If R_2 is open, what is the output voltage? _____

3. If a student used a potentiometer in the circuit of Figure 8–3(b) that was 10 kΩ instead of 1.0 kΩ, what would happen to the range of output voltages?

4. For the circuit in Figure 8–5, compute the output voltage for each position of the switch:
   V_A _____
   V_B _____
   V_C _____
   V_D _____

5. Compute the minimum and maximum voltage available from the circuit shown in Figure 8–6:

   $V_{MIN} =$ _____ $V_{MAX} =$ _____

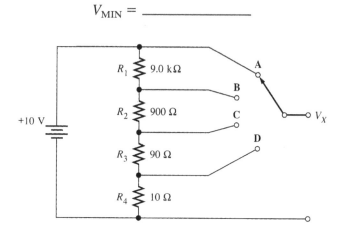

Figure 8–5

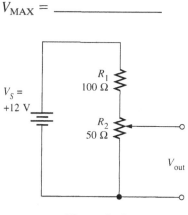

Figure 8–6

59

FOR FURTHER INVESTIGATION

The voltage dividers in this experiment were *unloaded*—that is, they were not required to furnish current to a load. If a load is put on the output, then current is supplied to the load and the output voltage of the divider changes. Investigate this effect by placing some load resistors on the voltage divider from this experiment (Figure 8–4). What size load resistor causes a 10% or less effect? Does the size of the resistors in the divider string affect your results? Why would you choose one set of resistors over another? Summarize your findings in a short laboratory report.

MULTISIM TROUBLESHOOTING

This experiment has four Multisim files on the website (www.prenhall.com/floyd). Three of the four files contain a simulated "fault"; one has "no fault". The file with no fault is named EXP8-3-nf. You may want to open this file to compare your results with the computer simulation. Then open each of the files with faults. Use the simulated instruments to investigate the circuit and determine the problem. The following are the filenames for circuits with troubleshooting problems for this experiment.

EXP8-3-f1

     Fault: _____

EXP8-3-f2

     Fault: _____

EXP8-3-f3

     Fault: _____

Application Assignment 4

Name _____
Date _____
Class _____

REFERENCE
Floyd, Chapter 4, Application Assignment: Putting Your Knowledge to Work

Step 1   Draw the schematic of the circuit.

Step 2   Determine the voltages.

	Specified (5%)	Computed
Pin 1:	0.0 V	
Pin 2:	2.8 V	
Pin 3:	12.0 V	
Pin 4:	10.4 V	
Pin 5:	8.0 V	
Pin 6:	7.3 V	
Pin 7:	6.2 V	

Step 3   Modify the existing circuit if necessary. Draw the schematic.

Step 4   Determine the life of the 6.5 Ah battery for your circuit.

Step 5   Step-by-step test procedure:

Step 6   Troubleshooting:
                Fault 1 (no voltage at any pin): _____
                Fault 2 (12 V at pins 3 and 4; all others have 0 V): _____
                Fault 3 (12 V at all pins except 0 V at pin 1): _____
                Fault 4 (12 V at pin 6 and 0 V at pin 7): _____
                Fault 5 (3.3 V at pin 2): _____

RELATED EXPERIMENT

MATERIALS NEEDED
Resistors:
        One 3.3 kΩ, one 6.8 kΩ, two 10 kΩ

DISCUSSION
Voltage dividers are commonly used to set up reference voltages. For example, a logic voltage can be compared to a specified threshold level to see if it is above or below the threshold. The voltage divider circuit shown in Figure AA–4–1 provides both positive and negative reference voltages. TTL (transistor-transistor logic) uses positive voltages, whereas ECL (emitter-coupled logic) uses negative voltages. The voltages required are shown and can be obtained from a single adjustable power supply. Use the resistors listed in the materials list to design a voltage divider that produces the voltages shown. Each voltage should be within 5% of the required voltage. Set up your circuit, and measure the voltages with respect to ground. Summarize your results in a short laboratory report.

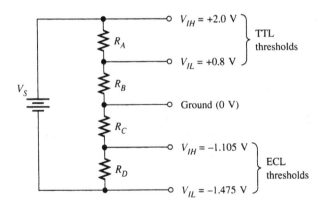

Figure AA–4–1

Checkup 4

Name _____
Date _____
Class _____

REFERENCE
Floyd, Chapter 4, and Buchla, Experiments 7 and 8

1. In a series circuit, all components have the same:
   (a) voltage drop (b) power (c) resistance (d) current

2. A 50 V power supply is connected to five 1.0 kΩ series resistors. The current in each resistor is:
   (a) 0.1 mA (b) 10 mA (c) 50 mA (d) 250 mA

3. Three equal value resistors are connected in series. If the total resistance is 10 kΩ, what is the value of each resistor?
   (a) 3.3 kΩ (b) 10 kΩ (c) 20 kΩ (d) 30 kΩ

4. The sum of the *IR* drops in a series circuit is:
   (a) smaller than the applied voltage (b) equal to the largest of the *IR* drops
   (c) greater than the applied voltage (d) equal to the applied voltage

5. A voltage source of 10 V is connected to two series resistors. The voltage across the first resistor is found to be 8.0 V. The voltage across the second resistor is:
   (a) 2.0 V (b) 8.0 V (c) 10 V (d) 18 V

6. A 10 V supply is available to operate a dc motor that requires 6.0 V at 0.25 A. A series dropping resistor is needed to drop the voltage to the required level for the motor. The resistance should be:
   (a) 1.5 Ω (b) 16 Ω (c) 24 Ω (d) 40 Ω

7. Two resistors are connected in series. The first resistor is found to have 5.0 V across it, and the second resistor is found to have 10 V across it. Which resistor has the greatest resistance?
   (a) the first (b) the second (c) neither (d) cannot be determined

8. Two resistors are connected in series. The first resistor has 5.0 V across it, and the second resistor has 10 V across it. Which resistor dissipates the greatest power?
   (a) the first (b) the second (c) neither (d) cannot be determined

9. A 75 W bulb is designed to operate from a 115 V source. If two 75 W bulbs are connected in series with a 115 V source, the total power dissipated by both bulbs is:
   (a) 37.5 W (b) 75 W (c) 150 W (d) 300 W

10. A 75 W bulb is designed to operate from a 115 V source. If two 75 W bulbs are connected in series with a 230 V source, the total power dissipated by both bulbs is:
    (a) 37.5 W (b) 75 W (c) 150 W (d) 300 W

11. Find the total resistance of the series combination of a 1.20 MΩ resistor, a 620 kΩ resistor, and a 150 kΩ resistor.

12. Assume you need a 36 V source but have only three 12 V batteries available. Draw the connection of the batteries to provide the required voltage.

13. Assume a faulty series circuit has no current due to an open circuit. How would you use a voltmeter to locate the open circuit?

14. A series circuit consists of three 50 Ω resistors, each rated for 250 mW.
    (a)   What is the largest voltage that can be applied before exceeding the power rating of any resistor?

    (b)   How much current is in the circuit at this voltage?

15. The total resistance of a series circuit is 2.2 kΩ. What fraction of the input voltage will appear across a 100 Ω resistor?

16. An 8 Ω series limiting resistor is used to limit the current in a bulb to 0.375 A with 12 V applied.
    (a)   Determine the resistance of the bulb.

    (b)   If the voltage source is increased to 15 V, what additional series resistance will limit the current to the same 0.375 A?

17. In Experiment 7 (Series Circuits), you used resistors that ranged in value from 330 Ω to 2.2 kΩ. How would your results have changed if all of the resistors were 20% larger than called for?

9 Parallel Circuits

Name _____

Date _____

Class _____

OBJECTIVES

After performing this experiment, you will be able to:
1.   Demonstrate that the total resistance in a parallel circuit decreases as resistors are added.
2.   Compute and measure resistance and currents in parallel circuits.
3.   Explain how to troubleshoot parallel circuits.

MATERIALS NEEDED

Resistors:

One 3.3 kΩ, one 4.7 kΩ, one 6.8 kΩ, one 10 kΩ

One dc ammeter, 0–10 mA

SUMMARY OF THEORY

A *parallel* circuit is one in which there is more than one path for current. Parallel circuits can be thought of as two parallel lines, representing conductors, with a voltage source and components connected between the lines. This idea is illustrated in Figure 9–1. The source voltage appears across each component. Each path for current is called a *branch*. The current in any branch is dependent only on the resistance of that branch and the source voltage.

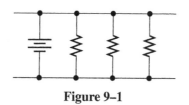

Figure 9–1

As more branches are added to a parallel circuit, the total resistance decreases. This is easy to see if you consider each added path in terms of conductance. Recall that conductance is the reciprocal of resistance. As parallel branches are added, new paths are provided for current, increasing the conductance. There is more total current in the circuit. If the total current in a circuit increases, with no change in source voltage, the total resistance must decrease according to Ohm's law. The total conductance of a parallel circuit is the sum of the individual conductances. This can be written:

$$G_T = G_1 + G_2 + G_3 + \ldots + G_n$$

By substituting the definition for resistance into the formula for conductance, the reciprocal formula for resistance in parallel circuits is obtained. It is:

$$\frac{1}{R_T} = \frac{1}{R_1} + \frac{1}{R_2} + \frac{1}{R_3} + \cdots + \frac{1}{R_n}$$

In parallel circuits, there are junctions where two or more components are connected. Figure 9–2 shows a circuit junction labeled A. Since electrical charge cannot accumulate at a point, the current into the junction must be equal to the current from the junction. In this case, $I_1 + I_2$ is equal to $I_3 + I_4$. This idea is expressed in Kirchhoff's current law, which is stated:

> The sum of the currents entering a circuit junction is equal to the sum of the currents leaving the junction.

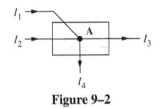

Figure 9–2

One important idea can be seen by applying Kirchhoff's current law to a point next to the source voltage. The current leaving the source must be equal to the sum of the individual branch currents. While Kirchhoff's voltage law is developed in the study of series circuits, and the current law is developed in the study of parallel circuits, both laws are applicable to any circuit.

In Experiment 8, you observed how a series circuit causes voltage to be divided between the various resistances. In parallel circuits, it is the *current* that is divided between the resistances. Keep in mind that the larger the resistance, the smaller the current. The general current divider rule can be written:

$$I_X = \left(\frac{R_T}{R_X}\right) I_T$$

Notice that the fraction R_T/R_X is always less than 1.0 and represents the fraction of the total current in R_X. This equation can be simplified for the special case of exactly two resistors. The special two-resistor current divider is written:

$$I_1 = \left(\frac{R_2}{R_1 + R_2}\right) I_T \qquad\qquad I_2 = \left(\frac{R_1}{R_1 + R_2}\right) I_T$$

PROCEDURE

1.   Obtain the resistors listed in Table 9–1. Measure and record the value of each resistor.

Application Assignment 5

REFERENCE

Floyd, Chapter 5, Application Assignment: Putting Your Knowledge to Work

■ Determine the maximum power dissipated by R_{SH} in Figure 5–55 for each range setting.

■ How much voltage is there from A to B in Figure 5–55 when the switch is set to the 2.5 A range and the current is 1 A?

■ The meter indicates 250 mA. How much does the voltage across the meter circuit from A to B change when the switch is moved from the 250 mA position to the 2.5 A position?

■ Assume the meter movement has a resistance of 4 Ω instead of 6 Ω. Specify any changes necessary in the circuit of Figure 5–55.

RELATED EXPERIMENT

MATERIALS NEEDED
Resistors:

Two 1.0 kΩ, one 1.5 kΩ, one 1.8 kΩ, one 2.2 kΩ

DISCUSSION
There are several ways of finding an open resistor in a parallel arrangement; presented here is a different method that you can investigate. The method is based on the voltage divider principle. A series 1.0 kΩ resistor is added to the parallel resistors, as shown in Figure AA–5–1. The parallel group represents an equivalent resistance in series with the 1.0 kΩ resistor. The voltage dropped across the parallel resistors will change if any resistor is open. Investigate this by connecting the circuit and measuring the voltage across the parallel group. Then, open one of the parallel resistors and measure the new voltage across the remaining group. Continue like this for each of the parallel resistors. Can you use your results to determine which resistor is open?

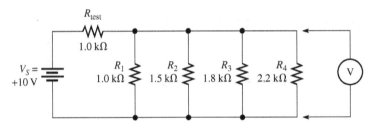

Figure AA–5–1

EXPERIMENTAL RESULTS

Checkup 5

REFERENCE

Floyd, Chap. 5, and Buchla, Experiment 9

1. In a parallel circuit, all components have the same:
   (a) voltage drop   (b) current   (c) power   (d) resistance

2. A 50 V power supply is connected to five 1.0 kΩ resistors connected in parallel. The total current from the source is:
   (a) 0.1 mA   (b) 10 mA   (c) 50 mA   (d) 250 mA

3. Three equal-value resistors are connected in parallel. If the total resistance is 10 kΩ, what is the value of each resistor?
   (a) 3.3 kΩ   (b) 10 kΩ   (c) 20 kΩ   (d) 30 kΩ

4. When a resistance path is added to a parallel circuit, the total resistance:
   (a) decreases   (b) remains the same   (c) increases

5. Assume a voltage of 27 V is connected across two equal parallel resistors. The current in the first resistor is 10 mA. The total resistance is:
   (a) 270 Ω   (b) 741 Ω   (c) 1.35 kΩ   (d) 2.7 kΩ

6. If one resistive branch of a parallel circuit is opened, the total current will:
   (a) decrease   (b) remain the same   (c) increase

7. Three resistors are connected in parallel. The first is 1.0 MΩ, the second is 2.0 MΩ, and the third is 10 kΩ. The total resistance is approximately:
   (a) 5 kΩ   (b) 10 kΩ   (c) 1 MΩ   (d) 3 MΩ

8. Three 75 W bulbs are connected in parallel across a 115 V line. The total power dissipated by the bulbs is:
   (a) 25 W   (b) 75 W   (c) 115 W   (d) 225 W

9. Assume an unknown resistor is in parallel with a 68 Ω resistor. The total resistance of the combination is 40.5 Ω. The resistance of the unknown resistor is:
   (a) 25 Ω   (b) 34 Ω   (c) 75 Ω   (d) 100 Ω

10. An ammeter with an internal resistance of 40 Ω and a full-scale deflection of 10 mA is needed to measure a full-scale current of 100 mA. The shunt resistor that will accomplish this has a value of:
    (a) 4.0 Ω   (b) 4.44 Ω   (c) 400 Ω   (d) 444 Ω

11.   In Experiment 9 (Parallel Circuits), you were asked to find the parallel resistance of a group of resistors as new ones were placed in the circuit. What was happening to the total *conductance* of the circuit as more resistors were placed in parallel? Why?

12.   Explain why electrical house wiring is done with parallel circuits.

13.   A 115 V source provides 30 A into a four-branch parallel circuit. The first three branch currents are 10 A, 8 A, and 5 A.
        (a)   What is the current in the fourth branch?

        (b)   What is the resistance of the fourth branch?

        (c)   What is the total resistance of the circuit?

14.   Assume there is a current of 350 μA into a parallel combination of two resistors, R_1 and R_2. The resistance of R_1 is 5.6 kΩ, and the resistance of R_2 is 8.2 kΩ. Compute the current in each resistor.

15.   Four 1.0 kΩ resistors are connected in parallel. The total power dissipated is 200 mW.
        (a)   What power is dissipated in each resistor?

        (b)   What is the source voltage?

16.   For the parallel circuit shown in Figure C–5–1, assume the ammeter reads 1.75 mA. What is the likely cause of trouble? Justify your answer.

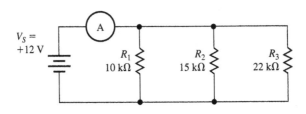

Figure C–5–1

74

10

Series-Parallel Combination Circuits

Name _____

Date _____

Class _____

OBJECTIVES

After performing this experiment, you will be able to:
1. Use the concept of equivalent circuits to simplify series-parallel circuit analysis.
2. Compute the currents and voltages in a series-parallel combination circuit and verify your computation with circuit measurements.

MATERIALS NEEDED

Resistors:
One 2.2 kΩ, one 4.7 kΩ, one 5.6 kΩ, one 10 kΩ

SUMMARY OF THEORY

Most electronic circuits are not just series or just parallel circuits. Instead they may contain combinations of components. Many circuits can be analyzed by applying the ideas developed for series and parallel circuits to them. Remember that in a *series* circuit the same current is through all components, and that the total resistance of series resistors is the sum of the individual resistors. By contrast, in *parallel* circuits, the applied voltage is the same across all branches and the total resistance is given by the reciprocals formula.

In this experiment, the circuit elements are connected in composite circuits containing both series and parallel combinations. The key to solving these circuits is to form equivalent circuits from the series or parallel elements. You need to recognize when circuit elements are connected in series or parallel in order to form the equivalent circuit. For example, in Figure 10–1(a) we see that the identical current must go through both R_2 and R_3. We conclude that these resistors are in series and could be replaced by an equivalent resistor equal to their sum. Figure 10–1(b) illustrates this idea. The circuit has been simplified to an equivalent parallel circuit. After finding the currents in the equivalent circuit, the results can be applied to the original circuit to complete the solution.

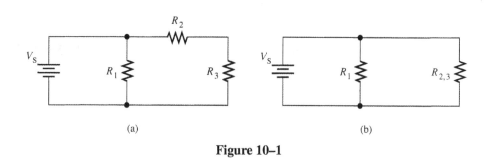

(a)   (b)

Figure 10–1

The answer to two questions will help you identify a series or parallel connection:
(1) Will the *identical* current go through both components? If the answer is yes, the components are in series. (2) Are *both ends* of one component connected directly to *both ends* of another component? If yes, the components are in parallel. The components that are in series or parallel may be replaced with an equivalent component. This process continues until the circuit is reduced to a simple series or parallel circuit. After solving the equivalent circuit, the process is reversed in order to apply the solution to the original circuit. This idea is studied in this experiment.

PROCEDURE

1. Measure and record the actual values of the four resistors listed in Table 10–1.

Table 10–1

Component	Listed Value	Measured Value
R_1	2.2 kΩ	
R_2	4.7 kΩ	
R_3	5.6 kΩ	
R_4	10.0 kΩ	

2. Connect the circuit shown in Figure 10–2. Then answer the following questions:

    (a) Are there any resistors for which the identical current will go through the resistors? Answer yes or no for each resistor:

    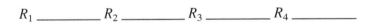
    R_1 _____ R_2 _____ R_3 _____ R_4 _____

    (b) Does any resistor have both ends connected directly to both ends of another resistor? Answer yes or no for each resistor:

    R_1 _____ R_2 _____ R_3 _____ R_4 _____

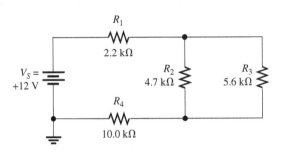

Figure 10–2

3.　　The answer to these questions should clarify in your mind which resistors are in series and which resistors are in parallel. You can begin solving for the currents and voltages in the circuit by replacing resistors that are either in series or in parallel with an equivalent resistor. In this case, begin by replacing R_2 and R_3 with an equivalent resistor labeled $R_{2,3}$. Draw the equivalent circuit in the space provided. Show the value of all components including $R_{2,3}$.

4.　　The equivalent circuit you drew in step 3 is a simple series circuit. Compute the total resistance of this equivalent circuit and enter it in the first two columns of Table 10–2. Then disconnect the power supply and measure the total resistance to confirm your calculation.

Table 10–2

	Computed		Measured
	Voltage Divider	Ohm's Law	
R_T			
I_T			
V_1			
$V_{2,3}$			
V_4			
I_2			
I_3			
V_T	12.0 V	12.0 V	

5.　　The voltage divider rule can be applied directly to the series equivalent circuit to find the voltages across R_1, $R_{2,3}$, and R_4. Find V_1, $V_{2,3}$, and V_4 using the voltage divider rule. Tabulate the results in Table 10–2 in the Voltage Divider column.

6.　　Find the total current, I_T, in the circuit by substituting the total voltage and the total resistance into Ohm's law. Enter the computed total current in Table 10–2 in the Ohm's Law column.

7.　　In the equivalent series circuit, the total current is through R_1, $R_{2,3}$, and R_4. The voltage drop across each of these resistors can be found by applying Ohm's law to each resistor. Compute V_1, $V_{2,3}$, and V_4 using this method. Enter the voltages in Table 10–2 in the Ohm's Law column.

8. Use $V_{2,3}$ and Ohm's law to compute the current in R_2 and R_3 of the original circuit. Enter the computed current in Table 10–2. As a check, verify that the computed sum of I_2 and I_3 is equal to the computed total current.

9. Measure the voltages V_1, $V_{2,3}$, and V_4. Enter the measured values in Table 10–2.

10. Change the original circuit to the new circuit shown in Figure 10–3. In the space provided below, draw an equivalent circuit by combining the resistors that are in series. Enter the values of the equivalent resistors on your schematic and in Table 10–3.

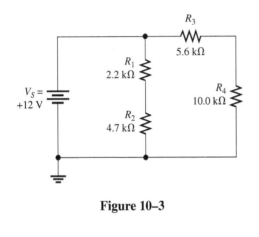

Figure 10–3

Table 10–3

	Computed	Measured
$R_{1,2}$		
$R_{3,4}$		
R_T		
I_T		
$I_{1,2}$		
$I_{3,4}$		
V_1		
V_2		
V_3		
V_4		

11. Compute the resistance of each branch ($R_{1,2}$ and $R_{3,4}$) for the equivalent circuit drawn in step 10. Then compute the total resistance, R_T, of the equivalent circuit. Apply Ohm's law to find the total current I_T. Enter the computed resistance for each branch and the total resistance, R_T, in Table 10–3.

12. Complete the computed values for the circuit by solving for the remaining currents and voltages listed in Table 10–3. Then measure the voltages across each resistor to confirm your computation.

CONCLUSION

EVALUATION AND REVIEW QUESTIONS

1. The voltage divider rule was developed for a series circuit, yet it was applied to the circuit in Figure 10–2.

   (a) Explain.

   (b) Could the voltage divider rule be applied to the circuit in Figure 10–3? Explain your answer.

2. As a check on your solution of the circuit in Figure 10–3, apply Kirchhoff's voltage law to each of two separate paths around the circuit. Show the application of the law.

3. Show the application of Kirchhoff's current law to the junction of R_2 and R_4 of the circuit in Figure 10–3.

4. In the circuit of Figure 10–3, assume you found that I_T was the same as the current in R_3 and R_4.

   (a) What are the possible problems?

   (b) How would you isolate the specific problem using only a voltmeter?

5. The circuit in Figure 10–4 has three equal resistors. If the voltmeter reads +8.0 V, find V_S.

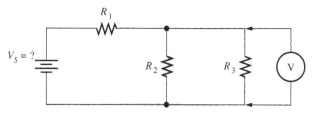

Figure 10–4

FOR FURTHER INVESTIGATION

Figure 10–5 illustrates another series-parallel circuit using the same resistors. Develop a procedure for solving the currents and voltages throughout the circuit. Summarize your procedure in a laboratory report. Confirm your method by computing and measuring the voltages in the circuit.

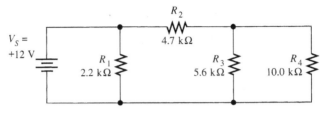

Figure 10–5

MULTISIM TROUBLESHOOTING

This experiment has four Multisim files on the website (www.prenhall.com/floyd). Three of the four files contain a simulated "fault"; one has "no fault". The file with no fault is named EXP10-2-nf. You may want to open this file to compare your results with the computer simulation. Then open each of the files with faults. Use the simulated instruments to investigate the circuit and determine the problem. The following are the filenames for circuits with troubleshooting problems for this experiment.

EXP10-2-f1

    Fault: _____

EXP10-2-f2

    Fault: _____

EXP10-2-f3

    Fault: _____

11 The Superposition Theorem

OBJECTIVES

After performing this experiment, you will be able to:

1.   Apply the superposition theorem to linear circuits with more than one voltage source.
2.   Construct a circuit with two voltage sources, solve for the currents and voltages throughout the circuit, and verify your computation by measurement.

MATERIALS NEEDED

Resistors:
        One 4.7 kΩ, one 6.8 kΩ, one 10.0 kΩ

SUMMARY OF THEORY

To superimpose something means to lay one thing on top of another. The superposition theorem is a means by which we can solve circuits that have more than one independent voltage source. Each source is taken, one at a time, as if it were the only source in the circuit. All other sources are replaced with their internal resistance. (The internal resistance of a dc power supply or battery can be considered to be zero.) The currents and voltages for the first source are computed. The results are marked on the schematic, and the process is repeated for each source in the circuit. When all sources have been taken, the overall circuit can be solved. The algebraic sum of the superimposed currents and voltages is computed. Currents that are in the same direction are added; those that are in opposing directions are subtracted with the sign of the larger applied to the result. Voltages are treated in a like manner.

        The superposition theorem will work for any number of sources *as long as you are consistent in accounting for the direction of currents and the polarity of voltages.* One way to keep the accounting straightforward is to assign a polarity, right or wrong, to each component. Tabulate any current which is in the same direction as the assignment as a positive current and any current which opposes the assigned direction as a negative current. When the final algebraic sum is completed, positive currents are in the assigned direction; negative currents are in the opposite direction of the assignment. In the process of replacing a voltage source with its zero internal resistance, you may completely short out a resistor in the circuit. If this occurs, there will be no current in that resistor for this part of the calculation. The final sum will still have the correct current.

PROCEDURE

1. Obtain the resistors listed in Table 11–1. Measure each resistor and record the measured value in Table 11–1.

2. Construct the circuit shown in Figure 11–1. This circuit has two voltage sources connected to a common reference ground.

Table 11–1

	Listed Value	Measured Value
R_1	4.7 kΩ	
R_2	6.8 kΩ	
R_3	10.0 kΩ	

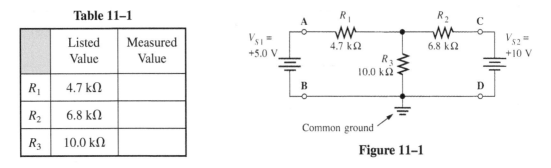

Figure 11–1

3. Remove the 10 V source and place a jumper between the points labeled **C** and **D**, as shown in Figure 11–2. This jumper represents the internal resistance of the 10 V power supply.

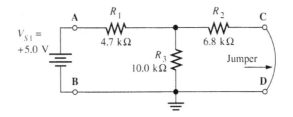

Figure 11–2

4. Compute the total resistance, R_T, seen by the +5.0 V source. Then temporarily remove the +5.0 V source and measure the resistance between points **A** and **B** to confirm your calculation. Record the computed and measured values in Table 11–2.

Table 11–2 Computed and measured resistances.

	Quantity	Computed	Measured
Step 4	R_T (V_{S1} operating alone)		
Step 7	R_T (V_{S2} operating alone)		

5. Use the source voltage, V_{S1}, and the total resistance to compute the total current, I_T, from the +5.0 V source. This current is through R_1, so record it as I_1 in Table 11–3. Use the current divider rule to determine the currents in R_2 and R_3. The current divider rule for I_2 and I_3 is:

$$I_2 = I_T\left(\frac{R_3}{R_2 + R_3}\right) \qquad I_3 = I_T\left(\frac{R_2}{R_2 + R_3}\right)$$

82

Table 11–3 Computed and measured current and voltage.

	Computed Current			Computed Voltage			Measured Voltage		
	I_1	I_2	I_3	V_1	V_2	V_3	V_1	V_2	V_3
Step 5									
Step 6									
Step 8									
Step 9									
Step 10 (totals)									

Record all three currents as *positive* values in Table 11–3. This will be the assigned direction of current. Mark the magnitude and direction of the current in Figure 11–2. Note that the current divider rules shown in this step are only valid for this particular circuit.

6. Use the currents computed in step 5 and the measured resistances to calculate the expected voltage across each resistor of Figure 11–2. Then connect the +5.0 V power supply and measure the actual voltages present in this circuit. Record the computed and measured voltages in Table 11–3. Since all currents in step 5 were considered *positive,* all voltages in this step are also *positive.*

7. Remove the +5.0 V source from the circuit and move the jumper from between points **C** and **D** to between points **A** and **B.** Compute the total resistance between points **C** and **D.** Measure the resistance to confirm your calculation. Record the computed and measured resistance in Table 11–2.

8. Compute the current through each resistor in Figure 11–3. Note that this time the total current is through R_2 and divides between R_1 and R_3. Mark the magnitude and direction of the current on Figure 11–3. *Important:* Record the current as a *positive* current if it is in the same direction as recorded in step 5 and as a *negative* current if it is in the opposite direction as in step 4. Record the computed currents in Table 11–3.

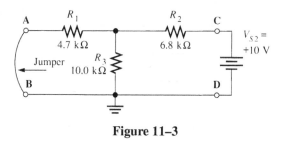

Figure 11–3

9. Use the currents computed in step 8 and the measured resistances to compute the voltage drops across each resistor. Record the computed voltage drops in Table 11–3. If the current through a resistor was a *positive* current, record the resistor's voltage as a *positive* voltage. If a current was a *negative* current, record the voltage as a *negative* voltage. Then connect the +10 V source as illustrated in Figure 11–3, measure, and record the voltages. The measured voltages should confirm your calculation.

83

10. Compute the algebraic sum of the currents and voltages listed in Table 11–3. Enter the computed sums in Table 11–3. Then replace the jumper between **A** and **B** with the +5.0 V source, as shown in the original circuit in Figure 11–1. Measure the voltage across each resistor in this circuit. The measured voltages should agree with the algebraic sums. Record the measured results in Table 11–3.

CONCLUSION

EVALUATION AND REVIEW QUESTIONS

1. (a) Prove that Kirchhoff's voltage law is valid for the circuit in Figure 11–1. Do this by substituting the measured algebraic sums from Table 11–3 into a loop equation written around the outside loop of the circuit.

   (b) Prove Kirchhoff's current law is valid for the circuit of Figure 11–1 by writing an equation showing the currents entering a junction are equal to the currents leaving the junction. Keep the assigned direction of current from step 5 and use the signed currents computed in step 10.

2. If an algebraic sum in Table 11–3 is negative, what does this indicate?

3. What would be the effect on the final result if you had been directed to record all currents in step 5 as negative currents instead of positive currents?

4.   In your own words, list the steps required to apply the superposition theorem.

5.   Use the superposition theorem to find the current in R_2 in Figure 11–4.

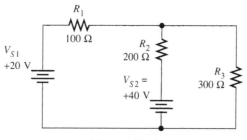

Figure 11–4

FOR FURTHER INVESTIGATION
Compute the power dissipated in each resistor in the circuits shown in Figures 11–1, 11–2, and 11–3. Using the computed results, find out if the superposition theorem is valid for power. Summarize your computations and conclusion.

MULTISIM TROUBLESHOOTING

This experiment has four Multisim files on the website (www.prenhall.com/floyd). Three of the four files contain a simulated "fault"; one has "no fault". The file with no fault is named EXP11-1-nf. You may want to open this file to compare your results with the computer simulation. Then open each of the files with faults. Use the simulated instruments to investigate the circuit and determine the problem. The following are the filenames for circuits with troubleshooting problems for this experiment.

EXP11-1-f1

        Fault: _____

EXP11-1-f2

        Fault: _____

EXP11-1-f3

        Fault: _____

13 The Wheatstone Bridge

OBJECTIVES

After performing this experiment, you will be able to:

1. Calculate the equivalent Thevenin circuit for a Wheatstone bridge circuit.
2. Verify that the Thevenin circuit determined in objective 1 enables you to compute the response to a load for the original circuit.
3. Balance a Wheatstone bridge and draw the Thevenin circuit for the balanced bridge.

MATERIALS NEEDED

Resistors:
        One 100 Ω, one 150 Ω, one 330 Ω, one 470 Ω
One 1 kΩ potentiometer
For Further Investigation:
   Wheatstone bridge sensitive to 0.1 Ω

SUMMARY OF THEORY

The Wheatstone bridge is a circuit with wide application in measurement systems. It can be used to accurately compare an unknown resistance with known precision resistors and is very sensitive to changes in the unknown resistance. The unknown resistance is frequently a transducer such as a strain gauge, in which very small changes in resistance are related to mechanical stress. The basic Wheatstone bridge is shown in Figure 13–1(a).

      Thevenin's theorem is very useful for analysis of the Wheatstone bridge, which is not a simple series-parallel combination circuit. From the perspective of the current in the load resistor, the method shown in Floyd's text is the most straightforward analysis technique. The following alternate method is very similar but preserves the ground reference point of the voltage source. This simplifies finding *all* of the currents in the bridge and finding the voltage at point **A** or **B** with respect to ground.

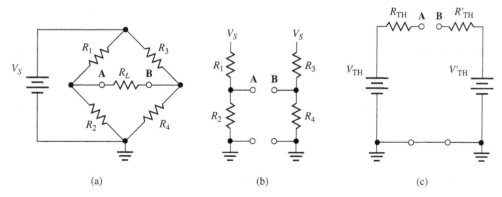

(a)   (b)   (c)

Figure 13–1

Begin by splitting the bridge into two independent voltage dividers as shown in Figure 13–1(b). Thevenin's theorem is applied between point **A** and ground for the left divider and between point **B** and ground for the right divider. V_A is the Thevenin voltage for the left divider, and V_B is the Thevenin voltage for the right divider. To find the Thevenin resistance, the source is replaced with a short, and the resistors on each side are seen to be in parallel. Two Thevenin circuits are then drawn as shown in Figure 13–1(c).

The load resistor can be added to the equivalent circuit as shown in Figure 13–2. Load current can be quickly found by the superposition theorem. The equations for the procedure are given for reference in Figure 13–2.

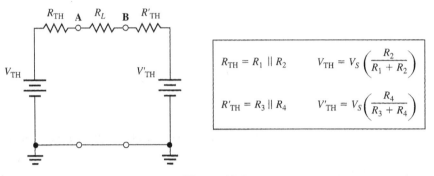

$$R_{TH} = R_1 \parallel R_2 \qquad V_{TH} = V_S \left(\frac{R_2}{R_1 + R_2} \right)$$

$$R'_{TH} = R_3 \parallel R_4 \qquad V'_{TH} = V_S \left(\frac{R_4}{R_3 + R_4} \right)$$

Figure 13–2

PROCEDURE

1. Measure and record the resistance of each of the four resistors listed in Table 13–1. R_4 is a 1 kΩ potentiometer. Set it for its maximum resistance and record this value.

Table 13–1

Component	Listed Value	Measured Value
R_1	100 Ω	
R_2	150 Ω	
R_3	330 Ω	
R_L	470 Ω	
R_4	1 kΩ pot.	

2. Construct the Wheatstone bridge circuit shown in Figure 13–3. R_4 should be set to its maximum resistance. Use the voltage divider rule to compute the voltage at point **A** with respect to ground and the voltage at **B** with respect to ground. Enter the computed V_A and V_B in Table 13–2.

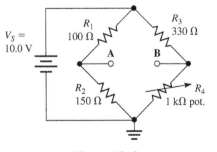

Figure 13–3

94

Table 13–2

	Computed	Measured
V_A		
V_B		
R_{TH}		
R'_{TH}		
V_L		

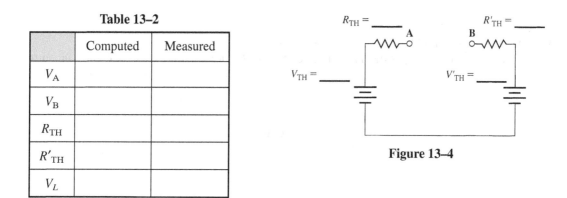

$R_{TH} =$ _____

$R'_{TH} =$ _____

A   B

$V_{TH} =$ _____ $V'_{TH} =$ _____

Figure 13–4

3. Measure V_A and V_B. Because these voltages are measured with no load, they are the Thevenin voltages for the bridge using the method illustrated in Figure 13–1. Enter the measured voltages in Table 13–2 and show them on Figure 13–4.

4. Compute the Thevenin resistance on the left side of the bridge in Figure 13–3 by mentally replacing V_S with a short. Notice that this causes R_1 to be in parallel with R_2. Repeat the process for the right side of the bridge. Enter the computed Thevenin resistances, R_{TH} and R'_{TH}, in Table 13–2 and on Figure 13–4. Then replace V_S with a short and measure R_{TH} and R'_{TH}.

5. Draw in the load resistor between the **A** and **B** terminals in the circuit of Figure 13–4. Show the value of the measured resistance of R_L. Use the superposition theorem to compute the expected voltage drop, V_L, across the load resistor. Enter the computed voltage drop in Table 13–2.

6. Place the load resistor across the **A** and **B** terminals of the bridge circuit (Figure 13–3) and measure the load voltage, V_L. If the measured value does not agree with the computed value, recheck your work. Enter the measured V_L in Table 13–2.

7. Monitor the voltage across the load resistor and carefully adjust R_4 until the bridge is balanced. When balance is achieved, remove the load resistor. Measure the voltage from **A** to ground and the voltage from **B** to ground. Since the load resistor has been removed, these measurements represent the Thevenin voltages of the balanced bridge. Enter the measured voltages on Figure 13–5.

8. Replace the voltage source with a short. With the short in place, measure the resistance from point **A** to ground and from point **B** to ground. Enter the measured resistances on Figure 13–5.

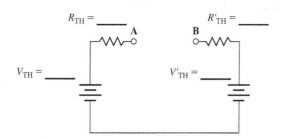

$R_{TH} =$ _____ $R'_{TH} =$ _____

A   B

$V_{TH} =$ _____ $V'_{TH} =$ _____

Figure 13–5 Thevenin circuit for balanced bridge.

9.   Use the superposition theorem to combine the two Thevenin sources into one equivalent circuit. Show the values of the single equivalent circuit on Figure 13–6.

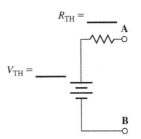

$R_{TH} = $ _____

$V_{TH} = $ _____

Figure 13–6 Net Thevenin circuit for balanced bridge.

CONCLUSION

EVALUATION AND REVIEW QUESTIONS

1.   If you doubled the load resistor in a Wheatstone bridge, the load current would *not* be half as much. Why not?

2.   (a)   Does a change in the load resistor change the currents in the arms of an *unbalanced* bridge?

        (b)   Does a change in the load resistor change the currents in the arms of a *balanced* bridge? Explain.

3. (a) What would happen to the load current of an *unbalanced* bridge if all the bridge resistors were doubled in size?

(b) What would happen to the load current of a *balanced* bridge if all the bridge resistors were doubled in size?

4. (a) What would happen to the load current of an *unbalanced* bridge if the source voltage were doubled?

(b) What would happen to the load current of a *balanced* bridge if the source voltage were doubled?

5. Compute the load current for the bridge in Figure 13–7. Show your work.

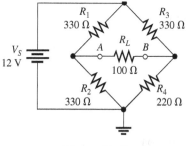

Figure 13–7

FOR FURTHER INVESTIGATION

To do this investigation, you will need a calibrated Wheatstone bridge, capable of making resistance measurements within 0.1 Ω or better. A Wheatstone bridge can determine the location of a short to ground in a multiple conductor cable. The bridge is connected to make a ratio measurement. Simulate a multiple conductor cable with two small diameter wires (#24 gauge or higher) at least 150 ft long. You will need an accurate total resistance of the wire, which you can obtain from the Wheatstone bridge or a sensitive ohmmeter. Place a short to ground at some arbitrary location along the wire. See Figure 13–8 for a diagram. The wire forms two legs of a Wheatstone bridge as illustrated.

Call the total resistance of the wire r (down and back) and the resistance of the wire to the fault a. The bridge is balanced, and the resistance a is determined by the equation shown in Figure 13–8. The fractional distance to the fault is the ratio of a to $(1/2)$ r. If you know the total length of the wire, you can find the distance to the fault by setting up a proportion. Investigate this and report on your results.

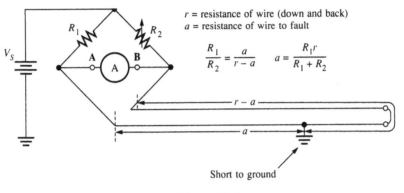

r = resistance of wire (down and back)
a = resistance of wire to fault

$$\frac{R_1}{R_2} = \frac{a}{r - a} \qquad a = \frac{R_1 r}{R_1 + R_2}$$

Short to ground

Figure 13–8

MULTISIM TROUBLESHOOTING

This experiment has four Multisim files on the website (www.prenhall.com/floyd). Three of the four files contain a simulated "fault"; one has "no fault". The file with no fault is named EXP13-7-nf. You may want to open this file to compare your results with the computer simulation. Then open each of the files with faults. Use the simulated instruments to investigate the circuit and determine the problem. The following are the filenames for circuits with troubleshooting problems for this experiment.

EXP13-7-f1
    Fault: _____

EXP13-7-f2
    Fault: _____

EXP13-7-f3
    Fault: _____

Application Assignment 6

Name _____
Date _____
Class _____

REFERENCE

Floyd, Chapter 6, Application Assignment: Putting Your Knowledge to Work

Step 1   Draw the schematic.

Step 2   Specify how to connect the power supply so that all resistors are in series and pin 2 has the highest voltage.

_____

Steps 3–6   Complete Table AA–6–1. Determine the unloaded output voltages, the loaded output voltages, the percent deviation between the loaded and unloaded voltages, and the load currents.

Table AA–6–1

10 MΩ Load	$V_{OUT\,(2)}$	$V_{OUT\,(3)}$	$V_{OUT\,(4)}$	% Deviation	$I_{LOAD\,(2)}$	$I_{LOAD\,(3)}$	$I_{LOAD\,(4)}$
None							
Pin 2 to ground							
Pin 3 to ground							
Pin 4 to ground							
Pin 2 to ground				2			
Pin 3 to ground				3			
Pin 2 to ground				2			
Pin 4 to ground				4			
Pin 3 to ground				3			
Pin 4 to ground				4			
Pin 2 to ground				2			
Pin 3 to ground				3			
Pin 4 to ground				4			

Specify the minimum value for the fuse: _____

Step 7 Troubleshooting:

Case 1: _____

Case 2: _____

Case 3: _____

Case 4: _____

Case 5: _____

Case 6: _____

Case 7: _____

Case 8: _____

RELATED EXPERIMENT

MATERIALS NEEDED

Resistors:

One 68 Ω, one 100 Ω, one 560 Ω

DISCUSSION

The application assignment involved determining the effects of a load on a voltage divider. Similar effects occur with a resistive matching network. A circuit is designed to match the resistance of a source and load. A circuit that performs this function is called an *attenuator pad*. The L-section shown in Figure AA–6–1 is a loaded voltage divider designed to match a higher resistance to a lower resistance. The load resistance is taken into account in the design of the divider network. The total resistance looking into the L-pad is very close to 600 Ω, the same as the source resistance.

Construct the circuit, and connect a 600 Ω source. The source can be a signal generator with an internal 600 Ω resistance set for a 1.0 kHz sine wave or a dc power supply with a series 600 Ω resistor. Set the source voltage to 5.0 V with a source open. Then connect the L-pad and load and observe V_{in} and V_{out}. What happens to V_{in} when the L-pad and load are connected? Compute and measure the attenuation (ratio of V_{out} to V_{in}). Is there a whole-number ratio between the output voltage and the input voltage? Write a short report on your results.

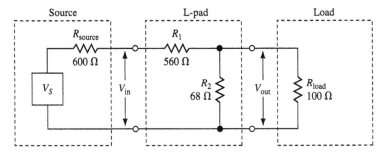

Figure AA–6–1

Checkup 6

Name _____

Date _____

Class _____

REFERENCE

Floyd, Chap. 6, and Buchla, Experiments 10, 11, 12, and 13

1. The term that best describes the analysis of a series-parallel circuit is:
   (a) one current   (b) same voltage   (c) equivalent circuits   (d) multiple sources

2. If two resistors in a series-parallel circuit are connected in series, the voltage across each will be:
   (a) the same   (b) proportional to the resistance
   (c) inversely proportional to the resistance   (d) equal to the source voltage

3. To minimize loading effects on a voltage divider, the load should be:
   (a) much smaller than the divider resistors   (b) equal to the smallest divider resistor
   (c) equal to the largest divider resistor   (d) much larger than the divider resistors

4. When a load resistor is connected to a voltage divider, the current from the source:
   (a) increases   (b) decreases   (c) stays the same

5. Assume a voltmeter has a sensitivity factor of 10,000 Ω/V. On the 10 V scale, the meter will have an internal resistance of:
   (a) 1000 Ω (b) 10,000 Ω (c) 100 kΩ (d) 1.0 MΩ

6. For the circuit shown in Figure C–6–1, the two resistors that are in series are:
   (a) R_1 and R_2 (b) R_2 and R_3 (c) R_2 and R_4 (d) R_3 and R_4

7. For the circuit shown in Figure C–6–1, the equivalent Thevenin voltage is:
   (a) 1.0 V   (b) 3.0 V   (c) 4.0 V   (d) 12 V

8. For the circuit shown in Figure C–6–1, the equivalent Thevenin resistance is:
   (a) 6.67 kΩ (b) 10 kΩ (c) 16.7 kΩ (d) 30 kΩ

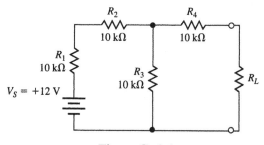

Figure C–6–1

9.   To apply the superposition theorem, each source is taken one at a time, as if it were the only source in the circuit. The remaining sources are replaced with:
        (a) their internal resistance   (b) a low resistance
        (c) a high resistance   (d) an open circuit

10.   To find the Thevenin voltage of a source, you could measure:
        (a) the voltage across the load   (b) the current in the load
        (c) the load resistance   (d) the open-circuit output voltage

11.   Assume a 15 kΩ load resistor is connected to the output terminals of the circuit shown in Figure C–6–1. Compute the voltage and current in the load.

12.   Determine the total resistance between the terminals for Figure C–6–2.

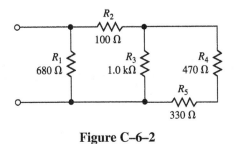

Figure C–6–2

13.   In Experiment 10 (Series-Parallel Combination Circuits), you were directed to solve a series-parallel circuit using two methods (Ohm's law and the voltage divider theorem). Why do you think this was requested?

14.   In Experiment 11 (The Superposition Theorem), you replaced each source with a jumper wire, one at a time. Is this valid for all sources? Explain.

15.   In Experiment 13 (The Wheatstone Bridge), you used Thevenin's theorem to compute parameters for a loaded bridge. Could the methods of Experiment 10 (Series-Parallel Combination Circuits) have been used instead? Why or why not?

14 Magnetic Devices

Name _____
Date _____
Class _____

OBJECTIVES

After performing this experiment, you will be able to:

1. Determine the pull-in voltage and release voltage for a relay.
2. Connect relay circuits including a relay latching circuit.
3. Explain the meaning of common relay terminology.

MATERIALS NEEDED

One DPDT relay with a low-voltage dc coil
Two LEDs: one red, one green
One SPST switch
Two 330 Ω resistors

SUMMARY OF THEORY

Magnetism plays an important role in a number of electronic components and devices including inductors, transformers, relays, solenoids, and transducers. Magnetic fields are associated with the movement of electric charges. By forming a coil, the magnetic field lines are concentrated, a fact that is used in most magnetic devices. Wrapping the coil on a core material such as iron, silicon steel, or permalloy provides two additional advantages. First, the magnetic flux is increased because the *permeability* of these materials is much higher than air. Permeability is a measure of how easily magnetic field lines pass through a material. Permeability is not a constant for a material but depends on the amount of flux in the material. The second advantage of using a magnetic core material is that the flux is more concentrated.

A common magnetic device is the *relay*. The relay is an electromagnetic switch with one or more sets of contacts used for controlling large currents or voltages. The switch contacts are controlled by an electromagnet, called the coil. Contacts are specified as either *normally open* (NO) or *normally closed* (NC) when no voltage is applied to the coil. Relays are *energized* by applying the rated voltage to the coil. This causes the contacts to either close or open.

Relays, like mechanical switches, are specified in terms of the number of independent switches (called *poles*) and the number of contacts (called *throws*). Thus, a single-pole double-throw (SPDT) relay has a single switch with two contacts—one normally open and one normally closed. An example of such a relay in a circuit is shown in Figure 14–1. With S_1 open, the motor is off and the light is on. When S_1 is closed, coil CR_1 is energized, causing the NO contacts to close and the NC contacts to open. This applies line voltage to the motor and at the same time removes line voltage from the light. Figure 14–1(a) is drawn in a manner similar to many industrial schematics, sometimes referred to as a ladder schematic. The NC contacts are indicated on this schematic with a diagonal line drawn through them. An alternative way of drawing the schematic is shown in Figure 14–1(b). In this drawing, the relay contacts are drawn as a switch.

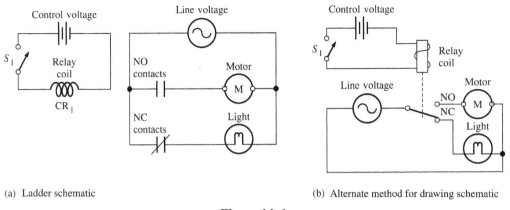

(a) Ladder schematic

(b) Alternate method for drawing schematic

Figure 14–1

Manufacturers specify relays in terms of the ratings for the coil voltage and current, maximum contact current, operating time, and so forth. The specification sheet shows the location of contacts and coil. If these are not available, a technician can determine the electrical wiring of contacts and coil by inspection and ohmmeter tests.

PROCEDURE

1. Obtain a double-pole double-throw (DPDT) relay with a low-voltage dc coil. The terminals should be numbered. Inspect the relay to determine which terminals are connected to the coil and which are connected to the contacts. The connection diagram is frequently drawn on the relay. Check the coil with an ohmmeter. It should indicate the coil resistance. Check contacts with the ohmmeter. NC contacts should read near zero ohms, and NO contacts should read infinite resistance. You may have difficulty determining which contact is movable until the coil is energized. In the space provided, draw a diagram of your relay, showing the coil, all contacts, and terminal numbers. Record the coil resistance on your drawing.

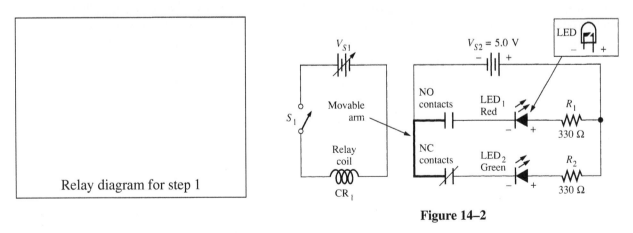

Relay diagram for step 1

Figure 14–2

2. Connect the circuit shown in Figure 14–2. In this circuit, only one pole of the relay is used. The movable arm is connected to the negative side of V_{S2}. Note carefully the direction of the light-emitting diodes (LEDs). LEDs are polarized and must be connected in the correct direction. V_{S1} is the control voltage and should be set to the specified coil voltage for the relay. V_{S2} represents a line voltage which is being controlled. For safety, a low voltage is used. Set V_{S2} for 5.0 V. If the circuit is correctly connected, the green LED should be on with S_1 open. Close S_1 and verify that the red LED turns on and the green LED goes off.

3. In this step, you will determine the *pull-in voltage* of the relay. The *pull-in voltage* is the minimum value of coil voltage which will cause the relay to switch. Turn V_{S1} to its lowest setting. With S_1 closed, gradually raise the voltage until the relay trips as indicated with the LEDs. Record the pull-in voltage in Table 14–1.

4. The *release voltage* is the value of the coil voltage at which the contacts return to the unenergized position. Gradually lower the voltage until the relay resets to the unenergized position as indicated by the LEDs. Record the release voltage in Table 14–1.

5. Repeat steps 3 and 4 for two more trials, entering the results of each trial in Table 14–1.

6. Compute the average pull-in voltage and the average release voltage. Enter the averages in Table 14–1.

7. In this step you will learn how to construct a latching relay. Connect the unused NO contacts from the other pole on the relay in parallel with S_1 as illustrated in Figure 14–3. Set V_{S1} for the rated coil voltage. Close and open S_1. Describe your observations.

_____

_____

Table 14–1

		Pull-in Voltage	Release Voltage
Steps 3 and 4	Trial 1		
Step 5	Trial 2		
	Trial 3		
Step 6	Average		

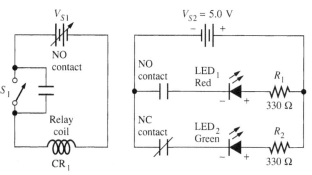

Figure 14–3

8. Remove the NO contact from around S_1. Connect the NC contact in series with S_1 as shown in Figure 14–4. Explain what happens.

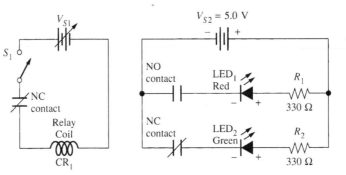

Figure 14–4

CONCLUSION

EVALUATION AND REVIEW QUESTIONS

1. Using the average pull-in voltage and the measured resistance of your relay coil, compute the average *pull-in current.* The pull-in current is defined as the minimum value of coil current at which the switching function is completed.

2. Repeat Question 1 for the *release current* using the average of the measured release voltage and the measured resistance of the coil.

3.   Hysteresis can be defined as the difference in response due to an increasing or decreasing signal. For a relay, it is the difference between the pull-in and the release voltage. Compute the hysteresis of your relay.

4.   (a)   Explain the difference between (a) SPDT and (b) DPST.

        (b)   Explain the meaning of NO and NC, as it applies to a relay.

5.   For the circuit of Figure 14–1, assume that when S_1 is closed, the light stays on and the motor remains off.
        (a)   Name two possible faults that could account for this.

        (b)   What procedure would you suggest to isolate the fault?

FOR FURTHER INVESTIGATION

A DPDT relay can be used to reverse a voltage—such as causing a dc motor to turn in the opposite direction. Consider the problem of reversing a 5.0 V power supply with a single-pole single-throw switch and a relay, as illustrated in the partial schematic in Figure 14–5. When the switch is closed, the red LED should be ON, but when it is opened, the voltage should reverse, causing the green LED to turn on. Complete the schematic that will accomplish the problem; then build and test your circuit.

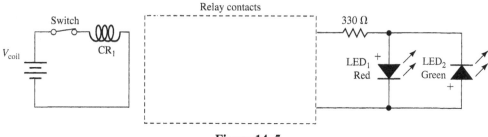

Figure 14–5

Application Assignment 7

Name _____

Date _____

Class _____

REFERENCE

Floyd, Chapter 7, Application Assignment: Putting Your Knowledge to Work

Step 1   Complete the diagram of the system and provide a wire list.

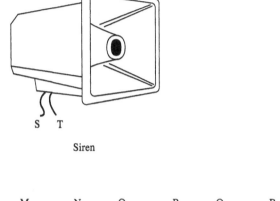

S   T

Siren

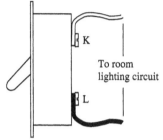

K

To room
lighting circuit

L

Wall switch

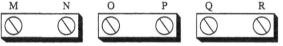

M   N   O   P   Q   R

Magnetic switches

2   1   3

U   V

System ON/OFF
toggle switch

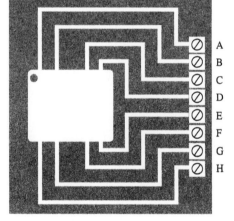

A
B
C
D
E
F
G
H

Relay terminal board

I   J

+   −

Battery

Figure AA–7–1

Wire list. (Two lines are given as an example.)

From	–	To	From	–	To
Relay board–pin A		Relay board–pin F			
Relay board–pin A		Magnetic switch–pin R			

Step 2   Develop a test procedure for the alarm system.

RELATED EXPERIMENT

MATERIALS NEEDED
One CdS photocell (Jameco 120299 or equivalent)
One DPDT relay with a low-voltage dc coil

DISCUSSION
Sometimes burglar alarms, such as the one you figured out in the application assignment, are constructed with a light sensor acting as a switch. Detection is accomplished by breaking a beam of light that is sensed by a photocell. A cadmium sulfide (CdS) photocell is a device that changes its resistance when light strikes it. This change in resistance can be used to energize a relay. Test this idea and devise a circuit in which a CdS cell controls the energizing of a relay. Show the schematic, the measurements you made, and conclusions about your circuit in a short report.

Checkup 7

Name _____

Date _____

Class _____

REFERENCE

Floyd, Chap. 7, and Buchla, Experiment 14

1. The magnetic field lines that surround a current-carrying wire are:
    (a) parallel to the current   (b) perpendicular toward the wire
    (c) perpendicular away from the wire (d) concentric circles surrounding the wire

2. The magnetic field strength of an electromagnet depends on:
    (a) current in the coil   (b) type of core material
    (c) number of turns of wire   (d) all of these

3. The magnetic unit most like resistance in an electrical circuit is:
    (a) reluctance   (b) magnetic flux   (c) permeability   (d) magnetomotive force

4. The magnetic unit most like current in an electrical circuit is:
    (a) reluctance   (b) magnetic flux
    (c) permeability   (d) magnetomotive force

5. The tesla is the unit of:
    (a) magnetizing force   (b) flux   (c) flux density   (d) reluctance

6. An electromagnetic device that normally is used to control contact closure in another circuit is a:
    (a) solenoid   (b) relay   (c) switch   (d) transistor

7. The effect that occurs when an increase in field intensity (H) produces little change in flux density (B) is called:
    (a) hysteresis   (b) saturation   (c) demagnetization   (d) permeability

8. The relative permeability of a substance is the ratio of absolute permeability to the permeability of:
    (a) a vacuum   (b) soft iron   (c) nickel   (d) glass

9. The flux density in an iron core depends on the field intensity and the:
    (a) area   (b) length   (c) permeability   (d) retentivity

10. Assume a coil with an mmf of 500 ampere-turns (At) has a flux of 100 μWb. The reluctance is:
    (a) 5×10^6 At/Wb   (b) 0.2×10^{-6} At/Wb
    (c) 0.5 At/Wb   (d) 5×10^{-6} At/Wb

11.   Show how to use one set of contacts on a DPDT relay to form a latching relay.

12.   In Experiment 14 (Magnetic Devices), you observed that the release voltage of a relay is less than the pull-in voltage. Explain why this is true.

13.   (a)   Compare the magnetic field strength of a 1000-turn coil that contains 100 mA of current with a 2000-turn coil that contains 50 mA of current.

       (b)   Compare the flux intensity of the two coils, assuming they are both the same length.

14.   Explain how Faraday's law accounts for the voltage from a basic dc generator.

15.   Assume a flux of 500 μWb is distributed evenly across a rectangular area that is 10 cm × 10 cm.
       (a)   What is the flux density?

       (b)   How much of the flux in (a) will pass through a 1 cm × 1 cm square?

15 Constructing and Observing a Circuit

Objectives

- Construct a circuit on a solderless circuit board.
- Identify parts used in the circuit including resistors, a capacitor, an integrated circuit, and LED.
- Given the equation for the operation, predict the time an LED will be on and off.
- Measure the total time (on and off) and compare it with your prediction.

Materials Needed

One solderless breadboard ("protoboard")
One 555 timer integrated circuit (IC)
One 100 µF capacitor
Resistors: one 680 Ω, two 4.7 kΩ
One red light-emitting diode (LED)
Optional – small 9 V battery and snap connector (or use 9 V power supply).

Summary of Theory

Solderless breadboards are a quick way to connect circuits for test. They are used in most of the experiments in this manual so you need to be familiar with how to wire circuits on them. Read over the explanation on breadboards in the Introduction to the Student before attempting to connect the circuit in this experiment.

This first circuit in this manual is an introductory experiment that will familiarize you with several components and how to wire them into a working circuit. The circuit is a light blinker and you will use an equation to calculate the approximate time it will be on. Don't worry about the detailed operation at this point.

The circuit uses an integrated circuit (IC), resistors, a capacitor, and an LED. These are described briefly here so that you can recognize them for the circuit. Later, you will learn more about these components. If possible, put the circuit on one end of your board.

Resistors are a fundamental component used in almost all electronic circuits. The purpose is to limit current by providing a certain amount of opposition. Resistors and the resistor color code are described in Experiment 16. The schematic symbol and appearance of a typical resistor is shown in Figure 15-1. In this experiment, the first three colors are given. A fourth color indicates the tolerance and will be either gold or silver on all of the resistors you use.

(a) Pictorial view   (b) Schematic symbol

Figure 15-1 Resistor.

Capacitors are components that are used to store charge temporarily. Electrolytic capacitors are polarized, meaning they must be put into the circuit in the proper direction, with the positive lead on the more positive voltage and the negative lead on the more negative voltage. An electrolytic capacitor is shown in Figure 15-2. On the symbol, the curved line represents the negative side.

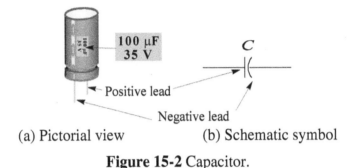

(a) Pictorial view   (b) Schematic symbol

Figure 15-2 Capacitor.

Light emitting diodes (LEDs) are devices that emit a specific color of light. All diodes are polarized, so attention must be given to the direction they are placed in a circuit. LEDs have a shorter lead on the negative side and a small flat spot on the diode on the same side. An LED is shown in Figure 15-3. The arrows on the schematic symbol represent light.

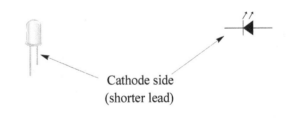

(a) Pictorial view   (b) Schematic symbol

Figure 15-3 Light-emitting diode (LED).

An integrated circuit is one that has multiple circuit elements in a single small package. The integrated circuit in this experiment is called a 555 timer. Most of the final circuit is internal to the 555 timer, but you will need to connect a few components to complete the circuit. The pictorial view and the schematic symbol for the 555 timer is illustrated in Figure 15-4. Notice on the pictorial view that the pins are counted counter-clockwise, starting from pin 1, which is next to a dot or other small mark. On the schematic symbol, pins are not shown in sequence; they are placed arbitrarily within the rectangle where it is most convenient for showing on a schematic.

Pins are numbered
by counting counter
clockwise.

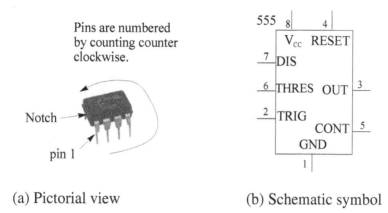

Notch

pin 1

(a) Pictorial view

(b) Schematic symbol

Figure 15-4

Procedure

1. Before constructing the circuit for a light blinker, calculate the time (in seconds) that the light should be *OFF* from the equation

$$t_{OFF} = 0.7 C_{EXT} (R_1 + R_2)$$

The value of C_{EXT} is 100 μF. This is entered in your calculator as 100EE –06. The value of the resistors are: R_1 = 4.7 kΩ and R_2 = 4.7 kΩ. Enter your calculated time off (t_{OFF}) in Table 15-1.

2. Calculate the time the light will be *ON* from the equation

$$t_{ON} = \left(\frac{R_1 + 2R_2}{R_1 + R_2} \right) t_{OFF} - t_{OFF}$$

You should find that the *ON* time is shorter the *OFF* time. Enter your calculated time on (t_{ON}) in Table 15-1.

3. Calculate the total time the light will be on and off. Enter the total time in Table 15-1.

Table 15-1

Quantity	Calculated	Measured
t_{OFF}		
t_{ON}		
t_{TOTAL}		

4. Construct the circuit shown in Figure 15-5. Try to keep wires no longer than necessary to make a neat circuit. Notice the orientation of the IC, the capacitor, and the LED. The circuit is shown constructed at one end of a small breadboard.

5. Connect power and ground to the circuit by connecting it to a power supply set to +9.0 V. Alternatively, you may use a small 9 V battery and battery connector. When you connect power, you should observe that the light blinks on and off.

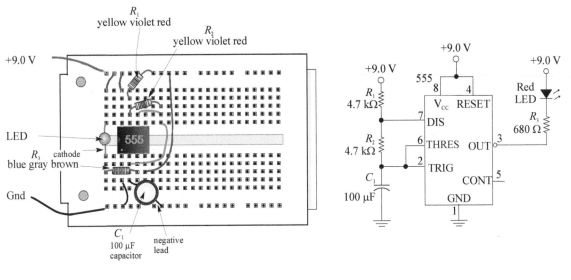

(a) Pictorial view   (b) Schematic

Figure 15-5 Light blinker. This figure is shown in color in Appendix C of the text.

6. Measure the total time (on and off) by counting the number of "blinks" in one minute. Calculate the total on and off time (in seconds) by dividing 60 seconds per minute by the observed "blinks" per minute. Enter this as the TOTAL time (on and off) in Table 15-1. Your measured result will not be exactly the same as the calculated value, but should agree within 10–20%, depending on the components used in the circuit.

Questions

1. From the equations in Steps 1 and 2, predict what will happen if C is smaller.

2. From the equations in Steps 1 and 2, predict what will happen if R_2 is 0 Ω.

3. What two changes would you suggest to make the ON time longer but not affect the OFF time?

A common problem is to locate parts and find the cost breakdown for a project. Assume you plan to build one prototype circuit and then you will consider how much you can build 1000 of the same circuit as part of a market analysis. Power will be supplied from an external source and is not part of the cost breakdown. Figure 15-6 shows a 3-D view of what the circuit board might look like. From the Materials Needed list, find the best price you can to build one prototype circuit on a solderless breadboard (Do not include the price of the breadboard in the analysis.) Then redo the analysis for constructing 1000 of these circuits on individual printed circuit boards. Assume the 1000 printed circuit boards can be supplied from a vendor for $1.22 each in quantities of 1000. Show the cost of parts for each board based on quantity discounts you can obtain.

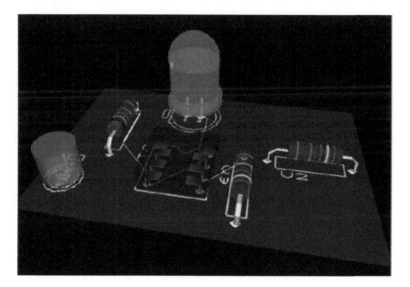

Figure 15-6 3-D View of the light blinker (Picture adapted from the computer program Ultiboard).

You can find many suppliers of electronic parts on the Internet. Some suppliers are:
    Allied Electronics (http://www.alliedelec.com)
    Electronix Express (http://www.elexp.com)
    Jameco Electronics (http://www.jameco.com)
    Mouser Electronics (http://www.mouser.com)

Part Description	Quantity needed	Cost each (1-10) (1000)		Supplier	Part Number

Summary:

16 Resistance

Objectives

- Use the resistor color code to determine the nominal resistance of resistors.
- Measure resistors with a DMM or VOM and compare the readings with the color-coded value.
- Test a basic circuit with different resistors and a potentiometer wired as a rheostat.

Materials Needed

Protoboard
Resistors (one of each): 470 Ω, 1.5 kΩ, 3.3 kΩ, 8.2 kΩ, 270 kΩ, 1.0 MΩ
One small 100 kΩ potentiometer for use in a protoboard
One red LED
One small screwdriver

Summary of Theory

Resistance is the opposition to current. Resistance is measured in units of *ohms* symbolized by the Greek letter Ω.

One of the most commonly used components for electronic circuits is the resistor, designed to provide a specific amount of resistance. Resistors are color-coded to indicate the amount of resistance, as described in the text. For reference, the resistor color code is shown in Table 16-1.

When you measure a resistor's value, you can use either a digital multimeter (DMM) or a Volt-Ohm-Milliammeter (VOM). If you use a DMM that is autoranging, the meter is simply set to the ohms scale (indicated by the Ω symbol). If the meter has different ranges, you can choose the range that will show the most number of significant digits. For a VOM, you should always check the Zero Adjust before making a measurement or after changing ranges. For any resistance measurement, the resistor must be isolated from other components. You may hold one end and a meter lead in one hand, but do not hold the resistor itself with the other hand, to avoid reading your body resistance.

In this experiment, you will measure a series of resistors. Then you will connect several different resistors in a basic circuit. It is important to use the specified resistors in this experiment to avoid burning out the light-emitting diode, used as an indicator or light. The red LED in this experiment is one that is useful in an astronomer's flashlight, for reading maps at night, and to avoid losing "night vision." A rheostat is introduced to show how you can control the current in the LED.

Table 16-1 Resistor color codes

Color	Digit	Multiplier	Tolerance
Black	0	10^0	
Brown	1	10^1	1% (five band)
Red	2	10^2	2% (five band)
Orange	3	10^3	
Yellow	4	10^4	
Green	5	10^5	
Blue	6	10^6	
Violet	7	10^7	
Gray	8	10^8	
White	9	10^9	
Gold	-	10^{-1}	5% (four band)
Silver	-	10^{-2}	10% (four band)

Procedure

1. Obtain the six resistors listed in the Materials Needed and organize them at your workbench in order of increasing resistance. Resistor R_1 will be the smallest-value resistor, and resistor R_6 will be the largest value.

2. Record the colors of each of the six resistors in Table 16-2. Use the color code to determine the nominal resistance. Nominal resistance is not the actual resistance – it is only what the color-coded value indicates. Then measure each resistor and show its measured resistance in the table. The first line is completed as an example for a resistor called R_0.

3. Compute the percent difference between the measured and color-coded values for each resistor and record it in Table 16-2. The percent difference for all resistors should be shown as a positive value. The equation for percent difference is

$$\% \text{ difference} = \frac{\left| R_{measured} - R_{color\,code} \right|}{R_{color\,code}} \times 100$$

The vertical bars surrounding the numerator indicate absolute (positive) value of the expression.

Table 16-2

Resistor	Color of Band				Color-Code Value	Measured Value	% Difference
	1st	2nd	3rd	4th			
0	brown	green	brown	silver	150 Ω ± 10%	146 Ω	2.7%
1							
2							
3							
4							
5							
6							

4. Construct the LED flashlight shown in Figure 16-1. This is essentially an LED flashlight but without a switch. Set the voltage to +9.0 V (or use a 9 V battery). R_1 limits current to avoid burning out the LED. Observe the LED; then replace R_1 with each of the other five resistors listed in the Materials Needed list, one at a time.

Observations:

_____

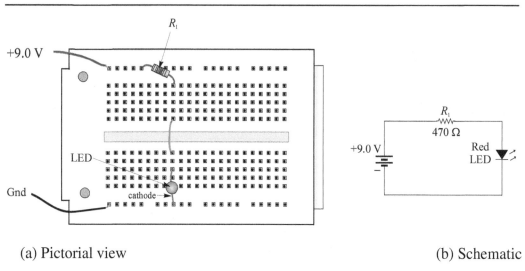

(a) Pictorial view   (b) Schematic

Figure 16-1

5. Obtain a 100 kΩ potentiometer and construct the circuit shown in Figure 16-2. Make sure each pin on the potentiometer is in a separate column on the protoboard. The first pin is in the same column as R_1, the middle pin is in the same column as the jumper wire. R_1 should be moved to place the potentiometer in the circuit. In this application, the potentiometer acts as a rheostat, a device that controls current. Turn the screw on the potentiometer and observe what happens.

Observations:

_____

121

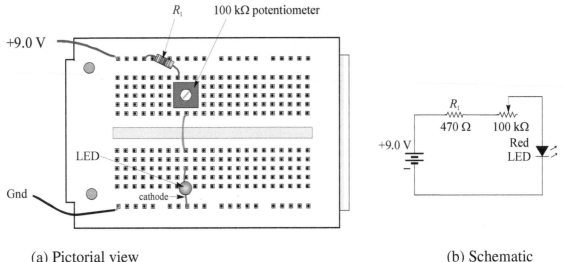

(a) Pictorial view   (b) Schematic

Figure 16-2

Questions

1. Were any resistors out of tolerance? If so, which one(s)?

2. What is the resistance of a resistor with the color bands as follows:
   (a) gray – red – yellow – silver _____
   (b) green – brown – green – gold _____
   (c) red – violet – black – silver _____
   (d) orange – blue – red – gold _____
   (e) brown – black – silver – gold _____

3. What are the color bands for each of the following resistors? Assume each resistor has a 5% tolerance.
   (a) 6.8 Ω _____
   (b) 100 Ω _____
   (c) 360 Ω _____
   (d) 560 kΩ _____
   (e) 1.5 MΩ _____

4. What is the difference between a potentiometer and a rheostat?

17 Power and Efficiency

Objectives

- Measure the input and output power from a 555 timer circuit when an LED is on.
- Measure the input power from a 555 timer circuit when an LED is off.
- Using the power data, determine the efficiency of the timer circuit when the LED is on.

Materials Needed

Materials from Experiment 15
One 47 kΩ resistor
One dc ammeter capable of measuring 15 mA (may use a DMM)

Summary of Theory

Power is the rate energy is transferred or converted to another form such as heat. All active devices in electronics convert dc power from a power supply to some form of output power. The 555 timer circuit that you have already used in earlier experiments is an example of an active device that you used to convert power from a power supply to light a small LED. Not all of the power from the power supply can go to the output; some is converted to heat by the 555 timer's internal circuitry.

In this experiment, you will modify the circuit from Experiment 15 to slow it down so you can measure input and output power when the LED is on and off. To determine the efficiency of the circuit when the LED is on, you will find the ratio of the output power to the input power. Of course, when the LED is off, there is no output power. Even so, the 555 timer will dissipate a small amount of power during this time. Keep in mind that the efficiency will change for different circuits.

Procedure

1. Replace R_2 in the circuit from Experiment 15 with a 47 kΩ resistor. Except for R_2, the schematic is identical to Figure 15-5(b). Place a dc ammeter (capable of reading 15 mA dc) in series (a single path) with the voltage source. The modified circuit and the schematic are shown in Figure 17-1. You should observe that the light blinks much slower than in Experiment 15. The blink rate is slowed to allow you to read the meter with the LED on and off.

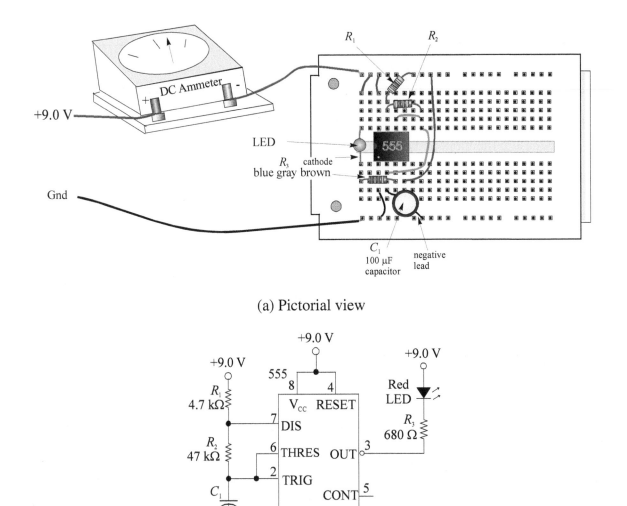

(a) Pictorial view

(b) Schematic

Figure 17-1 555 timer circuit with dc ammeter.

2. You should notice that the current from the power supply is much different when the LED is on than when it is off. Read the current in both instances and record the readings in Table 17-1.

3. Using your DMM, measure the voltage from the power supply. You may observe a very slight change in voltage when the LED blinks. Read the voltage in both instances and record the readings in Table 17-1.

4. From the measured current and voltage, calculate the input power (P_{in}) with the LED on and off. Record your calculated power in Table 17-1.

Table 17-1 Input power data.

Step	Parameter	Measured Value	Calculated Value
2	Current with LED off		
	Current with LED on		
3	Source voltage with LED off		
	Source voltage with LED on		
4	Input power with LED off, P_{in}		
	Input power with LED on, P_{in}		

5. In the following steps, you will need to know the resistance of R_3, the current limiting resistor that is in series with the LED. Turn off power, remove it from the circuit and measure its resistance. Record the resistance in Table 17-2, then restore the circuit to operating condition.

6. To find the power delivered to the load, you will first determine the current and voltage delivered to the load. In this case, assume the load is both the current limiting resistor (R_3) and the LED. Determine the current in the load when the LED is on by measuring the voltage across R_3 and applying Ohm's law. Enter the calculated current in Table 17-2.

Table 17-2 Output power data

Step	Parameter	Measured Value	Calculated Value
5	Resistance of R_3		
6	Load current with LED on		
7	Load voltage with LED on		
8	Output power with LED on, P_{out}		

7. Measure the voltage across the load (R_3 and the LED) when the LED is on. Enter the measured voltage in Table 17-2.

8. From the calculated current and measured voltage, calculate the output power (P_{out}) to the load. Enter the calculated output power delivered to the load in Table 17-2.

9. From your data, calculate the efficiency of the circuit when the LED is on. The equation for efficiency is given here for convenience. Use the value of P_{in} when the LED is on from Table 17-1 and the value of P_{out} when the LED is on from Table 17-2.

$$\text{Efficiency} = \frac{P_{out}}{P_{in}} \times 100\%$$

Efficiency of 555 timer circuit (with LED on) = _____

Questions

1. Why do you think you were instructed to determine the load current indirectly, instead of using an ammeter?

2. Do you think the efficiency of the 555 circuit will be more, less, or about the same if the supply voltage were increased to 12 V? Explain your answer.

3. If the voltage across a resistor doubles, what happens to the power it dissipates?

18 Voltage Dividers

Objectives

- Construct and test voltage dividers with both fixed outputs and variable outputs.
- Given a source voltage and resistors to select from, design a voltage divider that meets certain criteria.

Materials Needed

Protoboard
Resistors (one of each): 1.0 kΩ, 2.7 kΩ, 3.3 kΩ
One 1.0 kΩ potentiometer

Summary of Theory

This experiment uses series resistors to develop a voltage, which will always be less than the source voltage on any one resistor. The resistors "divide" the source voltage such that a larger resistor has a larger drop across it and a smaller resistor has a smaller drop across it.

The concept of dividing voltages in a series circuit between the various resistors is the basis of the name *voltage divider*. Voltage dividers are very useful for developing a particular voltage in many electronic circuits. In fact, the 555 timer that you investigated in earlier experiments, has an internal voltage divider to set certain voltages for comparison. In the 555 timer, three resistors (each 5 kΩ) are used to divide the power supply voltage in thirds. In general, a voltage divider consists of two or more resistors in series with a voltage source – the output is taken across one or more resistors.

As an example, consider the circuit shown in Figure 18-1. Because the two resistors are in series, the current is identical in both. Ohm's law tells us that this current will generate a larger voltage drop across the larger resistor and a smaller voltage drop across the smaller resistor. In fact, the voltage across any resistor in a series circuit is simply the fraction of the total resistance represented by the resistor in question. For example, if a given resistor has 20% of the total resistance, then it will have 20% of the source voltage across it.

To find the voltage across R_2, the ratio of R_2 to R_T is multiplied by the source voltage. That is,

$$V_2 = V_S \left(\frac{R_2}{R_T} \right)$$

Notice that the part of the expression within the parenthesis represents the fraction of the resistance for the resistor of interest.

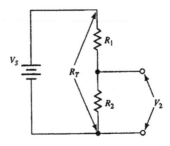

Figure 18-1

Sometimes it is useful to have a voltage dividers that has a range of voltage outputs, controlled by a potentiometer. In this experiment, you will start with a fixed divider, then change it so that is has a range of outputs.

Procedure

Test a voltage-divider

1. Obtain the resistors listed in Table 18-1. Measure each resistor and record the value in Table 18-1, column 3. When constructing electronic circuits, it is always a good idea to check values of resistors, to assure the resistance is correct before putting them in a circuit. Compute the total resistance of the series circuit by adding the actual measured values.

Table 18-1

Resistor	Listed Value	Measured Value
R_1	2.7 kΩ	
R_2	1.0 kΩ	
R_3	3.3 kΩ	
Total	7.0 kΩ	

2. Construct the circuit shown in Figure 18-2. Connect it to a power supply, which is set to +14 V. The divider is set up for three outputs labeled A, B, and C, as shown on the schematic. On the protoboard, these outputs are at the connection points between the resistors.

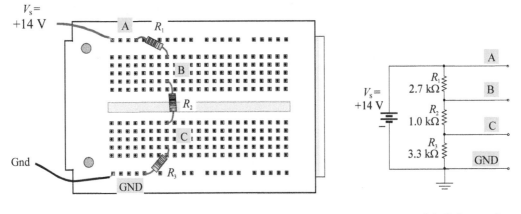

(a) Pictorial view   (b) Schematic

Figure 18-2

128

3. Using the voltage-divider rule, predict the voltage at points A, B, and C for the voltage-divider in Figure 18-2. Recall that a voltage designated with a single letter subscript is referenced to ground. Enter your predicted voltages in Table 18-2. For reference, the voltage divider rule is

$$V_X = V_S \left(\frac{R_X}{R_T} \right)$$

where V_X is the voltage across resistance R_X.

Table 18-2

Output Voltage	Predicted Value	Measured Value
V_A		
V_B		
V_C		

4. Measure the voltage at points A, B, and C with respect to ground. Enter the measured voltages in Table 18-2. Your results should be in good agreement with your predicted values.

Test a voltage-divider with a variable output
5. Change the circuit to one that will supply a variable output as shown in Figure 18-3. The potentiometer pins must be inserted into three different columns of the protoboard. The output is between the center pin and ground as shown.

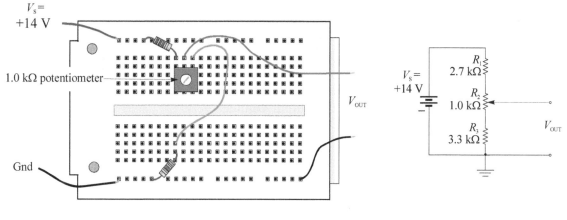

(a) Pictorial view   (b) Schematic

Figure 18-3

6. Predict the minimum and maximum output voltage for the voltage divider in Figure 18-3. Enter your predicted voltages in the second column of Table 18-3.

Table 18-3

Output Voltage	Predicted Value	Measured Value
$V_{OUT(MIN)}$		
$V_{OUT(MAX)}$		

7. Measure the minimum and maximum output voltage. Enter the measured voltages in the third column of Table 18-3. Your results should be in good agreement with your predicted values.

Questions

1. If all of the resistors in the voltage-divider in Figure 18-2 are ten times larger than specified, what happens to the output voltages? Explain your answer.

2. If R_1 and R_3 in Figure 18-3 are reversed, what is the new range of output voltage?

3. If a 10 kΩ potentiometer were used in place of the 1 kΩ potentiometer in the circuit in Figure 18-3, what is the new range of output voltage?

Design a Voltage Divider

Change the source voltage (power supply) to +5.0 V. This is a voltage commonly used in logic circuits (such as used in computers). Assume you need a voltage of +1.35 V to be used as a reference voltage in a logic circuit. From the fixed resistors in this experiment, choose two that can be set up as a voltage divider to give the required output. Show your design in the space provided. Test the design and indicate your results in a short report.

Calculations:

Circuit diagram:

Description:

19 Thevenin's Theorem

Objectives

- Find the equivalent Thevenin circuit for a resistive circuit.
- Prove that the equivalent circuit delivers the same current to a given load as the original circuit.

Materials Needed

Protoboard
Resistors (one of each): 330 Ω, 470 Ω, 560 Ω, 620 Ω, 820 Ω
One LED
Ammeter (0-15 mA)

Summary of Theory

In this experiment, you will use a method for forming an equivalent circuit called Thevenin's theorem.

Thevenin's theorem allows you to replace a complicated linear-circuit with a very simple circuit when there are two terminals of interest (usually the output terminals). The equivalent circuit is composed of a single voltage source and a series resistor. For example, a circuit such as the one shown in Figure 19-1(a) contains a resistive network. It can be simplified by Thevenin's theorem to the circuit shown in Figure 19-1(b), which will be equivalent from the standpoint of the load resistor.

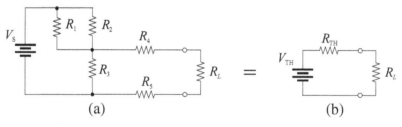

(a)   (b)

Figure 19-1

Two steps are required in order to simplify a circuit to its equivalent Thevenin circuit. The first step is to measure or compute the voltage at the output terminals with the load removed. This open-circuit voltage is the Thevenin voltage. The second step is to compute the resistance seen at the same open terminals if sources are replaced with their internal resistance. For voltage sources, the internal resistance is usually taken as zero, and for current sources, the internal resistance is infinite (open circuit). This resistance is the Thevenin resistance.

Procedure

1. Obtain the resistors listed in Table 19-1. Measure each resistor and record its actual resistance in Table 19-1.

Table 19-1

Resistor	Listed Value	Measured Value
R_1	330 Ω	
R_2	470 Ω	
R_3	620 Ω	
R_L	560 Ω	
R_{TH}	820 Ω	

2. Construct the circuit shown in Figure 18-2. The circuit is a three-resistor network with an LED load. Connect it to a power supply, which is set to +15 V. Measure the current in the LED load (I_{LED}) by reading the ammeter. Record the current in the space provided for the original circuit measurements in Table 19-2.

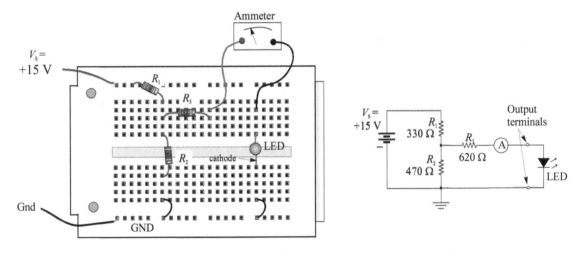

(a) Pictorial view   (b) Schematic

Figure 19-2 Original circuit.

Table 19-2

Quantity	Measured in Original Circuit	Measured in Thevenin Circuit
I_{LED}		
I_{RL}		

3. Replace the LED with a resistive load of 560 Ω. Measure the current in the resistive load (I_{RL}) and record it in Table 19-2.

134

Calculating the Thevenin Resistance

4. The Thevenin resistance and the Thevenin voltage are calculated with the load removed. To calculate the resistance, assume the voltage source (V_S) is replaced with a short (DO NOT actually do this). Then calculate the resistance (R_{TH}) looking from the output terminals looking back as illustrated in Figure 19-3. Use the measured values of your resistors to calculate the Thevenin resistance and enter the result in Table 19-3.

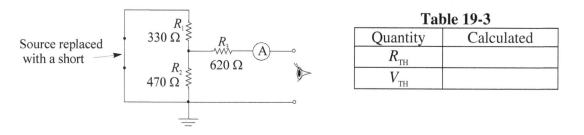

Table 19-3

Quantity	Calculated
R_{TH}	
V_{TH}	

Figure 19-3 Calculating the Thevenin resistance

Calculating the Thevenin Voltage

5. Calculate the Thevenin voltage by calculating the output voltage with no load. When the load is removed, there will be no current in R_3. For this reason, there is no voltage drop across R_3 and it is not part of the calculation of the Thevenin voltage. Apply the voltage-divider rule to R_1 and R_2 (using measured resistances) to calculate the voltage across R_2. This voltage is the same as the output voltage with no load and is therefore the Thevenin voltage (V_{TH}). Enter the calculated Thevenin voltage in Table 19-3.

6. From the calculated values in Table 19-3, draw the equivalent Thevenin circuit in the space below. Label the value of the Thevenin resistance and Thevenin voltage.

7. Remove the three resistors from the protoboard and construct the Thevenin circuit that you drew in step 6. Your calculated Thevenin resistance should be very close to 820 Ω, so use the 820 Ω resistor you measured in step 1 for the Thevenin resistance. Set the power supply to the voltage you calculated in step 5. Place the ammeter in series with the Thevenin resistance and the LED load as shown in Figure 19-4. Measure the current in the load and record it in Table 19-2 in the last column as I_{LED}.

8. Replace the LED with the 560 Ω resistor used as a load in the original circuit. Measure the current in the resistive load. Record the current in Table 19-2 as I_{RL} for the Thevenin circuit.

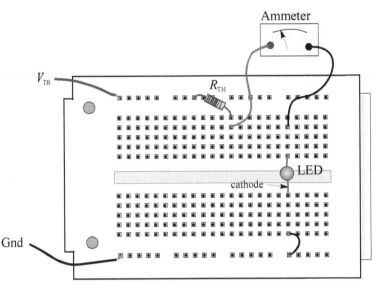

Figure 19-4 Thevenin circuit

Questions

1. (a) What voltage would you expect across a 1.0 kΩ load for the original circuit in this experiment?

   (b) What voltage would you expect across a 1.0 kΩ load for the Thevenin circuit in this experiment?

2. Assume a short is placed across the output terminals in the original circuit and the current is measured. Would you expect the current in the Thevenin circuit to be the same or different? Explain your answer.

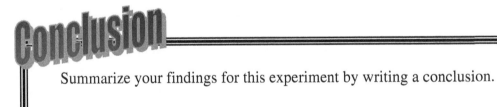

Summarize your findings for this experiment by writing a conclusion.

20 The Wheatstone Bridge

Objectives

- Calculate the load voltage for an unbalanced Wheatstone bridge.
- Construct the bridge circuit and confirm that the calculated voltage is nearly the same as the measured voltage.
- Use a 741C configured as a comparator to observe the effect of a temperature sensitive resistor.

Materials Needed

Protoboard

Resistors (one of each) 470 Ω, 680 Ω, 820 Ω, 1.5 kΩ

One small 1.0 kΩ potentiometer for use in a protoboard

Additional Materials Needed for Part 2

One 741C op-amp

Two LEDs – one red, one green

One 1.0 kΩ resistor

One thermistor 1 kΩ – Mouser part number 71-01C1001JP

Summary of Theory

The Wheatstone bridge is a circuit with wide application in measurement systems. It can be used to accurately compare an unknown resistance (in one of the arms of the bridge) with a standard adjustable resistor (in another arm). In the traditional Wheatstone bridge circuit, a galvanometer (a bidirectional sensitive ammeter) was used to detect any imbalance. The standard resistor would be adjusted until the galvanometer read zero, indicating balance. At balance, the setting of the standard resistance indicated the precise value of an unknown resistor. The traditional Wheatstone bridge, with R_3 as a variable resistor, is shown in Figure 20-1.

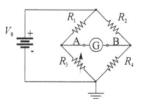

Figure 20-1 In the traditional bridge circuit, a galvanometer detected any imbalance.

A more sensitive way to detect when the bridge is balanced is with an electronic circuit called a *comparator*. This method is actually more sensitive than the traditional galvanometer and is cheaper. It is a simple circuit to set up, so it will be used to test for balance in Part 2 this experiment. You will use an op-amp as a comparator with LEDs as indicators of imbalance.

An unbalanced Wheatstone bridge is also used in certain instruments. This is a method used in most electronic scales; the resistance of one or more arms is controlled by the weight on the scale. The output voltage is calibrated to read the weight directly.

An unbalanced Wheatstone bridge can be solved application of Thevenin's theorem. In the first part of this experiment, you will calculate and measure the voltage across a load resistor in an unbalanced bridge. Then you will balance the bridge by adjusting it until there is no current (and thus no voltage) in the load resistor. Finally, you will add a thermistor (a temperature sensitive resistor) to one leg of the bridge, and observe what happens as it is warmed or cooled.

Procedure
Part 1

1. Measure and record the resistance of each of the four resistors listed in Table 20-1. R_3 is a 1 kΩ potentiometer. Set it for its maximum resistance and record this value.

Table 20-1

Component	Listed Value	Measured Value
R_1	680 Ω	
R_2	1.5 kΩ	
R_3	1 kΩ potentiometer	(max)
R_4	820 Ω	
R_L	470 Ω	

2. Construct the Wheatstone bridge circuit shown in Figure 20-2. R_3 should be set to its maximum resistance. Use the voltage divider rule to compute the voltage at points A and B. Enter the computed V_A and V_B in Table 20-2.

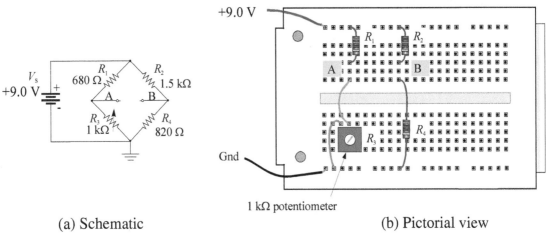

(a) Schematic   (b) Pictorial view

Figure 20-2

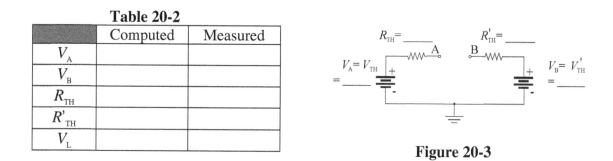

Table 20-2	Computed	Measured
V_A		
V_B		
R_{TH}		
R'_{TH}		
V_L		

Figure 20-3

3. Measure V_A and V_B. Because there is no load resistor, these voltages are the Thevenin voltages for each side of the bridge as shown in Figure 20-3. Enter the measured voltages in Table 20-2 and on Figure 20-3.

4. Calculate the Thevenin resistance for each side of the bridge by mentally replacing the dc voltage source with a short. Notice this places the resistors on each side in parallel as discussed in the text. Enter the computed R_{TH} and R'_{TH} in Table 20-2.

5. Replace V_S with a short and measure R_{TH} and R'_{TH}. Enter the measured values in Table 20-2 and on Figure 20-3.

6. Place the load resistor between points A and B. Calculate the voltage across the load. Then measure the load voltage. It should be in good agreement with your calculated value. Enter the calculated and measured values in Table 20-2.

7. Monitor the voltage across the load resistor and carefully adjust R_3 for no load voltage. When balance is achieved, remove the load resistor and measure the resistance of R_3. You will need to isolate R_3 from the rest of the circuit and measure only the resistance that was part of the bridge circuit.

    Resistance of R_3 for balanced bridge = _____

8. Prove that the products of the opposite diagonal resistances are equal in your balanced bridge.

Part 2: Adding a comparator to the bridge

9. Add the 741C op-amp configured as a comparator to the bridge as shown in Figure 20-4. Notice the location of pin 1 on the pictorial view. Pin numbers are shown on the schematic and are counted counterclockwise around the integrated circuit. Pin 4 is connected to –9 V and pin 7 is connected to +9 V.

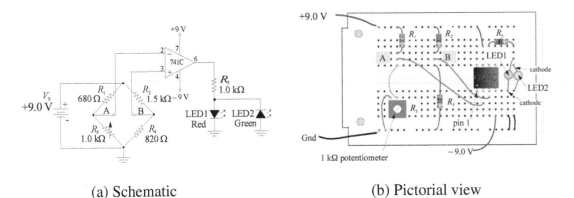

(a) Schematic   (b) Pictorial view

Figure 20-4 This figure is shown in color in Appendix C of the text.

10. The LEDs are so sensitive to an imbalance, it is not possible to adjust R_3 for the condition where both are on. Observe what happens as you adjust R_3 back and forth near balance.

Observations:

_____

11. Replace R_4 with the 1 kΩ thermistor. The thermistor is a temperature-sensitive resistor. Adjust R_3 for balance but leave it so that LED1 is just on at the threshold. Then hold the thermistor between your fingers and observe what happens. The heat from your hand changes the resistance of the thermistor.

Observations:

_____

Questions
1. Could the bridge be balanced if R_2 and R_4 were reversed? Explain your answer.

2. What effect would an increase in the source voltage have on a Wheatstone bridge?

21 Constructing a Reed-Switch Motor

Objectives

- Construct a reed-switch motor.
- Test the motor and discuss how you would improve it.

Materials Needed

One 1″ × 6″ board approximately 10 inches long
Three Popsicle sticks
One nylon round through –hole spacer ¾″ long, 0.14″ diameter hole
(Keystone part #888; website is *www.keyelco.com*)
One nylon washer for #6 screw (Keystone part #3054)
One 1″ long #6 screw, round head
One reed switch (George Risk Industries model PS-2020 3/8″ diameter enclosed
switch – website is *www.grisk.com*)
One electromagnet
Two ceramic magnets (Forcefield part #585; website is
www.wondermagnet.com)
Sandpaper #60 or #80 grit, ¼ sheet
Two pieces of ½″ stiff foam – about 1″ × ½″ for supporting coil and reed switch

Tools needed: Drill with ¼ inch bit, Hot glue gun, soldering iron,
small square, small fine tooth "hobby" saw

Summary of Theory

Motors exploit the forces between magnets to turn electrical energy into motion.
Electromagnets can be controlled, so they are used in some way in almost all motors.

In this experiment, you use an electromagnet to provide the field coil for the motor.
The field coil will be pulsed by the closure of the reed switch.

In this experiment, you will work with hot glue. Use caution when you work
with hot glue. Do not touch the glue until it cools (a few minutes).

Procedure

1. Locate a point 4 inches from the end of your board and drill a shallow ¼" hole that is just deep enough to accept the head of a #6 screw. Place a small amount of hot glue in the hole and quickly insert the head of the 1" long screw into the hole. Check that it is straight up and down with a small square before the glue has a chance to set up. See Figure 21-1.

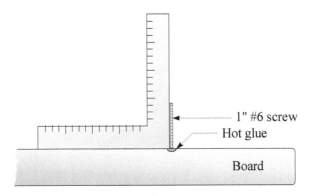

1" #6 screw

Hot glue

Board

Figure 21-1

2. Using a small piece of sand paper, square up the ends of two Popsicle sticks and sand the sticks so that they are the same length. Mark the center of the sticks with a line and hot glue the ¾" nylon spacer to one of the sticks so that it is flush with one side as shown in Figure 21-2. It is important that the spacer is centered and perpendicular to the Popsicle stick. This will become the rotor for your motor.

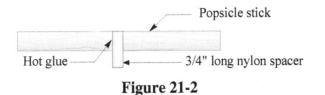

Popsicle stick

Hot glue ———— 3/4" long nylon spacer

Figure 21-2

3. Cut two ½" pieces of Popsicle sticks. You may want to use a small hobby saw to cut the Popsicle sticks; then lightly sand the ends. Hot glue the ½" pieces to the ends of the rotor to form the assembly shown in Figure 21-3.

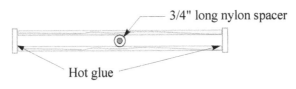

3/4" long nylon spacer

Hot glue

Figure 21-3

4. Hot glue two ceramic magnets with the south end to the outside. Place the small nylon washer over the screw and then place the rotor on the screw. Figure 21-4 shows the rotor at this stage of the motor project. The rotor should spin easily if you give it a small push.

Figure 21-4 Rotor assembly

5. Hot glue the reed switch to a small piece of ½″ foam spacer. Glue the assembly on the board just outside the radius of the rotor as shown in Figure 21-5. Hot glue a small ½″ foam spacer to the electromagnet, but do not glue it to the board yet.

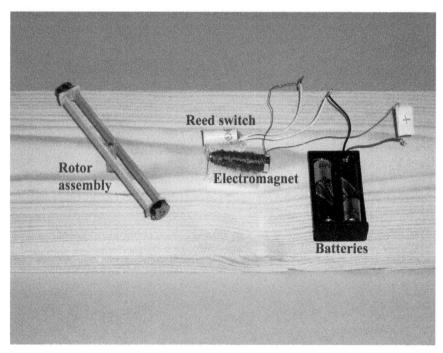

Figure 21-5 Final motor assembly

6. Wire the positive lead on the electromagnet to the positive lead of the batteries. Wire the negative lead from the batteries in series with the reed switch as shown in Figure 21-6. The electromagnet is positioned close to the reed switch with the head of the bolt (north) pointing away from the rotor. Spin the rotor; you can adjust the location of the electromagnet for best performance. Then glue the electromagnet and the battery pack in place and the motor is completed.

Observations:

_____

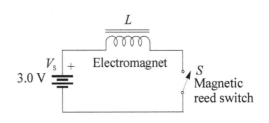

Figure 21-6 Schematic of motor.

Questions
1. Does the motor work because of attraction between magnets or repulsion? Explain how your answer.

2. Why doesn't the motor turn in either direction?

Design Problem

Describe with a diagram how you would improve the motor so that it had more speed and power. You can modify the motor so that it can support a small paper cylinder (such as the bottom part of a round ice cream container). Then convert the paper cylinder to a *Zoetrope*, an early way to view "moving pictures." Look up *Zoetrope* on the Internet and you will find various resources for constructing your own and using the motor to turn it.

PART II

AC Electronics Experiments

Introduction to the Student

PREPARING FOR LABORATORY WORK

The purpose of experimental work is to help you gain a better understanding of the principles of electronics and to give you experience with instruments and methods used by technicians and electronic engineers. You should begin each experiment with a clear idea of the purpose of the experiment and the theory behind the experiment. Each experiment requires you to use electronic instruments to measure various quantities. The measured data are to be recorded, and you need to interpret the measurements and draw conclusions about your work. The ability to measure, interpret, and communicate results is basic to electronic work.

Preparation before coming to the laboratory is an important part of experimental work. You should prepare in advance for every experiment by reading the *Reading, Objectives,* and *Summary of Theory* sections before coming to class. The *Summary of Theory* is *not* intended to replace the theory presented in the text—it is meant only as a short review to jog your memory of key concepts and to provide some insight to the experiment. You should also look over the *Procedure* for the experiment. This prelab preparation will enable you to work efficiently in the laboratory and enhance the value of the laboratory time.

This laboratory manual is designed to help you measure and record data as efficiently as possible. Techniques for using instruments are described in many experiments. Data tables are prepared and properly labeled to facilitate recording. Plots are provided where necessary. You will need to interpret and discuss the results in the section titled *Conclusion* and answer the *Evaluation and Review Questions.* The *Conclusion* to an experiment is a concise statement of your key findings from the experiment. Be careful of generalizations that are not supported by the data. The conclusion should be a specific statement that includes important findings with a brief discussion of problems, or revisions, or suggestions you may have for improving the circuit. It should directly relate to the objectives of the experiment. For example, if the objective of the experiment is to use the concept of equivalent circuits to simplify series-parallel circuit analysis, the conclusion can refer to the simplified circuit drawings and indicate that these circuits were used to compute the actual voltages and currents in the experiment. Then include a statement comparing the measured and computed results as evidence that the equivalent circuits you developed in the experiment were capable of simplifying the analysis.

THE LABORATORY NOTEBOOK

Your instructor may assign a formal laboratory report or a report may be assigned in the section titled *For Further Investigation.* A suggested format for formal reports is as follows:

1. *Title and date.*
2. *Purpose:* Give a statement of what you intend to determine as a result of the investigation.
3. *Equipment and materials:* Include a list of equipment model and serial numbers that can allow retracing if a defective or uncalibrated piece of equipment was used.
4. *Procedure:* Give a description of what you did and what measurements you made.
5. *Data:* Tabulate raw (unprocessed) data; data may be presented in graph form.
6. *Sample calculations:* Give the formulas that you applied to the raw data to transform them to processed data.
7. *Conclusion:* The conclusion is a specific statement supported by the experimental data. It should relate to the objectives for the experiment as described earlier. For example, if the purpose of the experiment is to determine the frequency response of a filter, the conclusion should describe the frequency response or contain a reference to an illustration of the response.

GRAPHING

A graph is a pictorial representation of data that enables you to see the effect of one variable on another. Graphs are widely used in experimental work to present information because they enable the reader to discern variations in magnitude, slope, and direction between two quantities. In this manual, you will graph data in many experiments. You should be aware of the following terms that are used with graphs:

abscissa: the horizontal or *x*-axis of a graph. Normally the independent variable is plotted along the abscissa.

dependent variable: a quantity that is influenced by changes in another quantity (the independent variable).

graph: a pictorial representation of a set of data constructed on a set of coordinates that are drawn at right angles to each other. The graph illustrates one variable's effect on another.

independent variable: the quantity that the experimenter can change.

ordinate: the vertical or *y*-axis of a graph. Normally the dependent variable is plotted along the ordinate.

scale: the value of each division along the *x*- or *y*- axis. In a linear scale, each division has equal weight. In a logarithmic scale, each division represents the same percentage change in the variable.

The following steps will guide you in preparing a graph:

1.   Determine the type of scale that will be used. A linear scale is the most frequently used and will be discussed here. Choose a scale factor that enables all of the data to be plotted on the graph without being cramped. The most common scales are 1, 2, 5, or 10 units per division. Start both axes from zero unless the data covers less than half of the length of the coordinate.

2.   Number the *major* divisions along each axis. Do not number each small division as it will make the graph appear cluttered. Each division must have equal weight. Note: The experimental data is *not* used to number the divisions.

3.   Label each axis to indicate the quantity being measured and the measurement units. Usually, the measurement units are given in parentheses.

4.   Plot the data points with a small dot with a small circle around each point. If additional sets of data are plotted, use other distinctive symbols (such as triangles) to identify each set.

5.   Draw a smooth line that represents the data trend. It is normal practice to consider data points but to ignore minor variations due to experimental errors. (Exception: calibration curves and other discontinuous data are connected "dot-to-dot.")

6.   Title the graph, indicating with the title what the graph represents. The completed graph should be self-explanatory.

SOLDERLESS BREADBOARDS

The solderless breadboard (also called "Experimenter Socket" or "protoboard") is a quick way to build circuits for test, so it is widely used in schools for building circuits such as those in this lab manual. Spring-loaded connectors are internal to the board and form groups of holes that are common connection points. There are different sizes and arrangements of solderless breadboards, but most are quite similar to the one described here (the Radio Shack #276–174).

Solderless breadboards are designed to connect small parts such as resistors, capacitors, or transistors together. Wires are also inserted in holes to connect them to parts or other wires. Wires should

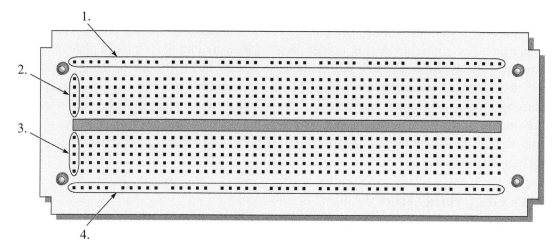

Figure II–1

be #22 or #24 solid core wire (not stranded) and be stripped about 3/8″. Figure II–1 shows a typical solderless breadboard. The following points are indicated on Figure II–1:

1. A horizontal row generally used by the experimenter for power or ground. These holes are all interconnected so that a wire or part inserted in any one is connected to all other holes in the row. Some boards have this row "broken" in the middle or have more than one long row.

2. A vertical column of five holes connected together internally with a spring-loaded connector. Any part inserted in any one of these holes can be joined to another part by inserting the second part into another of these holes. This group of five holes is isolated from all other groups of holes.

3. Another vertical column of five holes connected together internally. These are separate from the holes described in 2.

4. Another horizontal row with all of the holes connected together.

Figure II–2 shows an example of three resistors connected in series (one path). The choice of which holes to use is up to you but the ends of two resistors must be connected in holes that are joined in the board in order to connect them together. Other examples of wiring are given within the lab manual.

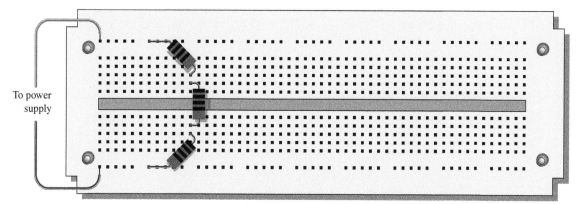

Figure II–2

WIRING HINTS

When wiring a circuit, you should keep wiring neat to be able to easily follow the layout. The best way to keep wiring neat is to cut wires to the size needed; don't make your circuit look like a plate of spaghetti. Don't force components with large leads into the holes in boards; this will cause the spring-loaded connectors to be permanently distorted and not hold other components properly. You can connect larger components by clipping an alligator lead between the component and a piece of #22 or #24 wire. Don't insert wires more than 1/4″ into the holes. When wires are inserted too far, they find a way to short another row or push the spring-loaded connectors out the back of the board. A "bad board" can be a troubleshooting nightmare.

SAFETY IN THE LABORATORY

The experiments in this lab book are designed for low voltages to minimize electric shock hazard; however, never assume that electric circuits are safe. A current of a few milliamps through the body can be lethal. In addition, electronic laboratories often contain other hazards such as chemicals and power tools. For your safety, you should review laboratory safety rules before beginning a course in electronics. In particular, you should

1. Avoid contact with *any* voltage source. Turn off power before you work on circuits.
2. Remove watches, jewelry, rings, and so forth before you work on circuits—even those circuits with low voltages—as burns can occur.
3. Know the location of the emergency power-off switch.
4. Never work alone in the laboratory.
5. Keep a neat work area and handle tools properly. Wear safety goggles or gloves when required.
6. Ensure that line cords are in good condition and grounding pins are not missing or bent. Do not defeat the three-wire ground system in order to make "floating" measurements.
7. Check that transformers and instruments that are plugged into utility lines are properly fused and have no exposed wiring. If you are not certain about procedure, check with your instructor first.
8. Report any unsafe condition to your instructor.
9. Be aware of and follow laboratory rules.

Circuit Simulation and Prototyping
Using Multisim and NI ELVIS

DESIGN, SIMULATION, PROTOTYPING, AND LAYOUT

Electronics has changed rapidly and has become a part of an increasing array of products. As circuits and systems become more advanced, circuit designers rely on computers to assist in the design process. The computer has become a vital part of this process. Producing a new circuit for a product can be broken into four main steps: design, simulation, prototyping, and layout. The last three steps usually involve a computer.

A circuit designer begins the development process with an idea for solving a problem. The idea is developed into a circuit, and the designer usually calculates the expected results by hand to get a good idea of circuit behavior. The second step is to enter the schematic into a computer (this is called "schematic capture") and test it with a circuit simulation program such as *Multisim*. The third step is to construct and test a prototype, which may reveal a hidden or unforeseen problem. Prototyping can also be computer aided as will be discussed. Sometimes the simulation and prototyping steps are repeated to refine the design. Finally, the design is ready to be implemented. This fourth step is done by transferring the circuit design to a printed circuit board (PCB) using a graphical layout tool like *Ultiboard* to determine the optimum placement and interconnection of the components.

The focus here is for two of the steps in the design process—simulation and prototyping. As a design aid, Multisim is one of the most widely used circuit design and simulation tools in industry. Multisim is also used in educational environments because it can simulate circuits quickly, including circuits with troubles. Many Multisim problems have been prepared for this lab manual and the text to introduce you to computer design and simulation tools and to give you troubleshooting practice in a simulated circuit. Although computer simulations are useful and allow you to test parameters that may be difficult, unsafe, or impossible to attain in the lab, they should not be considered a replacement for careful lab work.

The traditional circuit prototype in electronics classes is usually constructed on a solderless protoboard ("breadboard"). The prototype circuit can be tested with stand-alone instruments in the lab. Alternatively, the circuit can be tested with a complete prototyping system like National Instrument's Educational Laboratory and Virtual Instrumentation Suite (NI ELVIS). The NI ELVIS system has over 10 built-in instruments and an interface that can communicate with Multisim. Multisim can also simulate the NI ELVIS interface, as will be shown later.

MORE ABOUT MULTISIM

Electronics Workbench's Multisim provides an intuitive environment for schematic capture. You place "virtual" electrical components and wire them together into a schematic just as in the laboratory. The graphical circuit schematic capture tool within Multisim is built around a sophisticated industry standard SPICE simulator. Multisim provides built-in instruments that can be connected to schematic circuits in the same way they would connect to a real-world circuit. SPICE was developed at the University of California, Berkeley, and stands for "Simulation Program with Integrated Circuit Emphasis."

Multisim is available for the Windows operating system in a number of tiers for both students and educators. Once you have opened Multisim, you can create a new schematic such as the one shown in Figure II–3. This figure outlines the various elements of the Multisim environment.

Create circuits in the Circuit Window by placing components from the Component Toolbar. Clicking on the component toolbar will open the component browser. Choose the family of components,

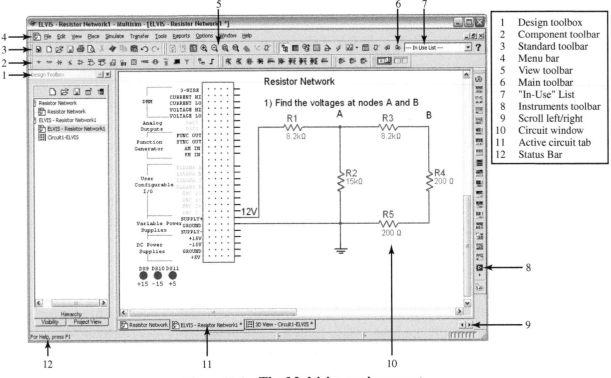

1	Design toolbox
2	Component toolbar
3	Standard toolbar
4	Menu bar
5	View toolbar
6	Main toolbar
7	"In-Use" List
8	Instruments toolbar
9	Scroll left/right
10	Circuit window
11	Active circuit tab
12	Status Bar

Figure II–3   The Multisim environment.

and select an individual component to place on the circuit window by double-clicking on it. Once you have selected a component, it will attach itself and "ghost" the mouse cursor. Clicking again on the desired location in the schematic will place the component. New users to Multisim should use the BASIC_VIRTUAL family of components, which can be assigned any arbitrary value.

The next step is to wire components together. Simply left-click on the source terminal and then left-click on the destination terminal. Multisim will automatically choose the best path for the virtual wire between the two terminals. Always be sure your circuit has a source and a ground or reference, which are components found in the sources group. Once the circuit has been fully captured, it can then be simulated. Results of the simulation can then be used as a comparison with the physical circuit.

As an example of a simple Multisim circuit, a resistor network is shown in Figure II–3. The network is connected to a virtual interface that represents inputs and outputs on the NI ELVIS station. To create this type of simulated circuit, first create a new NI ELVIS schematic by clicking File » New » ELVIS Schematic. Place virtual resistors by clicking on the resistor icon of the components toolbar. Change the values of the resistors to match Figure II–3. Wire the NI ELVIS positive supply and ground reference to your circuit, and the circuit is ready to simulate.

Alternatively, you can create a traditional schematic by clicking File » New » Schematic. If you do this, you will need to manually place power and ground components. This is useful if you are using traditional stand-alone instruments to analyze your circuit. Once you have drawn the circuit, there are many ways to analyze your design using the simulation software.

Assume you want to know the steady state voltages of points A and B in the circuit (V_A and V_B). For now, we'll assume you have come up with the prediction that $V_A = 4.81$ V and $V_B = 0.245$ V.

The easiest way to interact with your circuit in Multisim is using the measurement probe. Use the measurement probe to measure voltages and other important characteristics from a circuit while the

152

simulation is running. To use the measurement probe, click on the probe icon from the virtual instruments toolbar. The probe becomes attached to the mouse cursor and will display information about any node or wire that the mouse hovers above. To attach a probe to any particular wire, simply click on it. For this example, the measurement probe indicated that $V_A = 4.81$ V and $V_B = 0.245$ V, in precise agreement with the calculation.

MORE ABOUT NI ELVIS
NI ELVIS consists of LabVIEW virtual instruments, a multifunction data acquisition (DAQ) device, and a bench-top workstation. The combination of LabVIEW virtual instruments, a DAQ board, and prototyping workstation provides all the functions most commonly used in laboratories worldwide. Instructors and students can build customized instruments to suit their application using LabVIEW. Figure II–4 shows the components that make the NI ELVIS. The workstation can be customized by using different experiment boards such as the solderless protoboard shown.

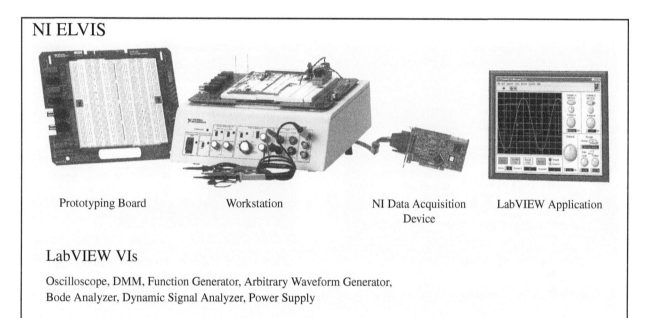

NI ELVIS

| Prototyping Board | Workstation | NI Data Acquisition Device | LabVIEW Application |

LabVIEW VIs

Oscilloscope, DMM, Function Generator, Arbitrary Waveform Generator, Bode Analyzer, Dynamic Signal Analyzer, Power Supply

Figure II–4   Components of NI ELVIS.

After a circuit has been simulated successfully and you are satisfied with its operation, you can build a prototype. Prototyping hardware and instruments are designed to allow you to quickly construct circuits and test them in the real world. Prototyping is valuable for verifying the operation of the design and for uncovering real-world inconsistencies that simulation was not able to predict. For example, the simulation might not show the effect of unexpected spikes from the wall power or interference from a cell phone. It is critically important that there is a high correlation between real-world measurements and simulation results. A close match assures you that the design will effectively solve the problem.

Your lab may be equipped with separate instruments or you may have them provided as a functional package, such as the NI ELVIS prototyping hardware system. The advantage of the NI ELVIS system is that it can aid in the prototyping process by allowing you to construct circuits first on a "virtual protoboard." After constructing the virtual circuit, you can transfer it to the hardware in the NI ELVIS system. The ideal electronics laboratory will provide an easy way for comparing measurements to simulations. The NI ELVIS system integrates naturally with Multisim to provide a seamless transition from design to prototyping. All the measured data is available in a single environment that allows for quick and easy comparison of simulations to real-world measurements.

ANALYZING THE RESISTOR NETWORK USING A REAL-WORLD PROTOTYPE

Returning to the resistor network introduced with Multisim as an example, you can continue to the prototyping step. You can build the circuit on a standard protoboard and test it with the laboratory instruments to complete the design.

Alternatively, you can repeat the simulation step but this time as a prototype using the 3D Virtual NI ELVIS from within Multisim. 3D prototyping allows you to learn more about using breadboards and experiment with your designs in a risk-free environment. To construct a 3D NI ELVIS prototype, open the 3D breadboard by clicking Tools » Show Breadboard. Place components and wires to build up your circuit. The corresponding connection points and symbols on the NI ELVIS schematic will turn green, indicating the 3D connections are correct. If you created a traditional schematic, you will see a standard breadboard. Figure II–5 shows the virtual NI ELVIS. Figure II–6 shows the circuit on NI ELVIS prototyped in Multisim and ready for construction. Once the layout of your circuit has been verified using the 3D virtual environment, it can be physically built on the NI ELVIS.

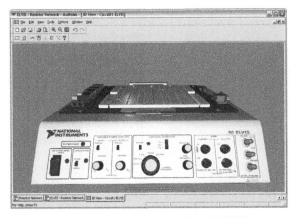

Figure II–5 3D Virtual NI ELVIS.	Figure II–6 Resistor network prototyped in Multisim.

Figure II–7 shows the resistor network on the NI ELVIS protoboard. The variable power supply is connected to the input of the resistor network. Connections to other instruments such as the oscilloscope, DMM, AM and FM modulator lines are also available on the breadboard for more advanced applications.

After you have wired the circuit, you can use the variable power supply provided by NI ELVIS to supply 12 volts (V_S) as needed by the experimental circuit and measure the voltages at A and B using interactive graphical software.

Figure II–8 shows the result of SignalExpress, an interactive measurement tool based on LabVIEW. SignalExpress provides a step-by-step interface to a computer to allow you to perform measurements. The screen shows the measured voltage on the prototype circuit displayed on the computer. If desired, it can be exported to an Excel file or saved for later reference.

The most important step in the laboratory procedure is to compare measurements of the actual circuit to the simulation. This will help you determine where potential errors exist in your design. For example, comparisons can help reveal inadequacies in the simulation model, or incorrect component values. After comparison with the theoretical values, you can revisit your design to improve it or prepare it for layout on a pc board.

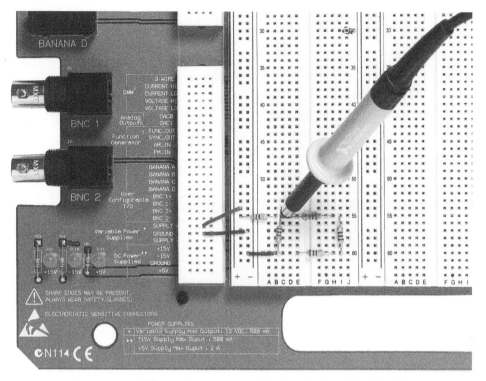

Figure II–7   The resistor network wired on an NI ELVIS.

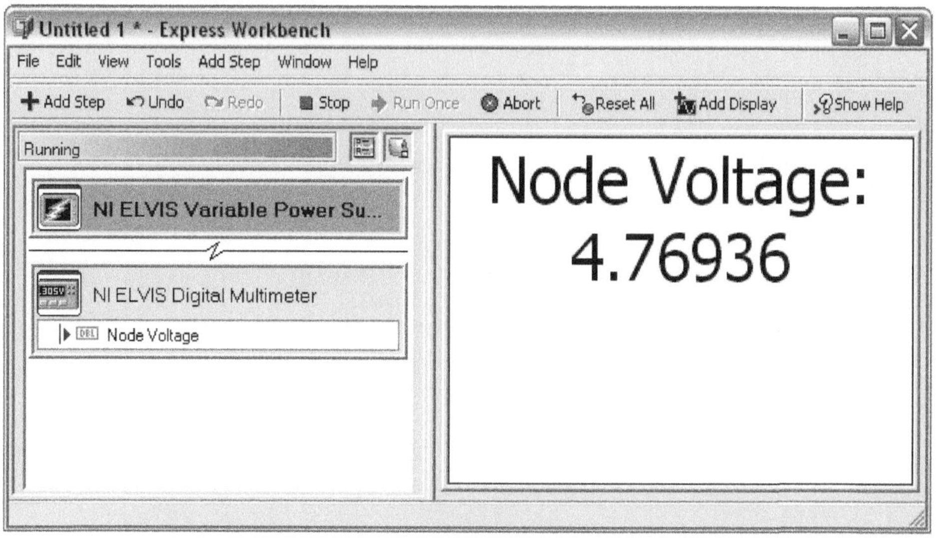

Node Voltage:
4.76936

Figure II–8   NI ELVIS measurements (voltage at node A).

To obtain your free Multisim Evaluation Version
Visit the Electronics Workbench website
http://www.electronicsworkbench.com/edu/eduprod_cd.html

To get your free 3-Hour Tutorial, contact
Electronics Workbench

Toll Free   800.263.5552
Fax   416.977.1818
Email   sales@electronicsworkbench.com
Web   www.electronicsworkbench.com/edu/floyd

For more on the NI ELVIS, contact
National Instruments

Toll Free   888.280.7645
Fax   512.683.8411
Email   sales@ni.com
Web   www.ni.com

To download NI ELVIS courseware and read technical papers on NI ELVIS/Multisim integration, visit
http://www.ni.com/academic/ni_elvis/ltb.htm

To view conference papers on NI ELVIS in Academia, go to
http://www.ni.com/academic/ni_elvis/conference_papers_on_nielvis.htm

Oscilloscope Guide
Analog and Digital Storage Oscilloscopes

The oscilloscope is the most widely used general-purpose measuring instrument because it allows you to see a graph of the voltage as a function of time in a circuit. Many circuits have specific timing requirements or phase relationships that can be readily measured with a two-channel oscilloscope. The voltage to be measured is converted into a visible display that is presented on a screen.

There are two basic types of oscilloscope: analog and digital. In general, they each have specific characteristics. Analog scopes are the classic "real-time" instruments that show the waveform on a cathode-ray tube (CRT). Digital oscilloscopes are rapidly replacing analog scopes because of their ability to store waveforms and because of measurement automation and many other features such as connections for computers. The storage function is so important that it is usually incorporated in the name as a Digital Storage Oscilloscope (DSO). Some higher-end DSOs can emulate an analog scope in a manner that blurs the distinction between the two types. Tektronix, for example, has a line of scopes called DPOs (Digital Phosphor Oscilloscopes) that can characterize a waveform with intensity gradients like an analog scope and gives the benefits of a digital oscilloscope for measurement automation.

Analog and digital scopes have similar functions, and the basic controls are essentially the same for both types (although certain enhanced features are not). In the descriptions that follow, the analog scope is introduced first to familiarize you with basic controls, then a specific digital storage oscilloscope is described (the Tektronix TDS1000 series).

ANALOG OSCILLOSCOPES
Block Diagram
The analog oscilloscope contains four functional blocks, as illustrated in Figure II–9. Shown within these blocks are the most important typical controls found on nearly all oscilloscopes.

Each of two input channels is connected to the vertical section, which can be set to attenuate or amplify the input signals to provide the proper voltage level to the vertical deflection plates of the CRT. In a dual-trace oscilloscope (the most common type), an electronic switch rapidly switches between channels to send one or the other to the display section.

The trigger section samples the input waveform and sends a synchronizing trigger signal at the proper time to the horizontal section. The trigger occurs at the same relative time, thus superimposing each succeeding trace on the previous trace. This action causes a repetitive signal to stop, allowing you to examine it.

The horizontal section contains the time-base (or sweep) generator, which produces a linear ramp, or "sweep," waveform that controls the rate the beam moves across the screen. The horizontal position of the beam is proportional to the time that elapsed from the start of the sweep, allowing the horizontal axis to be calibrated in units of time. The output of the horizontal section is applied to the horizontal deflection plates of the CRT.

Finally, the display section contains the CRT and beam controls. It enables the user to obtain a sharp presentation with the proper intensity. The display section usually contains other features such as a probe compensation jack and a beam finder.

Controls
Generally, controls for each section of the oscilloscope are grouped together according to function. Frequently, there are color clues to help you identify groups of controls. Details of these controls are

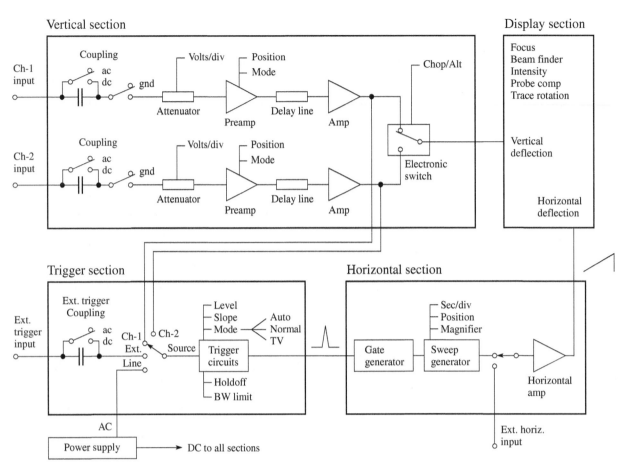

Figure II–9   Block diagram of a basic analog oscilloscope.

explained in the operator's manual for the oscilloscope; however, a brief description of frequently used controls is given in the following paragraphs. The important controls are shown on the block diagram of Figure II–9.

Display Controls   The display system contains controls for adjusting the electron beam, including FOCUS and INTENSITY controls. FOCUS and INTENSITY are adjusted for a comfortable viewing level with a sharp focus. The display section may also contain the BEAM FINDER, a control used in combination with the horizontal and vertical POSITION controls to bring the trace on the screen. Another control over the beam intensity is the z-axis input. A control voltage on the z-axis input can be used to turn the beam on or off or adjust its brightness. Some oscilloscopes also include the TRACE ROTATION control in the display section. TRACE ROTATION is used to align the sweep with a horizontal graticule line. This control is usually adjusted with a screwdriver to avoid accidental adjustment. Usually a PROBE COMP connection point is included in the display group of controls. Its purpose is to allow a quick qualitative check on the frequency response of the probe-scope system.

Vertical Controls   The vertical controls include the VOLTS/DIV (vertical sensitivity) control and its vernier, the input COUPLING switch, and the vertical POSITION control. There is a duplicate set of these controls for each channel and various switches for selecting channels or other vertical operating modes. The vertical inputs are connected through a selectable attenuator to a high input impedance dc amplifier. The VOLTS/DIV control on each channel selects a combination of attenuation/gain to determine the vertical sensitivity. For example, a low-level signal will need more gain and less attenuation than a higher level signal. The vertical sensitivity is adjusted in fixed VOLTS/DIV increments to allow the user to make calibrated voltage measurements. In addition, a concentric vernier control is usually provided to allow a continuous range of sensitivity. This knob must be in the detent (calibrated) position to make voltage measurements. The detent position can be felt by the user as the knob is turned because the knob tends to "lock" in the detent position. Some oscilloscopes have a warning light or message when the vernier is not in its detent position.

The input coupling switch is a multiple-position switch that can be set for AC, GND, or DC and sometimes includes a 50 Ω position. The GND position of the switch internally disconnects the signal from the scope and grounds the input amplifier. This position is useful if you want to set a ground reference level on the screen for measuring the dc component of a waveform. The AC and DC positions are high-impedance inputs, typically 1 MΩ shunted by 15 pF of capacitance. High-impedance inputs are useful for general probing at frequencies below about 1 MHz. At higher frequencies, the shunt capacitance can load the signal source excessively, causing measurement error. Attenuating divider probes are good for high-frequency probing because they have very high impedance (typically 10 MΩ) with very low shunt capacitance (as low as 2.5 pF).

The AC position of the coupling switch inserts a series capacitor before the input attenuator, causing dc components of the signal to be blocked. This position is useful if you want to measure a small ac signal riding on top of a large dc signal—power supply ripple, for example. The DC position is used when you want to view both the AC and DC components of a signal. This position is best when viewing digital signals because the input *RC* circuit forms a differentiating network. The AC position can distort the digital waveform because of this differentiating circuit. The 50 Ω position places an accurate 50 Ω load to ground. This position provides the proper termination for probing in 50 Ω systems and reduces the effect of a variable load which can occur in high impedance termination. The effect of source loading must be taken into account when using a 50 Ω input. It is important not to overload the 50 Ω input because the resistor is normally rated for only 2 W, implying a maximum of 10 V of signal can be applied to the input.

The vertical POSITION control varies the dc voltage on the vertical deflection plates, allowing you to position the trace anywhere on the screen. Each channel has its own vertical POSITION control, enabling you to separate the two channels on the screen. You can use vertical POSITION when the coupling switch is in the GND position to set an arbitrary level on the screen as ground reference.

There are two types of dual-channel oscilloscope: dual beam and dual trace. A dual-beam oscilloscope has two independent beams in the CRT and independent vertical deflection systems, allowing both signals to be viewed at the same time. A dual-trace oscilloscope has only one beam and one deflection system; it uses electronic switching to show the two signals. Dual-beam oscilloscopes are generally restricted to high-performance research instruments and are much more expensive than dual-trace oscilloscopes. The block diagram in Figure II–9 is for a typical dual-trace oscilloscope.

A dual-trace oscilloscope has user controls labeled CHOP or ALTERNATE to switch the beam between the channels so that the signals appear to occur simultaneously. The CHOP mode rapidly switches the beam between the two channels at a fixed high speed rate, so the two channels appear to be displayed at the same time. The ALTERNATE mode first completes the sweep for one of the channels and then displays the other channel on the next (or alternate) sweep. When viewing slow signals, the CHOP mode is best because it reduces the flicker that would otherwise be observed. High-speed signals can usually be observed best in ALTERNATE mode to avoid seeing the chop frequency.

Another feature on most dual-trace oscilloscopes is the ability to show the algebraic sum and difference of the two channels. For most measurements, you should have the vertical sensitivity

(VOLTS/DIV) on the same setting for both channels. You can use the algebraic sum if you want to compare the balance on push-pull amplifiers, for example. Each amplifier should have identical out-of-phase signals. When the signals are added, the resulting display should be a straight line, indicating balance. You can use the algebraic difference when you want to measure the waveform across an ungrounded component. The probes are connected across the ungrounded component with probe ground connected to circuit ground. Again, the vertical sensitivity (VOLTS/DIV) setting should be the same for each channel. The display will show the algebraic difference in the two signals. The algebraic difference mode also allows you to cancel any unwanted signal that is equal in amplitude and phase and is common to both channels.

Dual-trace oscilloscopes also have an X-Y mode, which causes one of the channels to be graphed on the X-axis and the other channel to be graphed on the Y-axis. This is necessary if you want to change the oscilloscope base line to represent a quantity other than time. Applications include viewing a transfer characteristic (output voltage as a function of input voltage), swept frequency measurements, or showing Lissajous figures for phase measurements. Lissajous figures are patterns formed when sinusoidal waves drive both channels and are described in Experiment 10, For Further Investigation.

Horizontal Controls   The horizontal controls include the SEC/DIV control and its vernier, the horizontal magnifier, and the horizontal POSITION control. In addition, the horizontal section may include delayed sweep controls. The SEC/DIV control sets the sweep speed, which controls how fast the electron beam is moved across the screen. The control has a number of calibrated positions divided into steps of 1-2-5 multiples which allow you to set the exact time interval that you view the input signal. For example, if the graticule has 10 horizontal divisions and the SEC/DIV control is set to 1.0 ms/div, then the screen will show a total time of 10 ms. The SEC/DIV control usually has a concentric vernier control that allows you to adjust the sweep speed continuously between the calibrated steps. This control must be in the detent position in order to make calibrated time measurements. Many scopes are also equipped with a horizontal magnifier that affects the time base. The magnifier increases the sweep time by the magnification factor, giving you increased resolution of signal details. Any portion of the original sweep can be viewed using the horizontal POSITION control in conjunction with the magnifier. This control actually speeds the sweep time by the magnification factor and therefore affects the calibration of the time base set on the SEC/DIV control. For example, if you are using a 10× magnifier, the SEC/DIV dial setting must be divided by 10.

Trigger Controls   The trigger section is the source of most difficulties when learning to operate an oscilloscope. These controls determine the proper time for the sweep to begin in order to produce a stable display. The trigger controls include the MODE switch, SOURCE switch, trigger LEVEL, SLOPE, COUPLING, and variable HOLDOFF controls. In addition, the trigger section includes a connector for applying an EXTERNAL trigger to start the sweep. Trigger controls may include HIGH or LOW FREQUENCY REJECT switches and BANDWIDTH LIMITING.

The MODE switch is a multiple-position switch that selects either AUTO or NORMAL (sometimes called TRIGGERED) and may have other positions such as TV or SINGLE sweep. In the AUTO position, the trigger generator selects an internal oscillator that will trigger the sweep generator as long as no other trigger is available. This mode ensures that a sweep will occur even in the absence of a signal because the trigger circuits will "free-run" in this mode. This allows you to obtain a baseline for adjusting ground reference level or for adjusting the display controls. In the NORMAL or TRIGGERED mode, a trigger is generated from one of three sources selected by the SOURCE switch—the INTERNAL signal, an EXTERNAL trigger source, or the AC LINE. If you are using the internal signal to obtain a trigger, the normal mode will provide a trigger only if a signal is present and other trigger conditions (level, slope) are met. This mode is more versatile than AUTO as it can provide stable triggering for very low to very high frequency signals. The TV position is used for synchronizing either television fields or lines and SINGLE is used primarily for photographing the display.

The trigger LEVEL and SLOPE controls are used to select a specific point on either the rising or falling edge of the input signal for generating a trigger. The trigger SLOPE control determines which edge will generate a trigger, whereas the LEVEL control allows the user to determine the voltage level on the input signal which will start the sweep circuits.

The SOURCE switch selects the trigger source—either from the CH-1 signal, the CH-2 signal, an EXTERNAL trigger source, or the AC LINE. In the CH-1 position, a sample of the signal from channel-1 is used to start the sweep. In the EXTERNAL position, a time-related external signal is used for triggering. The external trigger can be coupled with either AC or DC COUPLING. The trigger signal can be coupled with AC COUPLING if the trigger signal is riding on a dc voltage. DC COUPLING is used if the triggers can occur at a frequency of less than about 20 Hz. The LINE position causes the trigger to be derived from the ac power source. This synchronizes the sweep with signals that are related to the power line frequency.

The variable HOLDOFF control allows you to exclude otherwise valid triggers until the holdoff time has elapsed. For some signals, particularly complex waveforms or digital pulse trains, obtaining a stable trigger can be a problem. This can occur when one or more valid trigger points occur before the signal repetition time. If every event that the trigger circuits qualified as a trigger were allowed to start a sweep, the display could appear to be unsynchronized. By adjusting the variable HOLDOFF control, the trigger point can be made to coincide with the signal-repetition point.

OSCILLOSCOPE PROBES
Signals should always be coupled into the oscilloscope through a probe. A probe is used to pick off a signal and couple it to the input with a minimum loading effect on the circuit under test. Various types of probes are provided by manufacturers but the most common type is a 10:1 attenuating probe that is shipped with most general-purpose oscilloscopes. These probes have a short ground lead that should be connected to a nearby circuit ground point to avoid oscillation and power line interference. The ground lead makes a mechanical connection to the test circuit and passes the signal through a flexible, shielded cable to the oscilloscope. The shielding helps protect the signal from external noise pickup.

Begin any session with the oscilloscope by checking the probe compensation on each channel. Adjust the probe for a flat-topped square wave while observing the scope's calibrator output. This is a good signal to check the focus and intensity and verify trace alignment. Check the front-panel controls for the type of measurement you are going to make. Normally, the variable controls (VOLTS/DIV and SEC/DIV) should be in the calibrated (detent) position. The vertical coupling switch is usually placed in the DC position unless the waveform in which you are interested has a large dc offset. Trigger holdoff should be in the minimum position unless it is necessary to delay the trigger to obtain a stable sweep.

DIGITAL STORAGE OSCILLOSCOPES
Block Diagram
The digital storage oscilloscope (DSO) uses a fast analog-to-digital converter (ADC) on each channel (typically two or four channels) to convert the input voltage into numbers that can be stored in a memory. The digitizer samples the input at a uniform rate called the sample rate; the optimum sample rate depends on the speed of the signal. The process of digitizing the waveform has many advantages for accuracy, triggering, viewing hard-to-see events, and for waveform analysis. Although the method of acquiring and displaying the waveform is quite different than analog scopes, the basic controls on the instrument are similar.

A block diagram of the basic DSO is shown in Figure II–10. As you can see, functionally, the block diagram is similar to the analog scope. As in the analog oscilloscope, the vertical and horizontal controls include position and sensitivity, which are used to set up the display for the proper scaling.

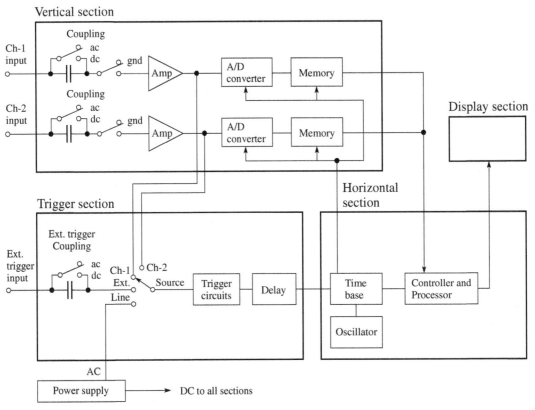

Figure II–10   Block diagram of a basic digital storage oscilloscope.

Specifications   Important parameters with DSOs include the resolution, maximum digitizing rate, and the size of the acquisition memory as well as the available analysis options. The resolution is determined by the number of bits digitized by the ADC. A low-resolution DSO may use only six bits (one part in 64). A typical DSO may use 8 bits, with each channel sampled simultaneously. High-end DSOs may use 12 bits. The maximum digitizing rate is important to capture rapidly changing signals; typically the maximum rate is 1 Gsample/s. The size of the memory determines the length of time the sample can be taken; it is also important in certain waveform measurement functions.

Triggering   One useful feature of digital storage oscilloscopes is their ability to capture waveforms either before or after the trigger event. Any segment of the waveform, either before or after the trigger event, can be captured for analysis. **Pretrigger capture** refers to acquisition of data that occurs *before* a trigger event. This is possible because the data are digitized continuously, and a trigger event can be selected to stop the data collection at some point in the sample window. With pretrigger capture, the scope can be triggered on the fault condition, and the signals that preceded the fault condition can be observed. For example, troubleshooting an occasional glitch in a system is one of the most difficult troubleshooting jobs; by employing pretrigger capture, trouble leading to the fault can be analyzed. A similar application of pretrigger capture is in material failure studies where the events leading to failure are most interesting but the failure itself causes the scope triggering.

Besides pretrigger capture, posttriggering can also be set to capture data that occur some time after a trigger event. The record that is acquired can begin after the trigger event by some amount of time or by a specific number of events as determined by a counter. A low-level response to a strong stimulus signal is an example of when posttriggering is useful.

A Specific DSO   Because of the large number of functions that can be accomplished by even basic DSOs, manufacturers have largely replaced the plethora of controls with menu options, similar to computer menus and detailed displays that show the controls as well as measurement parameters. CRTs have been replaced by liquid crystal displays, similar to those on laptop computers. As an example, the display for a Tektronix TDS1000 and 2000 series digital storage oscilloscope is shown in Figure II–11. Although this is a basic scope, the information available to the user right on the display is impressive.

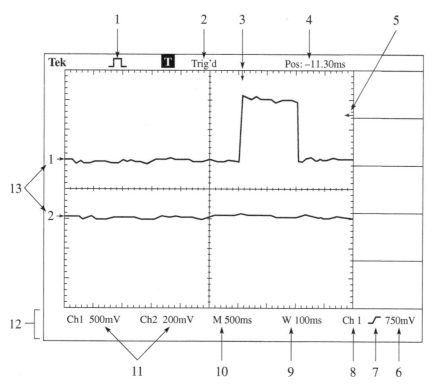

Figure II–11   The display area for Tektronix TDS1000 and 2000 series oscilloscope (courtesy of Tektronix, Inc.).

The numbers on the display in Figure II–11 refer to the following parameters:
1. Icon display shows acquisition mode.
    ⊓ Sample mode
    ⋀ Peak detect mode
    ⊓ Average mode
2. Trigger status shows if there is an adequate trigger source or if the acquisition is stopped.
3. Marker shows horizontal trigger position. This also indicates the horizontal position since the Horizontal Position control actually moves the trigger position horizontally.

163

4. Trigger position display shows the difference (in time) between the center graticule and the trigger position. Center screen equals zero.

5. Marker shows trigger level.

6. Readout shows numeric value of the trigger level.

7. Icon shows selected trigger slope for edge triggering.

8. Readout shows trigger source used for triggering.

9. Readout shows window zone time-base setting.

10. Readout shows main time-base setting.

11. Readout shows channels 1 and 2 vertical scale factors.

12. Display area shows on-line messages momentarily.

13. On-screen markers show the ground reference points of the displayed waveforms. No marker indicates the channel is not displayed.

A front view of the TDS1000 and 2000 series is shown in Figure II–12. Operation is similar to that of an analog scope except more of the functions are menu controlled; in the TDS1000 and 2000 series, 12 different menus are accessed to select various controls and options. For example, the MEASURE function brings up a menu that the user can select from five automated measurements including voltage, frequency, period, and averaging to name a few.

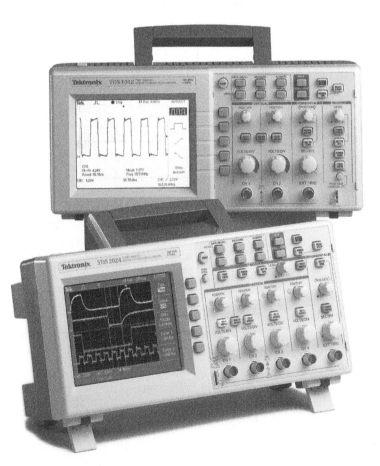

Figure II–12   The Tektronix TDS1000 and 2000 series oscilloscope (courtesy of Tektronix, Inc.).

The Technical Report

EFFECTIVE WRITING

The purpose of technical reports is to communicate technical information in a way that is easy for the reader to understand. Effective writing requires that you know your reader's background. You must be able to put yourself in the reader's place and anticipate what information you must convey to have the reader understand what you are trying to say. When you are writing experimental results for a person working in your field, such as an engineer, your writing style may contain words or ideas that are unfamiliar to a layperson. If your report is intended for persons outside your field, you will need to provide background information.

WORDS AND SENTENCES

You need to choose words that have clear meaning to a general audience or define every term, including acronyms, that does not have a well-established meaning. Keep sentences short and to the point. Short sentences are easier for the reader to comprehend. Avoid stringing a series of adjectives or modifiers together. For example, the meaning of this figure caption is unclear:

Operational amplifier constant-current source schematic

The noun *schematic* is described by two modifiers, each of which has its own modifier. By changing the order and adding natural connectors such as *of, using,* and *an,* the meaning can be clarified:

Schematic of a constant-current source using an operational amplifier

PARAGRAPHS

Paragraphs need to contain a unit of thought. Excessively long paragraphs suffer from the same weakness that afflict overly long sentences. The reader is asked to digest too much material at once, causing comprehension to diminish. Paragraphs should organize your thoughts in a logical format. Look for natural breaks in your ideas. Each paragraph should have one central idea and contribute to the development of the entire report.

Good organization is the key to a well-written report. Outlining in advance will help organize your ideas. The use of headings and subheadings for paragraphs or sections can help steer the reader through the report. Subheadings also prepare the reader for what is ahead and make the report easier to understand.

FIGURES AND TABLES

Figures and tables are effective ways to present information. Figures should be kept simple and to the point. Often a graph can make clear the relationship of data. Comparisons of different data drawn on the same graph make the results more obvious to the reader. Figures should be labeled with a figure number and a brief label. Don't forget to label both axes of graphs.

Data tables are useful for presenting data. Usually data presented in a graph or figure should not also be included in a data table. Data tables should be labeled with a table number and short title. The data table should contain enough information that its meaning is clear to the reader without having to refer to the text. If the purpose of the table is to compare information, then form the data in columns rather than rows. Information in columns is easier for people to compare. Table footnotes are a useful method of clarifying some point about the data. Footnotes should appear at the bottom of the table with a key to where the footnote applies.

Data should appear throughout your report in consistent units of measurement. Most sciences use the metric system; however, the English (or customary) system is still sometimes used. The metric system uses derived units that are cgs (centimeter-gram-second) or mks (meter-kilogram-second). It is best to use consistent metric units throughout your report.

Tabular data should be shown with a number of significant digits consistent with the precision of the measurement.

Reporting numbers using powers of 10 can be a sticky point with reference to tables. Table II–1 shows four methods of abbreviating numbers in tabular form. The first column is unambiguous; the number is presented in conventional form. This requires more space than if the information is presented in scientific notation. In column 2, the same data are shown with a metric prefix used for the unit. In column 3, the power of 10 is shown. Each of the first three columns shows the measurement unit and is not subject to misinterpretation. Column 4, on the other hand, is wrong. In this case, the author is trying to tell us what operation was performed on the numbers to obtain the values in the column. This is incorrect because the column heading should contain the unit of measurement for the numbers in the column.

Table II–1 Reporting numbers in tabular data.

Column 1	Column 2	Column 3	Column 4
Resistance ohms	Resistance $k\Omega$	Resistance $\times 10^3$ ohms	Resistance ohms $\times 10^{-3}$
470,000	470	470	470
8,200	8.2	8.2	8.2
1,200,000	1,200	1,200	1,200
330	0.33	0.33	0.33
	Correct		Wrong

SUGGESTED FORMAT

1. *Title.* A good title needs to convey the substance of your report by using key words that provide the reader with enough information to decide if the report should be investigated further.

2. *Contents.* Key headings throughout the report are listed with page numbers.

3. *Abstract.* The abstract is a brief summary of the work with principal facts and results stated in concentrated form. It is a key factor in helping a reader to determine if he or she should read further.

4. *Introduction.* The introduction orients a reader. It should briefly state what you did and give the reader a sense of the purpose of the report. It may tell the reader what to expect and briefly describe the report's organization.

5. *Body of the report.* The report can be made clearer to the reader if you use headings and subheadings to mark major divisions through your report. The headings and subheadings can be generated from the outline of your report. Figures and tables should be labeled and referenced in the body of the report.

6. *Conclusion.* The conclusion summarizes important points or results. It may refer to figures or tables previously discussed in the body of the report to add emphasis to significant points. In some cases, the primary reasons for the report are contained within the body and a conclusion is deemed to be unnecessary.

7. *References.* References are cited to enable the reader to find information used in developing your report or work that supports your report. The references should include names of all authors, in the order shown in the original document. Use quotation marks around portions of a complete document such as a journal article or a chapter of a book. Books, journals, or other complete documents should be underlined. Finally, list the publisher, city, date, and page numbers.

1 The Oscilloscope

Name _____
Date _____
Class _____

READING
Floyd, Section 8–9
Oscilloscope Guide, pages 157 through 164 of this manual

OBJECTIVES
After performing this experiment, you will be able to:
1.   Explain the four functional blocks on an oscilloscope and describe the major controls within each block.
2.   Use an oscilloscope to measure ac and dc voltages.

MATERIALS NEEDED
None

SUMMARY OF THEORY
The oscilloscope is an extremely versatile instrument that lets you see a picture of the voltage in a circuit as a function of time. There are two basic types of oscilloscopes—analog oscilloscopes and digital storage oscilloscopes (DSOs). DSOs are rapidly replacing older analog scopes because they offer significant advantages in measurement capabilities including waveform processing, automated measurements, waveform storage, and printing, as well as many other features. Operation of either type is similar; however, most digital scopes tend to have menus and typically provide the user with information on the display and may have automatic setup provisions.

There is not room in this Summary of Theory to describe all of the controls and features of oscilloscopes, so this is by necessity a limited description. You are encouraged to read the Oscilloscope Guide at the beginning of this manual, which describes the controls in some detail and highlights some of the key differences between analog scopes and DSOs. You can obtain further information from the User Manual packaged with your scope and from manufacturers' websites.

Both analog and digital oscilloscopes have a basic set of four functional groups of controls that you need to be completely familiar with, even if you are using a scope with automated measurements. In this experiment, a generic analog scope is described. Keep in mind, that if you are using a DSO, the controls referred to operate in much the same way but you may see some small operating differences.

Although the process for waveform display is very different between an analog oscilloscope and a DSO, the four main functional blocks and primary controls are equivalent. Figure 1–1 shows a basic analog oscilloscope block diagram which illustrates these four main functional blocks. These blocks are broken down further in the Oscilloscope Guide for both types of scope.

Controls for each of the functional blocks are usually grouped together. Frequently, there are color clues to help you identify groups of controls. Look for the controls for each functional group on your oscilloscope. The display controls include INTENSITY, FOCUS, and BEAM FINDER. The vertical controls include input COUPLING, VOLTS/DIV, vertical POSITION, and channel selection (CH1, CH2, DUAL, ALT, CHOP). The triggering controls include MODE, SOURCE, trigger COUPLING, trigger LEVEL, and others. The horizontal controls include the SEC/DIV, MAGNIFIER, and horizontal POSITION controls. Details of these controls are explained in the referenced reading and in the operator's manual for the oscilloscope.

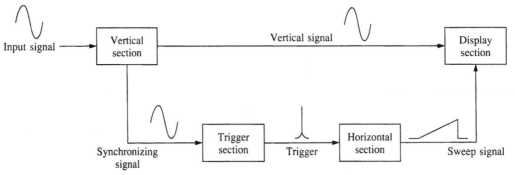

Figure 1–1 Block diagram of an analog oscilloscope

With all the controls to learn, you may experience difficulty obtaining a trace on an analog oscilloscope. If you do not see a trace, start by setting the SEC/DIV control to 0.1 ms/div, select AUTO triggering, select CH1, and press the BEAM FINDER. Keep the BEAM FINDER button depressed and use the vertical and horizontal POSITION controls to center the trace. If you still have trouble, check the INTENSITY control. Note that it's hard to lose the trace on a digital scope, so there is no BEAM FINDER.

Because the oscilloscope can show a voltage-versus-time presentation, it is easy to make ac voltage measurements with a scope. However, care must be taken to equate these measurements with meter readings. Typical digital multimeters show the *rms* (root-mean-square) value of a sinusoidal waveform. This value represents the effective value of an ac waveform when compared to a dc voltage when both produce the same heat (power) in a given load. Usually the *peak-to-peak* value is easiest to read on an oscilloscope. The relationship between the ac waveform as viewed on the oscilloscope and the equivalent rms reading that a DMM will give is illustrated in Figure 1–2.

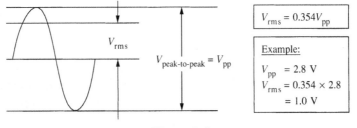

Figure 1–2

Many automated oscilloscopes can measure peak-to-peak or even rms readings of waveforms directly on the screen. They may include horizontal and vertical cursors. Be careful using an automated rms measurement of a sine wave. It may include any dc offset present. If you want to avoid including the dc component, ac couple the signal.

Waveforms that are not sinusoidal cannot be directly compared with an oscilloscope and DMM except for the dc component. The dc level of any waveform can be represented by a horizontal line which splits the waveform into equal areas above and below the line. For a sinusoidal wave, the dc level is always halfway between the maximum and minimum excursions. The dc component can be correctly read by a DMM no matter what the shape of the wave when it is in the DC volts mode.

The amplitude of any periodic waveform can be expressed in one of four ways: the peak-to-peak, the peak, the rms, or the average value. The peak-to-peak value of any waveform is the total magnitude of the change and is *independent* of the zero position. The peak value is the maximum excursion of the wave and is usually referenced to the dc level of the wave. To indicate that a reported value includes a dc offset, you need to state both the maximum and minimum excursions of the waveform.

An important part of any oscilloscope measurement is the oscilloscope probe. The type of probe that is generally furnished with an oscilloscope by the manufacturer is called an *attenuator probe* because it attenuates the input by a known factor. The most common attenuator probe is the 10× probe, because it reduces the input signal by a factor of 10. It is a good idea, before making any measurement, to check that the probe is properly compensated, meaning that the frequency response of the probe/scope system is flat. Probes have a small variable capacitor either in the probe tip or a small box that is part of the input connector. This capacitor is adjusted while observing a square wave to ensure that the displayed waveform has vertical sides and square corners. Most oscilloscopes have the square-wave generator built in for the purpose of compensating the probe.

PROCEDURE

1. Review the front panel controls in each of the major groups. Then turn on the oscilloscope, select CH1, set the SEC/DIV to 0.1 ms/div, select AUTO triggering, and obtain a line across the face of the CRT. Although many of the measurements described in this experiment are automated in newer scopes, it is useful to learn to make these measurements manually.

2. Turn on your power supply and use the DMM to set the output for 1.0 V. Now we will use the oscilloscope to measure this dc voltage from the power supply. The following steps will guide you:
   (a) Place the vertical COUPLING (AC-GND-DC) in the GND position. This disconnects the input to the oscilloscope. Use the vertical POSITION control to set the ground reference level on a convenient graticule line near the bottom of the screen.
   (b) Set the CH1 VOLTS/DIV control to 0.2 V/div. Check that the vernier control is in the CAL position or your measurement will not be accurate. Note that digital scopes do not have a vernier control. For fine adjustments, the VOLTS/DIV control can be changed to a more sensitive setting that remains calibrated.
   (c) Place the oscilloscope probe on the positive side of the power supply. Place the oscilloscope ground on the power supply common. Move the vertical coupling to the DC position. The line should jump up on the screen by 5 divisions. *Note that 5 divisions times 0.2 V per division is equal to 1.0 V (the supply voltage)*. Multiplication of the number of divisions of deflection times volts per division is equal to the voltage measurement.

3. Set the power supply to each voltage listed in Table 1–1. Measure each voltage using the above steps as a guide. The first line of the table has been completed as an example. To obtain accurate readings with the oscilloscope, it is necessary to select the VOLTS/DIV that gives several divisions of change between the ground reference and the voltage to be measured. The readings on the oscilloscope and meter should agree with each other within approximately 3%.

Table 1–1

Power Supply Setting	VOLTS/DIV Setting	Number of Divisions of Deflection	Oscilloscope (measured voltage)	DMM (measured voltage)
1.0 V	0.2 V/DIV	5.0 DIV	1.0 V	1.0 V
2.5 V				
4.5 V				
8.3 V				

171

4. Before viewing ac signals, it is a good idea to check the probe compensation for your oscilloscope. To check the probe compensation, set the VOLT/DIV control to 0.1 V/div, the AC-GND-DC coupling control to DC, and the SEC/DIV control to 2 ms/div. Touch the probe tip to the PROBE COMP connector. You should observe a square wave with a flat top and square corners. If necessary, adjust the compensation to achieve a good square wave.

5. Set the function generator for an ac waveform with a frequency of 1.0 kHz. Adjust the amplitude of the function generator for 1.0 V_{rms} as read on your DMM. Set the SEC/DIV control to 0.2 ms/div and the VOLTS/DIV to 0.5 V/div. Connect the scope probe and its ground to the function generator. Adjust the vertical POSITION control and the trigger LEVEL control for a stable display near the center of the screen. You should observe approximately two cycles of an ac waveform with a peak-to-peak amplitude of 2.8 V. This represents 1.0 V_{rms}, as shown in Figure 1–3.

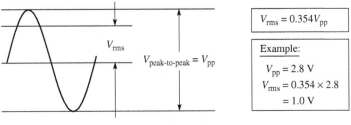

Figure 1–3

6. Use the DMM to set the function generator amplitude to each value listed in Table 1–2. Repeat the ac voltage measurement as outlined in step 5. The first line of the table has been completed as an example. Remember, to obtain accurate readings with the oscilloscope, you should select a VOLTS/DIV setting that gives several divisions of deflection on the screen.

Table 1–2

Signal Generator Amplitude	VOLTS/DIV Setting	Number of Divisions (peak-to-peak)	Oscilloscope Measured (peak-to-peak)	Oscilloscope Measured (rms)
1.0 V_{rms}	0.5 V/DIV	5.6 DIV	2.8 V_{pp}	1.0 V_{rms}
2.2 V_{rms}				
3.7 V_{rms}				
4.8 V_{rms}				

7. Do this step only if you are using an analog oscilloscope. You can observe both the power supply and the function generator at the same time. Select both channels (marked DUAL on some scopes). Each channel can be displayed with its own ground reference point. You will need to leave the trigger SOURCE on channel 2 because the ac waveform is connected to that channel. You can select either ALTernate or CHOP mode to view the waveforms. To really see the effects of this control, slow the function generator to 10 Hz and change the horizontal SEC/DIV control to 20 ms/div. Compare the display using ALTernate and CHOP. At this slow frequency, it is easier to see the waveforms using the CHOP mode; at high frequencies the ALTernate mode is generally preferred.

CONCLUSION

EVALUATION AND REVIEW QUESTIONS

1.   (a)   Compute the percent difference between the DMM measurement and the oscilloscope measurement for each dc voltage measurement summarized in Table 1–1.

       (b)   Which do you think is most accurate? Why?

2.   Describe the four major groups of controls on the oscilloscope and the purpose of each group.

3.   If you are having difficulty obtaining a stable display, which group of controls should you adjust?

4.   (a)   If an ac waveform has 3.4 divisions from peak to peak and the VOLTS/DIV control is set to 5.0 V/div, what is the peak-to-peak voltage?

       (b)   What is the rms voltage?

5.   If you wanted to view an ac waveform that was 20.0 V_{rms}, what setting of the VOLTS/DIV control would be best?

6.   Most analog oscilloscopes have a single beam, which is shared with two signals. If you are using an analog oscilloscope, when should you select ALTernate and when should you choose CHOP?

FOR FURTHER INVESTIGATION

Most function generators have a control that allows you to add or subtract a dc offset voltage to the signal. Set up the function generator for a 1.0 kHz sine wave signal, as shown in Figure 1–4. To do this, the AC-GND-DC coupling switch on the oscilloscope should be in the DC position and the offset control should be adjusted on the function generator. When you have the signal displayed on the oscilloscope face, switch the AC-GND-DC coupling switch into the AC position. Explain what this control does. Then measure the signal with your DMM. First measure it in the AC VOLTAGE position; then measure in the DC VOLTAGE position. How does this control differ from the AC-GND-DC coupling switch on the oscilloscope? Summarize your findings.

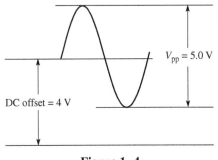

Figure 1–4

2 Sine Wave Measurements

Name _____

Date _____

Class _____

READING
Floyd, Sections 8–1 through 8–7

OBJECTIVES
After performing this experiment, you will be able to:
1.   Measure the period and frequency of a sine wave using an oscilloscope.
2.   Measure across ungrounded components using the difference function of an oscilloscope.

MATERIALS NEEDED
Resistors:

   One 2.7 kΩ, one 6.8 kΩ

SUMMARY OF THEORY
Imagine a weight suspended from a spring. If you stretch the spring and then release it, it will bob up and down with a regular motion. The distance from the rest point to the highest (or lowest) point is called the *amplitude* of the motion. As the weight moves up and down, the time for one complete cycle is called a *period,* and the number of cycles it moves in a second is called the *frequency*. This cyclic motion is called *simple harmonic motion*. A graph of simple harmonic motion as a function of time produces a sine wave, the most fundamental waveform in nature. It is also the waveform from an ac generator. Figure 2–1 illustrates these definitions.

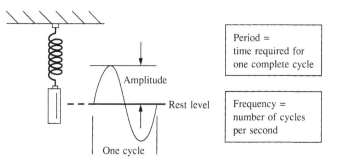

Figure 2–1

Sine waves can also be generated from uniform circular motion. Imagine a circle turning at a constant rate. The *projection* of the endpoint of the radius vector moves with simple harmonic motion. If the end point is plotted along the *x*-axis, the resulting curve is a sine wave, as illustrated in Floyd's text. This method is frequently used to show the phase relationship between two sine waves of the same frequency.

The sine wave has another interesting property. Different sine waves can be added together to give new waveforms. In fact, any repeating waveform such as a ramp or square wave can be made up of a group of sine waves. This property is useful in the study of the response of circuits to various waveforms.

The Oscilloscope

As you have seen, there are two basic types of oscilloscopes—analog and digital. In this experiment, you will use an oscilloscope to characterize sine waves. You may want to review the function of the controls on your oscilloscope in the section at the front of this manual entitled Oscilloscope Guide—Analog and Digital Storage Oscilloscopes. Although the method of presenting a waveform is different, the controls such as SEC/DIV are similar in function and should be thoroughly understood. You will make periodic measurements on sine waves in this experiment. Assuming you are not using automated measurements, you need to count the number of divisions for a full cycle and multiply by the SEC/DIV setting to determine the period of the wave. Other measurement techniques will be explained in the Procedure section.

The Function Generator

The basic function generator is used to produce sine, square, and triangle waveforms and may also have a pulse output for testing digital logic circuits. Function generators normally have controls that allow you to select the type of waveform and other controls to adjust the amplitude and dc level. The peak-to-peak voltage is adjusted by the AMPLITUDE control. The dc level is adjusted by a control labeled DC OFFSET; this enables you to add or subtract a dc component to the waveform. These controls are generally not calibrated, so amplitude and dc level settings need to be verified with an oscilloscope or multimeter.

The frequency may be selected with a combination of a range switch and vernier control. The range is selected by a decade frequency switch or pushbuttons that enable you to select the frequency in decade increments (factors of 10) up to about 1 MHz. The vernier control is usually a multiplier dial for adjusting the precise frequency needed.

The output level of a function generator will drop from its open-circuit voltage when it is connected to a circuit. Depending on the conditions, you generally will need to readjust the amplitude level of the generator after it is connected to the circuit. This is because there is effectively an internal generator resistance that will affect the circuit under test.

PROCEDURE

1. Set the signal generator for a 1.0 V_{pp} sine wave at a frequency of 1.25 kHz. Then set the oscilloscope SEC/DIV control to 0.1 ms/div in order to show one complete cycle on the screen. *The expected time for one cycle (the period) is the reciprocal of 1.25 kHz, which is 0.8 ms.* With the SEC/DIV control at 0.1 ms/div, one cycle requires 8.0 divisions across the screen. This is presented as an example in line 1 of Table 2–1.

2. Change the signal generator to each frequency listed in Table 2–1. Complete the table by computing the expected period and then measuring the period with the oscilloscope. Adjust the SEC/DIV control to show between one and two cycles across the screen for each frequency.

Table 2–1

Signal Generator Dial Frequency	Computed Period	Oscilloscope SEC/DIV	Number of Divisions	Measured Period
1.25 kHz	0.8 ms	0.1 ms/div	8.0 div	0.8 ms
1.90 kHz				
24.5 kHz				
83.0 kHz				
600.0 kHz				

176

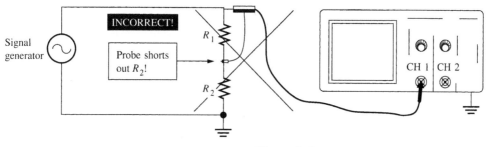

Figure 2–2

3.	In this step you will need to use a two-channel oscilloscope with two probes. Frequently, a voltage measurement is needed across an ungrounded component. If the oscilloscope ground is at the same potential as the circuit ground, then the process of connecting the probe will put an undesired ground path in the circuit. Figure 2–2 illustrates this.

The correct way to measure the voltage across the ungrounded component is to use two channels and select the subtract mode—sometimes called the *difference function*—as illustrated in Figure 2–3. The difference function subtracts the voltage measured on channel 2 from the voltage measured on channel 1. It is important that both channels have the same vertical sensitivity—that is, that the VOLTS/DIV setting is the same on both channels and they are both calibrated.

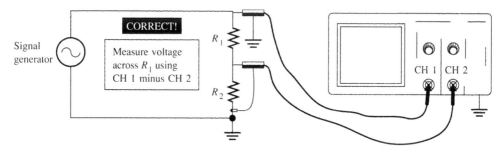

Figure 2–3

Connect the circuit shown in Figure 2–3. Use a 2.7 kΩ resistor for R_1 and a 6.8 kΩ resistor for R_2. Set the signal generator for a 1.0 V$_{pp}$ sine wave at 10 kHz. Channel 1 will show the voltage from the signal generator. Channel 2 will show the voltage across R_2. The difference function (CH1 subtract CH2) will show the voltage across R_1. Some oscilloscopes require that you ADD the channels and INVERT channel 2 in order to measure the difference.[1] Others may have the difference function shown on the Math menu. Complete Table 2–2 for the voltage measurements. Use the voltage divider rule to check that your measured voltages are reasonable.

Table 2–2

	Signal Gen. Voltage	Voltage across R_1	Voltage across R_2
Measured			
Computed	1.0 V$_{pp}$		

[1]If you do not have difference channel capability, then temporarily reverse the components to put R_1 at circuit ground. This can be accomplished with a lab breadboard but is not practical in a manufactured circuit.

CONCLUSION

EVALUATION AND REVIEW QUESTIONS

1.   (a)   Compare the computed and measured periods for the sine waves in Table 2–1. Calculate the percent difference for each row of the table.

      (b)   What measurement errors account for the percent differences?

2.   Using the measured voltages in Table 2–2, show that Kirchhoff's voltage law is satisfied.

3.   An oscilloscope display shows one complete cycle of a sine wave in 6.3 divisions. The SEC/DIV control is set to 20 ms/div.

      (a)   What is the period? _____

      (b)   What is the frequency? _____

4.   You wish to display a 10 kHz sine wave on the oscilloscope. What setting of the SEC/DIV control will show one complete cycle in 10 divisions?

      SEC/DIV = _____

5.   Explain how to measure the voltage across an ungrounded component.

FOR FURTHER INVESTIGATION

It is relatively easy to obtain a stable display on the oscilloscope at higher frequencies. It is more difficult to obtain a stable display with slower signals on an analog oscilloscope, especially those with very small amplitude. Set the signal generator on a frequency of 5.0 Hz. Try to obtain a stable display. You will probably have to use NORMAL triggering and carefully adjust the trigger LEVEL control. After you obtain a stable display, try turning the amplitude of the signal generator to its lowest setting. Can you still obtain a stable display?

3 Pulse Measurements

READING
Floyd, Sections 8–8 and 8–9

OBJECTIVES
After performing this experiment, you will be able to:
1. Measure rise time, fall time, pulse repetition time, pulse width, and duty cycle for a pulse waveform.
2. Explain the limitations of instrumentation in making pulse measurements.
3. Compute the oscilloscope bandwidth necessary to make a rise time measurement with an accuracy of 3%.

MATERIALS NEEDED
One 1000 pF capacitor

SUMMARY OF THEORY
A pulse is a signal that rises from one level to another, remains at the second level for some time, and then returns to the original level. Definitions for pulses are illustrated in Figure 3–1. The time from one pulse to the next is the period, *T*. This is often referred to as the *pulse repetition time.* The reciprocal of period is the *frequency.* The time required for a pulse to rise from 10% to 90% of its maximum level is called the *rise time,* and the time to return from 90% to 10% of the maximum level is called the *fall time.* Pulse width, abbreviated t_w, is measured at the 50% level, as illustrated. The duty cycle is the ratio of the pulse width to the period and is usually expressed as a percentage:

$$\text{Percent duty cycle} = \frac{t_w}{T} \times 100\%$$

Actual pulses differ from the idealized model shown in Figure 3–1(a). They may have *sag, overshoot,* or *undershoot,* as illustrated in Figure 3–1(b). In addition, if cables are mismatched in the system, *ringing* may be observed. Ringing is the appearance of a short oscillatory transient that appears at the top and bottom of a pulse, as illustrated in Figure 3–1(c).

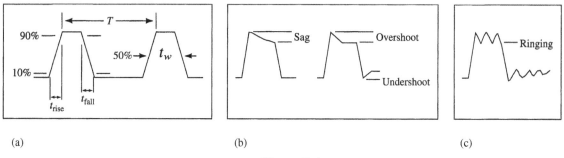

(a)   (b)   (c)

Figure 3–1

All measurements involve some error due to the limitations of the measurement instrument. In this experiment, you will be concerned with rise time measurements. The rise time of the oscilloscope's vertical amplifier (or digitizer's amplifier on a DSO) can distort the measured rise time of a signal. The oscilloscope's rise time is determined by the range of frequencies that can be passed through the vertical amplifier (or digitizing amplifier). This range of frequencies is called the bandwidth, an important specification generally found on the front panel of the scope. Both analog and digital oscilloscopes have internal amplifiers that affect rise time.

If the oscilloscope's internal amplifiers are too slow, rise time distortion may occur, leading to erroneous results. The oscilloscope rise time should be at least four times faster than the signal's rise time if the observed rise time is to have less than 3% error. If the oscilloscope rise time is only twice as fast as the measured rise time, the measurement error rises to over 12%! To find the rise time of an oscilloscope when the bandwidth is known, the following approximate relationship is useful:

$$t_{(r)\text{scope}} = \frac{0.35}{BW}$$

where $t_{(r)\text{scope}}$ is the rise time of the oscilloscope in microseconds and BW is the bandwidth in megahertz. For example, an oscilloscope with a 60 MHz bandwidth has a rise time of approximately 0.006 μs or 6 ns. Measurements of pulses with rise times faster than about 24 ns on this oscilloscope will have measurable error. A correction to the measured value can be applied to obtain the actual rise time of a pulse. The correction formula is

$$t_{(r)\text{true}} = \sqrt{t_{(r)\text{displayed}}^2 + t_{(r)\text{scope}}^2}$$

where $t_{(r)\text{true}}$ is the actual rise time of the pulse, $t_{(r)\text{displayed}}$ is the observed rise time, and $t_{(r)\text{scope}}$ is the rise time of the oscilloscope. This formula can be applied to correct observed rise times by 10% or less.

In addition to the rise time of the amplifier or digitizer, digital scopes have another specification that can affect the usable bandwidth. This specification is the maximum sampling rate. The required sampling rate for a given function depends on a number of variables, but an approximate formula for rise time measurements is

$$\text{Usable bandwidth} = \frac{\text{Maximum sampling rate}}{4.6}$$

From this formula, a 1 GHz sampling rate (1 GSa/s) will have a maximum usable bandwidth of 217 MHz. If the digitizer amplifier's bandwidth is less than this, then it should be used to determine the equivalent rise time of the scope.

Measurement of pulses normally should be done with the input signal coupled to the scope using dc coupling. This directly couples the signal to the oscilloscope and avoids causing pulse sag which can cause measurement error. Probe compensation should be checked before making pulse measurements. It is particularly important in rise time measurements to check probe compensation. This check is described in this experiment. For analog oscilloscopes, it is also important to check that variable knobs are in their calibrated position.

PROCEDURE

1. From the manufacturer's specifications, find the bandwidth of the oscilloscope you are using. Normally the bandwidth is specified with a 10× probe connected to the input. You should make oscilloscope measurements with the 10× probe connected to avoid bandwidth reduction. Use the specific bandwidth to compute the rise time of the oscilloscope as explained in the Summary of Theory. This will give you an idea of the limitations of the oscilloscope you are using to make accurate rise time measurements. Enter the bandwidth and rise time of the scope in Table 3–1.

2. Look on your oscilloscope for a probe compensation output. This output provides an internally generated square wave, usually at a frequency of 1.0 kHz. It is a good idea to check this signal when starting with an instrument to be sure that the probe is properly compensated. To compensate the probe, set the VOLTS/DIV control to view the square wave over several divisions of the display. An adjustment screw on the probe is used to obtain a good square wave with a flat top. An improperly compensated oscilloscope will produce inaccurate measurements. If directed by your instructor, adjust the probe compensation.

3. Set the signal generator for a square wave at a frequency of 100 kHz and an amplitude of 4.0 V. A square wave cannot be measured accurately with your meter—you will need to measure the voltage with an oscilloscope. Check the zero volt level on the oscilloscope and adjust the generator to go from zero volts to 4.0 V. Most signal generators have a separate control to adjust the dc level of the signal.

4. Measure the parameters listed in Table 3–2 for the square wave from the signal generator. Be sure the oscilloscope's SEC/DIV is in its calibrated position. If your oscilloscope has percent markers etched on the front gradicule, you may want to *uncalibrate* the VOLTS/DIV when making rise and fall time measurements. Use the vertical POSITION control and VOLTS/DIV vernier to position the waveform between the 0% and 100% markers on the oscilloscope display. Then measure the time between the 10% and 90% markers.[1]

5. To obtain practice measuring rise time, place a 1000 pF capacitor across the generator output. Measure the new rise and fall times. Record your results in Table 3–3.

Table 3–1
Oscilloscope.

BW	
$t_{(r)}$	

Table 3–2
Signal Generator.
(square wave output)

Rise time, $t_{(r)}$	
Fall time, $t_{(f)}$	
Period, T	
Pulse width, t_w	
Percent duty cycle	

Table 3–3
Signal Generator.
(with 1000 pF capacitor across output)

Rise time, $t_{(r)}$	
Fall time, $t_{(f)}$	

[1]If your oscilloscope has cursor measurements, the rise time can be read directly when the cursors are positioned on the 10% and 90% levels.

6. If you have a separate pulse output from your signal generator, measure the pulse characteristics listed in Table 3–4. To obtain good results with fast signals, the generator should be terminated in its characteristic impedance (typically 50 Ω). You will need to use the fastest sweep time available on your oscilloscope. Record your results in Table 3–4.

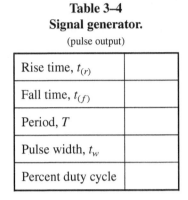

Table 3–4
Signal generator.
(pulse output)

Rise time, $t_{(r)}$	
Fall time, $t_{(f)}$	
Period, T	
Pulse width, t_w	
Percent duty cycle	

CONCLUSION

EVALUATION AND REVIEW QUESTIONS

1. Were any of the measurements limited by the bandwidth of the oscilloscope? If so, which ones?

2. If you need to measure a pulse with a predicted rise time of 10 ns, what bandwidth should the oscilloscope have to measure the time within 3%?

3. The SEC/DIV control on many oscilloscopes has a ×10 magnifier. When the magnifier is ON, the time scale must be divided by 10. Explain.

182

4.   An oscilloscope presentation has the SEC/DIV control set to 2.0 ms/div and the ×10 magnifier is OFF. Determine the rise time of the pulse shown in Figure 3–2.

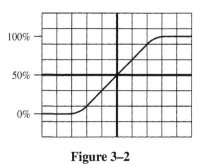

Figure 3–2

5.   Repeat Question 4 for the ×10 magnifier ON.

FOR FURTHER INVESTIGATION

In many applications, it is important to measure time differences. One important technique for doing this with analog oscilloscopes is to use *delayed sweep* measurements. If your scope is equipped with delayed sweep, you can trigger from a signal and view a magnified portion of the signal at a later time. With dual time base oscilloscopes, delayed sweep offers increased timing accuracy. If you have a *calibrated* DELAY TIME POSITION dial, you can make differential delay time measurements between two different signals. Most delayed sweep oscilloscopes will have a HORIZONTAL MODE switch which allows you to view either the A sweep, the B sweep, or A intensified by B. The sweep speeds for A and B can be separately controlled, often by concentric rings on the SEC/DIV control. Consult the operator's manual for your oscilloscope to determine the exact procedure.[2] Then practice by measuring the rise time of the pulse generator using delayed sweep. Summarize your procedure and results.

---

[2]An excellent source of information can be found at http://www.tek.com/. Search for *XYZs of Oscilloscopes,* and several related pdf files will be found.

Application Assignment 1

REFERENCE
Floyd, Chapter 8, Application Assignment: Putting Your Knowledge to Work

Step 1   Review the operation and controls of the function generator.

Step 2   Measure the sinusoidal output of the function generator.
From Figure 8–70(a)
    minimum amplitude: peak: _____ rms: _____
    minimum frequency _____

From Figure 8–70(b)
    maximum amplitude: peak: _____ rms: _____
    maximum frequency _____

Step 3   Measure the DC offset of the function generator.
From Figure 8–71(a)
    maximum positive dc offset: _____

From Figure 8–71(b)
    maximum negative dc offset: _____

Step 4   Measure the triangular output of the function generator.
From Figure 8–72(a)
    minimum amplitude: _____   minimum frequency _____

From Figure 8–72(b)
    maximum amplitude: _____   maximum frequency _____

Step 5   Measure the pulse output of the function generator.
From Figure 8–73(a)
    minimum amplitude: _____   minimum frequency _____
    duty cycle: _____

From Figure 8–73(b)
    maximum amplitude: _____   maximum frequency _____
    duty cycle: _____

RELATED EXPERIMENT

This application requires you to set up the oscilloscope for optimum settings to measure the period and amplitude of different waveforms. When you measure the period of a signal, choose the lowest SEC/DIV setting that shows at least one full cycle on the display. When measuring amplitude, use the lowest VOLT/DIV setting that shows the entire vertical portion of the waveform. Table AA–1–1 lists waveforms to measure. Before making the measurement, consider the best settings of the controls, and enter the settings in the predicted columns. Set up each signal, measure it, and enter the measured values in the table. Then sketch each waveform on the plots shown, showing the oscilloscope display.

EXPERIMENTAL RESULTS

Table AA–1–1

Function Generator Waveform	Required Amplitude	Required Frequency	VOLTS/DIV Setting (predicted)	SEC/DIV Setting (predicted)	Measured Values of Signal:		
					Horizontal Divisions	Vertical Divisions	Plot Number
Sine wave	$1.0\,V_{rms}$	30 Hz					See Plot AA–1–1
Sine wave	$5.0\,V_{pp}$	30 kHz					See Plot AA–1–2
Pulse	4.0 V	2.5 kHz					See Plot AA–1–3
Pulse	0.5 V	75 kHz					See Plot AA–1–4
Sawtooth	$2.0\,V_{pp}$	400 Hz					See Plot AA–1–5
Sawtooth	$9.0\,V_{pp}$	10 kHz					See Plot AA–1–6

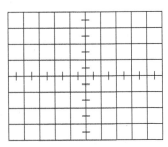

Plot AA–1–1

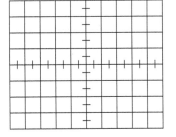

Plot AA–1–2

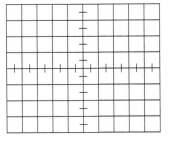

Plot AA–1–3

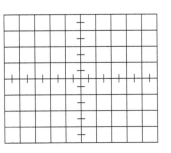

Plot AA–1–4

Plot AA–1–5

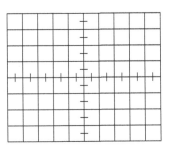

Plot AA–1–6

Checkup 1

REFERENCE

Floyd, Chap. 8, and Buchla, Experiments 15, 16, and 17

1. A sine wave has a peak-to-peak voltage of 25 V. The rms voltage is:
    (a) 8.83 V   (b) 12.5 V   (c) 17.7 V   (d) 35.4 V

2. The number of radians in one-fourth cycle is:
    (a) 57.3   (b) $\pi/2$ (c) π (d) 2π

3. Assume a sine wave has 100 complete cycles in 10 s. The period is:
    (a) 0.1 s   (b) 1 s   (c) 10 s   (d) 100 s

4. Assume a series resistive circuit contains three equal resistors. The source voltage is a sinusoidal waveform of 30 V_{pp}. What is the rms voltage drop across each resistor?
    (a) 3.54 V   (b) 5.0 V   (c) 10 V   (d) 21.2 V

5. Pulse width is normally measured at the:
    (a) 10% level   (b) 50% level   (c) 90% level   (d) baseline

6. A waveform characterized by positive and negative ramps of equal slope is called a:
    (a) triangle   (b) sawtooth   (c) sweep   (d) step

7. A repetitive pulse train has a pulse width of 2.5 μs and a frequency of 100 kHz. The duty cycle is:
    (a) 2.5%   (b) 10%   (c) 25%   (d) 40%

8. The oscilloscope section that determines when it begins to trace a waveform is:
    (a) horizontal   (b) vertical   (c) trigger   (d) display

9. The oscilloscope control that determines how fast the electron beam moves along the *x*-axis is:
    (a) SLOPE   (b) HOLDOFF   (c) VOLTS/DIV   (d) SEC/DIV

10. Measurement of pulses should be done with the input signal coupled to the oscilloscope using
    (a) AC coupling   (b) DC coupling   (c) either ac or dc coupling

11. A standard utility voltage is 115 V at a frequency of 60 Hz.
    (a) What is the peak-to-peak voltage?

    (b) What is the period?

12. How many cycles of a 40 MHz sine wave occur in 0.2 ms?

13. A sinusoidal waveform is represented by the equation $v = 40 \sin(\theta - 35°)$.
    (a) What is the peak voltage?

    (b) What is the phase shift?

14. Figure C–1–1 illustrates an oscilloscope display showing the time relationship between two sine waves. Assume the VOLTS/DIV control is set to 1.0 V/div. Draw a phasor diagram showing the relationship between the two waves.

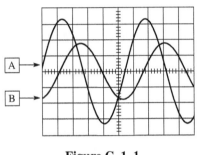

Figure C–1–1

15. A digital oscilloscope has a 1.5 GSa/s sampling rate. What is the usable bandwidth based on the sampling rate?

16. An analog oscilloscope with a bandwidth of 60 MHz is used to measure a pulse with a rise time of 8 ns.
    (a) What is the equivalent rise time of the scope?

    (b) What is the approximate displayed rise time?

17. Why should pulse measurements normally be made with a ×10 probe?

4 Capacitors

Name _____
Date _____
Class _____

READING
Floyd, Sections 9–1 through 9–5

OBJECTIVES
After performing this experiment, you will be able to:
1. Compare total capacitance, charge, and voltage drop for capacitors connected in series and in parallel.
2. Test capacitors with an ohmmeter and a voltmeter.
3. Determine the value of small capacitors from coded markings.

MATERIALS NEEDED:
Two LEDs
Resistors:
    Two 1.0 kΩ
Capacitors:
    One of each : 100 μF, 47 μF, 1.0 μF, 0.1 μF, 0.01 μF (35 WV or greater)

SUMMARY OF THEORY
A capacitor is formed whenever two conductors are separated by an insulating material. When a voltage exists between the conductors, there will be an electric charge between the conductors. The ability to store an electric charge is a fundamental property of capacitors and affects both dc and ac circuits. Capacitors are made with large flat conductors called *plates*. The plates are separated with an insulating material called a *dielectric*. The ability to store charge increases with larger plate size and closer separation.

    When a voltage is connected across a capacitor, charge will flow in the external circuit until the voltage across the capacitor is equal to the applied voltage. The charge that flows is proportional to the size of the capacitor and the applied voltage. This is a fundamental concept for capacitors and is given by the equation

$$Q = CV$$

where Q is the charge in coulombs, C is the capacitance in farads, and V is the applied voltage. An analogous situation is that of putting compressed air into a bottle. The quantity of air is directly proportional to the capacity of the bottle and the applied pressure. (In this analogy, pressure is like voltage, the capacity of the bottle is like capacitance, and the amount of air is like charge.)

    Recall that current is defined as charge per time. That is,

$$I = \frac{Q}{t}$$

where I is the current in amperes, Q is the charge in coulombs, and t is the time in seconds. This equation can be rearranged as

$$Q = It$$

If we connect two capacitors in series with a voltage source, the same charging current is through both capacitors. Since this current is for the same amount of time, the total charge, Q_T, must be the same as the charge on each capacitor. That is,

$$Q_T = Q_1 = Q_2$$

Charging capacitors in series causes the same charge to be across each capacitor; however, as shown in Floyd's text, the total capacitance *decreases*. In a series circuit, the total capacitance is given by the formula:

$$\frac{1}{C_T} = \frac{1}{C_1} + \frac{1}{C_2} + \ldots + \frac{1}{C_n}$$

Now consider capacitors in parallel. In a parallel circuit, the total current is equal to the sum of the currents in each branch as stated by Kirchhoff's current law. If this current is for the same amount of time, the total charge leaving the voltage source will equal the sum of the charges which flow in each branch. That is,

$$Q_T = Q_1 + Q_2 + \ldots + Q_n$$

Capacitors connected in parallel will raise the total capacitance because more charge is stored at the same voltage. The equation for the total capacitance of parallel capacitors is:

$$C_T = C_1 + C_2 + \ldots + C_n$$

There are two quick tests you can make to check capacitors. The first is an ohmmeter test, useful for capacitors larger than 0.01 µF. This test is best done with an analog ohmmeter rather than a digital meter. The test will sometimes indicate a faulty capacitor is good; however, you can be sure that if a capacitor fails the test, it is bad. The test is done as follows:

(a)   Remove one end of the capacitor from the circuit and discharge it by placing a short across its terminals.

(b)   Set the ohmmeter on a high-resistance scale and place the negative lead from an ohmmeter on the negative terminal of the capacitor. You must connect the ohmmeter with the proper polarity. *Do not assume the common lead from the ohmmeter is the negative side!*

(c)   Touch the other lead of the ohmmeter onto the remaining terminal of the capacitor. The meter should indicate very low resistance and then gradually increase resistance. If you put the meter in a higher range, the ohmmeter charges the capacitor slower and the capacitance "kick" will be emphasized. For small capacitors (under 0.01 µF), this charge may not be seen. Large electrolytic capacitors require more time to charge, so use a lower range on your ohmmeter. Capacitors should never remain near zero resistance, as this indicates a short. An immediate high resistance reading indicates an open for larger capacitors.

A capacitor that passes the ohmmeter test may still fail when voltage is applied. A voltmeter can be used to check a capacitor with voltage applied. The voltmeter is connected in *series* with the capacitor.

When voltage is first applied, the capacitor charges. As it charges, voltage will appear across it, and the voltmeter indication should be a very small voltage. Large electrolytic capacitors may have leakage current that makes them appear bad, especially with a very high impedance voltmeter. As in the case of the ohmmeter test, small capacitors may charge so quickly they appear bad. In these cases, use the test as a relative test, comparing the reading with a similar capacitor that you know is good. Ohmmeter and voltmeter tests are never considered comprehensive tests but are indicative that a capacitor is capable of being charged.

Capacitor Identification

There are many types of capacitors available with a wide variety of specifications for size, voltage rating, frequency range, temperature stability, leakage current, and so forth. For general-purpose applications, small capacitors are constructed with paper, ceramic, or other insulation material and are not polarized. Three common methods for showing the value of a small capacitor are shown in Figure 4–1. In Figure 4–1(a), a coded number is stamped on the capacitor that is read in pF. The first two digits represent the first two digits, the third number is a multiplier. For example, the number 473 is a 47000 pF capacitor. Figure 4–1(b) shows the actual value stamped on the capacitor in μF. In the example shown, .047 μF is the same as 47000 pF. In Figure 4–1(c), a ceramic color-coded capacitor is shown that is read in pF. Generally, when 5 colors are shown, the first is a temperature coefficient (in ppm/°C with special meanings to each color). The second, third, and fourth colors are read as digit 1, digit 2, and a multiplier. The last color is the tolerance. Thus a 47000 pF capacitor will have a color representing the temperature coefficient followed by yellow, violet, and orange bands representing the value. Unlike resistors, the tolerance band is generally green for 5% and white for 10%. More information on capacitor color codes is given in the text in Appendix B.

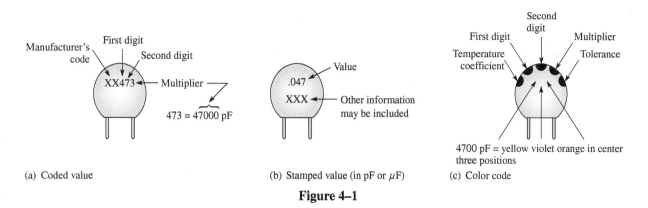

(a) Coded value   (b) Stamped value (in pF or μF)   (c) Color code

Figure 4–1

Larger electrolytic capacitors will generally have their value printed in uncoded form on the capacitor and a mark indicating either the positive or negative lead. They also have a maximum working voltage printed on them which must not be exceeded. Electrolytic capacitors are always polarized, and it is very important to place them into a circuit in the correct direction based on the polarity shown on the capacitor. They can overheat and explode if placed in the circuit backwards.

PROCEDURE

1. Obtain five capacitors as listed in Table 4–1. Check each capacitor using the ohmmeter test described in the Summary of Theory. Record the results of the test in Table 4–1.

2. Test each capacitor using the voltmeter test as illustrated in Figure 4–2. Large electrolytic capacitors or very small capacitors may appear to fail this test, as mentioned in the Summary of Theory. Check the voltage rating on the capacitor to be sure it is not exceeded. The working voltage is the maximum voltage that can safely be applied to the capacitor. Record your results in Table 4–1.

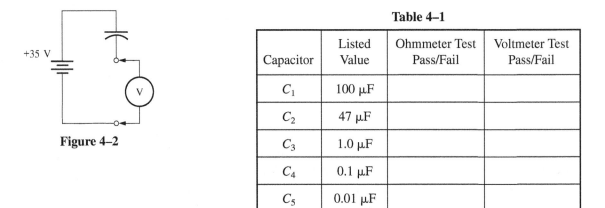

Figure 4–2

Table 4–1

Capacitor	Listed Value	Ohmmeter Test Pass/Fail	Voltmeter Test Pass/Fail
C_1	100 μF		
C_2	47 μF		
C_3	1.0 μF		
C_4	0.1 μF		
C_5	0.01 μF		

3. Connect the circuit shown in Figure 4–3. The switches can be made from jumper wires. Leave both switches open. The light-emitting diodes (LEDs) and the capacitor are both polarized components—they must be connected in the correct direction in order to work properly.

4. Close S_1 and observe the LEDs. Describe your observation.

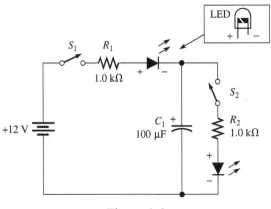

Figure 4–3

192

5.   Open S_1 and close S_2. What happens?

6.   Now connect C_2 in series with C_1. Open S_2. Make certain the capacitors are fully discharged by shorting them with a piece of wire; then close S_1. Measure the voltage across each capacitor. Do this quickly to prevent the meter from causing the capacitors to discharge. Record the voltages and describe your observations.

$V_1 =$ _____ $V_2 =$ _____

Observations:

7.   Using the measured voltage, compute the charge on each capacitor.

$Q_1 =$ _____ $Q_2 =$ _____

Then open S_1 and close S_2. Observe the result.

8.   Change the capacitors from series to parallel. Ensure that the capacitors are fully discharged. Open S_2 and close S_1. Measure the voltage (quickly) across the capacitors. Record the voltages and describe your observations.

$V_1 =$ _____ $V_2 =$ _____

Observations:

9.   Using the measured voltage, calculate the charge across each capacitor.

$Q_1 =$ _____ $Q_2 =$ _____

10. Replace the 12 V dc source with a signal generator. Close both S_1 and S_2. Set the signal generator to a square wave and set the amplitude to 12 V_{pp}. Set the frequency to 10 Hz. Notice the difference in the LED pulses. This demonstrates one of the principal applications of large capacitors—that of filtering. Explain your observations.

CONCLUSION

EVALUATION AND REVIEW QUESTIONS

1. Why did the LEDs flash for a shorter time in step 6 than in steps 4 and 5?

2. What would happen if you added more series capacitance in step 6?

3. (a) What is the total capacitance when a 1.0 μF capacitor is connected in parallel with a 2.0 μF capacitor?

   (b) If the capacitors are connected in series, what is the total capacitance?

   (c) In the series connection, which capacitor has the greater voltage across it?

4. Determine the value in pF and μF for each small capacitor with the coded numbers as shown:

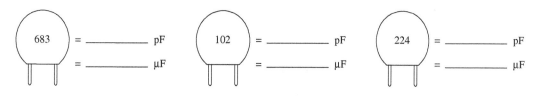

683 = _____ pF
= _____ μF

102 = _____ pF
= _____ μF

224 = _____ pF
= _____ μF

5. Write the coded number that should appear on each capacitor for the values shown:

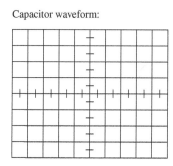

= ___47___ pF

= __10,000__ pF

= ___0.033___ μF

FOR FURTHER INVESTIGATION

Use the oscilloscope to measure the waveforms across the capacitors and the LEDs in step 10. Try speeding up the signal generator and observe the waveforms. Use the two-channel difference measurement explained in Experiment 2 to see the waveform across the ungrounded LED. Draw and label the waveforms.

Capacitor waveform:

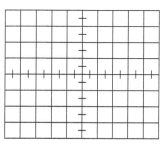

Plot 4–1

LED waveform:

Plot 4–2

5 Capacitive Reactance

Name _____

Date _____

Class _____

READING
Floyd, Sections 9–6 and 9–7

OBJECTIVES
After performing this experiment, you will be able to:
1. Measure the capacitive reactance of a capacitor at a specified frequency.
2. Compare the reactance of capacitors connected in series and parallel.

MATERIALS NEEDED
One 1.0 kΩ resistor
Two 0.1 µF capacitors
For Further Investigation:
   Two 100 µF capacitors, two LEDs, one 100 kΩ resistor

SUMMARY OF THEORY
If a resistor is connected across a sine wave generator, the current is *in phase* with the applied voltage. If, instead of a resistor, we connect a capacitor across the generator, the current is not in phase with the voltage. This is illustrated in Figure 5–1. Note that the current and voltage have exactly the same frequency, but the current is *leading* the voltage by 1/4 cycle.

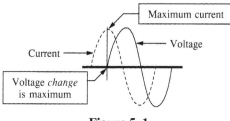

Figure 5–1

Current in the capacitor is directly proportional to the capacitance and the rate of change of voltage. The largest current is when the voltage *change* is a maximum. If the capacitance is increased or the frequency is increased, there is more current. This is why a capacitor is sometimes thought of as a high-frequency short.

Reactance is the opposition to ac current and is measured in ohms, like resistance. Capacitive reactance is written with the symbol X_C. It can be defined as:

$$X_C = \frac{1}{2\pi fC}$$

where f is the generator frequency in hertz and C is the capacitance in farads.

Ohm's law can be generalized to ac circuits. For a capacitor, we can find the voltage across the capacitor using the current and the capacitive reactance. Ohm's law for the voltage across a capacitor is

$$V_C = IX_C$$

PROCEDURE

1. Obtain two capacitors with the values shown in Table 5–1. If you have a capacitance bridge available, measure their capacitance and record in Table 5–1; otherwise, record the listed value of the capacitors. Measure and record the value of resistor R_1.

2. Set up the circuit shown in Figure 5–2. Set the generator for a 1.0 kHz sine wave with a 1.0 V rms output. Measure the rms voltage with your DMM while it is connected to the circuit.[1] Check the frequency and voltage with the oscilloscope. Note: $1.0\ V_{rms} = 2.828\ V_{pp}$.

Table 5–1

Component	Listed Value	Measured Value
C_1	0.1 μF	
C_2	0.1 μF	
R_1	1.0 kΩ	

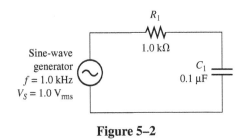

Sine-wave generator
$f = 1.0$ kHz
$V_S = 1.0\ V_{rms}$

R_1
1.0 kΩ

C_1
0.1 μF

Figure 5–2

3. The circuit is a series circuit, so the current in the resistor is the identical current seen by the capacitor. You can find this current easily by applying Ohm's law to the resistor. Measure the voltage across the resistor, V_R, using the DMM. Record the measured voltage in Table 5–2 in the column labeled Capacitor C_1. Compute the current in the circuit by dividing the measured voltage by the resistance of R_1 and enter in Table 5–2.

Table 5–2

	Capacitor C_1	Capacitor C_2
Voltage across R_1, V_R		
Total current, I		
Voltage across C, V_C		
Capacitive reactance, X_C		
Computed capacitance, C		

---

[1] DMMs have a relatively low bandwidth, although most can measure 1.0 kHz. Verify that the DMM you are using has at least a 1.0 kHz bandwidth; if it does not, use the oscilloscope for all voltage measurements.

4. Measure the rms voltage across the capacitor, V_C. Record this voltage in Table 5–2. Then use this voltage to compute the capacitive reactance using Ohm's law:

$$X_C = \frac{V_C}{I}$$

Enter this value as the capacitive reactance in Table 5–2.

5. Using the capacitive reactance found in step 4, compute the capacitance using the equation

$$C = \frac{1}{2\pi f X_C}$$

Enter the computed capacitance in Table 5–2. This value should agree with the value marked on the capacitor and measured in step 1 within experimental tolerances.

6. Repeat steps 3, 4, and 5 using capacitor C_2. Enter the data in Table 5–2 in the column labeled Capacitor C_2.

7. Now connect C_1 in series with C_2. The equivalent capacitive reactance and capacitance can be found for the series connection by measuring across both capacitors as if they were one capacitor. Enter the data in Table 5–3 in the column labeled Series Capacitors. The following steps will guide you:
   (a) Check that the generator is set to 1.0 V rms. Find the current in the circuit by measuring the voltage across the resistor as before and dividing by the resistance. Enter the measured voltage and the current you found in Table 5–3.
   (b) Measure the voltage across *both* capacitors. Enter this voltage in Table 5–3.
   (c) Use Ohm's law to find the capacitive reactance of both capacitors. Use the voltage measured in step (b) and the current measured in step (a).
   (d) Compute the total capacitance by using the equation

$$C_T = \frac{1}{2\pi f X_{CT}}$$

8. Connect the capacitors in parallel and repeat step 7. Assume the parallel capacitors are one equivalent capacitor for the measurements. Enter the data in Table 5–3 in the column labeled Parallel Capacitors.

Table 5–3

Step		Series Capacitors	Parallel Capacitors
(a)	Voltage across R_1, V_R		
	Total current, I		
(b)	Voltage across capacitors, V_C		
(c)	Capacitive reactance, X_{CT}		
(d)	Computed capacitance, C_T		

CONCLUSION

EVALUATION AND REVIEW QUESTIONS

1. Compare the capacitive reactance of the series capacitors with the capacitive reactance of the parallel capacitors. Use your data in Table 5–3.

2. Compare the total capacitance of the series capacitors with the total capacitance of the parallel capacitors.

3. If someone had mistakenly used too small a capacitor in a circuit, what would happen to the capacitive reactance?

4. How could you apply the method used in this experiment to find the value of the unknown capacitor?

5. Compute the capacitive reactance for an 800 pF capacitor at a frequency of 250 kHz.

FOR FURTHER INVESTIGATION

A voltage multiplier is a circuit that uses diodes and capacitors to increase the peak value of a sine wave. Voltage multipliers can produce high voltages without requiring a high-voltage transformer. The circuit illustrated in Figure 5–3 is a full-wave voltage doubler. The circuit is drawn as a bridge with diodes in two arms and capacitors in two arms. The diodes allow current in only one direction, charging the capacitors to near the peak voltage of the sine wave. Generally, voltage doublers are used with 60 Hz power line frequencies and with ordinary diodes, but in order to clarify the operation of this circuit, you can use the LEDs that were used in this experiment. (Note that this causes the output voltage to be reduced slightly.) Connect the circuit, setting the function generator to 20 V_{pp} sine wave at a frequency of 1.0 Hz. (If you cannot obtain a 20 V_{pp} signal, use the largest signal you can obtain from your generator.) Observe the operation of the circuit, then try speeding up the generator. Look at the waveform across the load resistor with your oscilloscope using the two-channel difference method. What is the dc voltage across the load resistor? What happens to the output as the generator is speeded up? Try a smaller load resistor. Can you explain your observations?

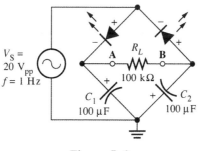

Figure 5–3

MULTISIM TROUBLESHOOTING

This experiment has four Multisim files on the website (www.prenhall.com/floyd). To simulate the winding resistance of the inductor, a 100 Ω resistor has been added in series in the computer simulations. The resistance of coils varies widely with the size of the coil and the wiring used to make the coil, so you may have found a much different resistance in the experiment. The frequency response has been plotted on the Bode plotter, a fictitious instrument but with characteristics similar to a spectrum analyzer.

Three of the four files contain a simulated "fault"; one has "no fault". The file with no fault is named EXP19-2-nf. You may want to open this file to compare your results with the computer simulation. Then open each of the files with faults. Use the simulated instruments to investigate the circuit and determine the problem. The following are the filenames for circuits with troubleshooting problems for this experiment.

EXP19-2-f1

    Fault: _____

EXP19-2-f2

    Fault: _____

EXP19-2-f3

    Fault: _____

Application Assignment 2

Name _____
Date _____
Class _____

REFERENCE
Floyd, Chapter 9, Application Assignment: Putting Your Knowledge to Work

Step 1   Compare the PC board with the schematic. Do they agree?

Step 2   Test the input to amplifier board 1. If incorrect, specify the likely fault:

Step 3   Test the input to amplifier board 2. If incorrect, specify the likely fault:

Step 4   Test the input to amplifier board 3. If incorrect, specify the likely fault:

RELATED EXPERIMENT

MATERIALS NEEDED
Resistors:
        One 1.0 kΩ, two 10 kΩ
Capacitors:
        One 0.1 μF, 1.0 μF

DISCUSSION
The capacitor tests described in Experiment 4 can be conducted only on a capacitor that has been removed from the circuit under test. Usually there are other components that could account for a circuit failure; you need to have an idea of the reason for the failure before you randomly check parts. If a capacitor fails because it is open, it has no effect on the dc voltages but will not pass ac. If it fails because it is shorted, both dc and ac paths are affected. Other failures (such as the wrong size component) may produce a partial failure.

        The circuit shown in Figure AA–2–1 is similar to the problem presented in the text. Capacitor C_1 represents a coupling capacitor and R_1 and R_2 set up the bias conditions needed for an amplifier. R_3

represents additional source resistance. Start by investigating the circuit when it is operating normally. Find the ac and dc voltage drops across each component. Then open C_1 and check circuit operation. Are there any changes to the dc voltages with the open capacitor? Then test the circuit with a short across C_1 (use a jumper). Finally, assume a capacitor that is too small was accidentally put in the circuit. Replace C_1 with a 0.1 μF capacitor and test the circuit. Table AA–2–1 is set up to record your data. Write a conclusion for your observations.

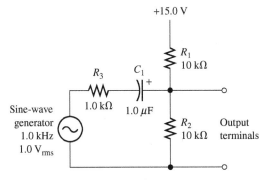

Figure AA–2–1

Table AA–2–1

Condition	Measured Voltages							
	V_{R1}		V_{R2}		V_{R3}		V_{C1}	
	dc	ac	dc	ac	dc	ac	dc	ac
Normal								
C_1 Open								
C_1 Shorted								
C_1 Wrong value								

EXPERIMENTAL RESULTS

Checkup 2

REFERENCE
Floyd, Chap. 9, and Buchla, Experiments 18 and 19

1.   Assume two capacitors have the same voltage across them but capacitor *A* has twice the charge of capacitor *B*. From this we can conclude that:
(a) *A* is larger.   (b) They are equal.
(c) *B* is larger.   (d) No conclusion can be made.

2.   Assume two capacitors have equal capacitances, but capacitor *A* has twice the voltage of capacitor *B*. From this we can conclude that:
(a) *A* has larger plates.   (b) *A* has smaller plates.
(c) *A* has a greater charge.   (d) *A* has less charge.

3.   Assume capacitor *A* is larger than capacitor *B*. If they are connected in series, the total capacitance will be:
(a) larger than *A*   (b) smaller than *B*
(c) larger than *B*   (d) between *A* and *B*

4.   Compared to any one capacitor, the total capacitance of three equal parallel capacitors is:
(a) one-third   (b) the same   (c) double   (d) three times

5.   Assume a 100 μF capacitor is charged to 10 V. The stored charge is:
(a) 10 μC   (b) 100 μC   (c) 110 μC   (d) 1000 μC

6.   In a series *RC* circuit, the time required for a capacitor to go from no charge to full charge (99%) is:
(a) one time constant   (b) three time constants
(c) five time constants   (d) 100 ms

7.   A sinusoidal voltage waveform is applied to a capacitor. The amount of current is inversely proportional to the:
(a) reactance   (b) capacitance   (c) frequency   (d) resistance

8.   A sinusoidal voltage waveform is applied to a capacitor. If the frequency of the waveform is increased, the capacitance:
(a) increases   (b) does not change   (c) decreases

9.   The unit of measurement for capacitive reactance is the:
(a) volt   (b) ohm   (c) farad   (d) coulomb

The power that is stored or returned to the circuit from a capacitor is called:

(a) stored power

(b) apparent power

(c) true power

(d) reactive power

11. The time constant of an RC circuit is measured with an oscilloscope and found to require 7.6 divisions to change from 0 to 63% of the final value. The SEC/DIV control is set to 20 μs/div.

(a) If the resistance is 4.7 kΩ, what is the measured value of the capacitance?

(b) How long after charging begins does it take the capacitor to reach full charge?

12. Assume you want to check a 100 μF capacitor to see if it is capable of storing a charge. What simple test would you perform?

13. Consider the circuit shown in Figure C–2–1, which is the same as Figure 5–2. You should have measured a larger voltage across C_1 than across R_1. What does this immediately tell you about the capacitive reactance at this frequency?

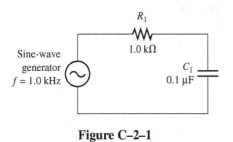

Figure C–2–1

14. Consider the circuit shown in Figure C–2–2. C_1 is known to be 0.047 μF, but the value of C_2 is unknown. Assume you measure 6.8 V$_{rms}$ across C_2. What is its capacitance?

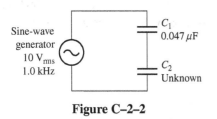

Figure C–2–2

15. A capacitor is marked 221. What is its value in pF and in μF?

6 Series *RC* Circuits

Name _____

Date _____

Class _____

READING
Floyd, Sections 10–1 through 10–3

OBJECTIVES
After performing this experiment, you will be able to:
1. Compute the capacitive reactance of a capacitor from voltage measurements in a series *RC* circuit.
2. Draw the impedance and voltage phasor diagrams for a series *RC* circuit.
3. Explain how frequency affects the impedance and voltage phasors in a series *RC* circuit.

MATERIALS NEEDED
One 6.8 kΩ resistor
One 0.01 µF capacitor

SUMMARY OF THEORY
When a sine wave at some frequency drives a circuit that contains only linear elements (resistors, capacitors, and inductors), the waveforms throughout the circuit are also sine waves at that same frequency. To understand the relationship between the sinusoidal voltages and currents, we can represent ac waveforms as phasor quantities. A *phasor* is a complex number used to represent a sine wave's amplitude and phase. A graphical representation of the phasors in a circuit is a useful tool for visualizing the amplitude and phase relationship of the various waveforms. The algebra of complex numbers can then be used to perform arithmetic operations on sine waves.

Figure 6–1(a) shows an *RC* circuit with its impedance phasor diagram plotted in Figure 6–1(b). The total impedance is 5 kΩ, producing a current in this example of 1.0 mA. In any series circuit, the same current is throughout the circuit. By multiplying each of the phasors in the impedance diagram by the current in the circuit, we arrive at the voltage phasor diagram illustrated in Figure 6–1(c). It is convenient to use current as the reference for comparing voltage phasors because the current is the same throughout. Notice the direction of current. The voltage and the current are in the same direction across the resistor because they are in phase, but the voltage across the capacitor lags the current by 90°. The generator voltage is the phasor sum of the voltage across the resistor and the voltage across the capacitor.

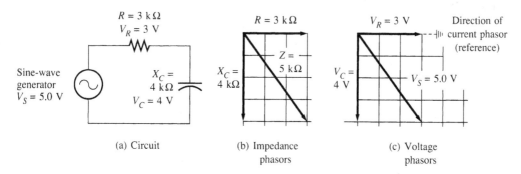

(a) Circuit

(b) Impedance phasors

(c) Voltage phasors

Figure 6–1

The phasor diagram illustrated by Figure 6–1 is correct only at one frequency. This is because the reactance of a capacitor is frequency dependent as given by the equation:

$$X_C = \frac{1}{2\pi f C}$$

As the frequency is raised, the reactance (X_C) of the capacitor decreases. This changes the phase angle and voltages across the components. These changes are investigated in this experiment.

PROCEDURE

1. Measure the actual capacitance of a 0.01 μF capacitor and a 6.8 kΩ resistor. Enter the measured values in Table 6–1. If you cannot measure the capacitor, use the listed value.

2. Connect the series *RC* circuit shown in Figure 6–2. Set the signal generator for a 500 Hz sine wave at 3.0 V_{pp}. The voltage should be measured with the circuit connected. Set the voltage with a voltmeter, and check both voltage and frequency with the oscilloscope. Record all voltages and currents throughout this experiment as peak-to-peak values.

Table 6–1

Component	Listed Value	Measured Value
C_1	0.01 μF	0.01
R_1	6.8 kΩ	6.68

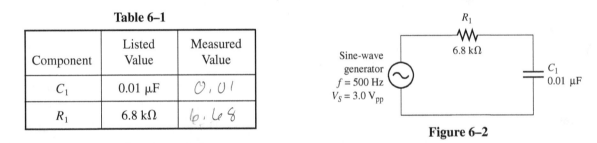

Figure 6–2

3. Using the two-channel-difference technique described in Experiment 2, measure the peak-to-peak voltage across the resistor (V_R). Then measure the peak-to-peak voltage across the capacitor (V_C). Record the voltage readings on the first line of Table 6–2.

4. Compute the peak-to-peak current in the circuit by applying Ohm's law to the measured value of the resistor:

   Ch 1 = Voltage across the hole thing

   ch2 = Vc

   add 1-2 = .5 at $\frac{1.3}{1} \times \frac{1}{2} = .65$ $I = \dfrac{V_R}{R}$

   Since the current is the same throughout a series circuit, this is a simple method for finding the current in both the resistor and the capacitor. Enter this computed current in Table 6–2.

5. Compute the capacitive reactance, X_C, by applying Ohm's law to the capacitor. The reactance is found by dividing the voltage across the capacitor (step 3) by the current in the circuit (step 4). Enter the capacitive reactance in Table 6–2.

851.1824
272.7260
108.6224

$$Z = \sqrt{R^2 + X_c^2}$$

845.8124

6.67k

Table 6–2

Frequency	V_R	V_C	I	X_C	Z
500 Hz	.65	2.75v	97 mA	28.4k	29.9k
1000 Hz	1.15	2.6v	172.15 mA	15.k	16.5k
1500 Hz	1.6	2.4v	239.5	10k	12.k
2000 Hz	1.85	2.2v	277 mA	8k	10.4
4000 Hz	2.4	1.45v	359 mA	4k	8k
8000 Hz	2.75	.85v	412. mA	2k	7k

6. Compute the total impedance of the circuit by applying Ohm's law to the entire circuit. Use the generator voltage set in step 2 and the current determined in step 4. Enter the computed impedance in Table 6–2.

7. Change the frequency of the generator to 1000 Hz. Check the generator voltage and reset it to 3.0 V_{pp} if necessary. Repeat steps 3 through 6, entering the data in Table 6–2. Continue in this manner for each frequency listed in Table 6–2.

8. From the data in Table 6–2 and the measured value of R_1, draw the impedance phasors for the circuit at a frequency of 1000 Hz on Plot 6–1(a) and the voltage phasors on Plot 6–1(b).

R 61.68 V_R 1.15

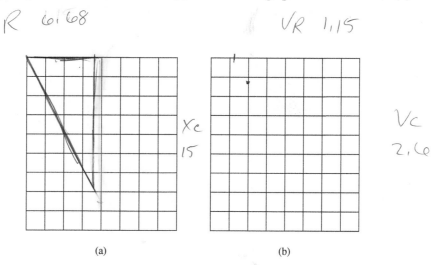

X_c
15

V_c
2.6

(a)   (b)

Plot 6–1

9. Repeat step 8 for a frequency of 4000 Hz. Draw the impedance phasors on Plot 6–2(a) and the voltage phasors on Plot 6–2(b).

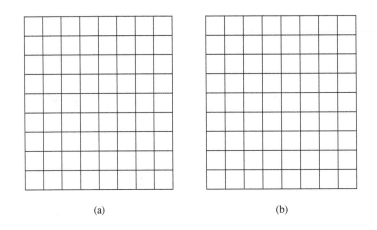

(a)　　　　　　　　　　　　(b)

Plot 6–2

10. The phasor drawings reveal how the impedance and voltage phasors change with frequency. Investigate the frequency effect further by graphing both the voltage across the capacitor and the voltage across the resistor as a function of frequency. Label each curve. Use Plot 6–3.

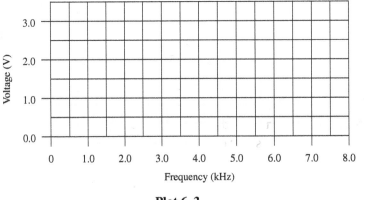

Plot 6–3

CONCLUSION

EVALUATION AND REVIEW QUESTIONS

1. The Pythagorean theorem can be applied to the phasors drawn in Plots 6–1 and 6–2. Show that the data in both plots satisfy the following equations

$$Z = \sqrt{R^2 + X_C^2}$$

$$V_S = \sqrt{V_R^2 + V_C^2}$$

210

2. Assume you needed to pass high frequencies through an *RC* filter but block low frequencies. From the data in Plot 6–3, should you connect the output across the capacitor or across the resistor? Explain your answer.

3. (a) What happens to the total impedance of a series *RC* circuit as the frequency is increased?

    (b) Explain why the phase angle between the generator voltage and the resistor voltage decreases as the frequency is increased.

4. A student accidentally used a capacitor that was ten times larger than required in the experiment. Predict what happens to the frequency response shown in Plot 6–3 with the larger capacitor.

5. Assume there was no current in the series *RC* circuit because of an open circuit. How could you quickly determine if the resistor or the capacitor were open?

FOR FURTHER INVESTIGATION

This experiment showed that the voltage phasor diagram can be obtained by multiplying each quantity on the impedance phasor diagram by the current in the circuit. In turn, if each of the voltage phasors is multiplied by the current, the resulting diagram is the power phasor diagram. Using the data from Table 6–2, convert the current and source voltage to an rms value. Then determine the true power, the reactive power, and the apparent power in the *RC* circuit at a frequency of 1000 Hz and a frequency of 4000 Hz. On Plot 6–4, draw the power phasor diagrams. (See Section 3–7 of Floyd's text for further discussion of the power phasors.)

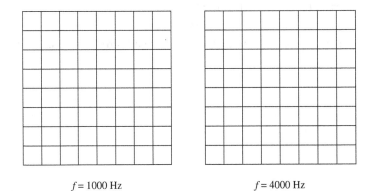

f = 1000 Hz f = 4000 Hz

Plot 6–4

MULTISIM TROUBLESHOOTING

This experiment has four Multisim files on the website (www.prenhall.com/floyd). Three of the four files contain a simulated "fault"; one has "no fault". The file with no fault is named EXP20-2-nf. You may want to open this file to compare your results with the computer simulation. Then open each of the files with faults. Use the simulated instruments to investigate the circuit and determine the problem. The following are the filenames for circuits with troubleshooting problems for this experiment.

EXP20-2-f1
     Fault: _____

EXP20-2-f2
     Fault: _____

EXP20-2-f3
     Fault: _____

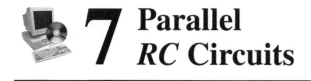

7 Parallel RC Circuits

Name _____
Date _____
Class _____

READING
Floyd, Sections 10–4 through 10–9

OBJECTIVES
After performing this experiment, you will be able to:
1. Measure the current phasors for a parallel *RC* circuit.
2. Explain how the current phasors and phase angle are affected by a change in frequency for parallel *RC* circuits.

MATERIALS NEEDED
Resistors:
    One 100 kΩ, two 1.0 kΩ
Capacitors:
    One 1000 pF

SUMMARY OF THEORY
In a series circuit, the same *current* is in all components. For this reason, current is generally used as the reference. By contrast, in parallel, the same *voltage* is across all components. The voltage is therefore the reference. Current in each branch is compared to the circuit voltage. In parallel circuits, Kirchhoff's current law applies to any junction but care must be taken to add the currents as phasors. The current entering a junction is always equal to the current leaving the junction.

Figure 7–1 illustrates a parallel *RC* circuit. If the impedance of each branch is known, the current in that branch can be determined directly from Ohm's law. The current phasor diagram can then be constructed. The total current can be found as the phasor sum of the currents in each branch. The current in the capacitor is shown at +90° from the voltage reference because the current leads the voltage in a capacitor. The current in the resistor is along the *x*-axis because current and voltage are in phase in a resistor. The Pythagorean theorem can be applied to the current phasors, resulting in the equation

$$I_T = \sqrt{I_R^2 + I_C^2}$$

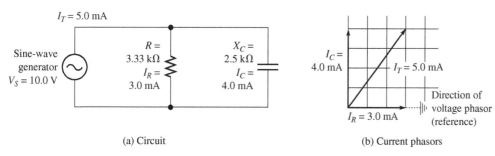

(a) Circuit   (b) Current phasors

Figure 7–1

In this experiment, two extra 1.0 kΩ resistors are added to "sense" current and provide a small voltage drop that can be measured. These resistors are much smaller than the parallel branch impedance, so their resistance can be ignored in the computation of circuit impedance.

PROCEDURE

1. Measure a resistor with a color-code value of 100 kΩ and each of two current-sense resistors (R_{S1} and R_{S2}) with color-code values of 1.0 kΩ. Measure the capacitance of a 1000 pF capacitor. Use the listed value if a measurement cannot be made. Record the measured values in Table 7–1.

Table 7–1   (f = 1.0 kHz)

	Listed Value	Measured Value	Voltage Drop	Computed Current
R_1	100 kΩ			
R_{S1}	1.0 kΩ			
R_{S2}	1.0 kΩ			
C_1	1000 pF			

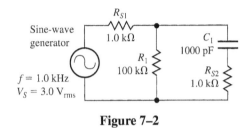

Figure 7–2

2. Construct the circuit shown in Figure 7–2. Set the generator to a voltage of 3.0 V_{rms} at 1.0 kHz. Check the voltage and frequency with your oscilloscope.

3. Using a voltmeter, measure the voltage drop across each resistor. The voltage drops are small, so measure as accurately as possible. You should keep three significant figures in your measurement. Record the voltage drops in Table 7–1.

4. Compute the current in each resistor using Ohm's law. Record the computed current in Table 7–1.

5. Draw the current phasors I_{R1}, I_{C1}, and the total current I_T on Plot 7–1. The total current is through sense resistor R_{S1}. The current I_{C1} is through sense resistor R_{S2}. Ignore the small effect of the sense resistors on the phasor diagram. Note carefully the direction of the phasors. Label each of the current phasors.

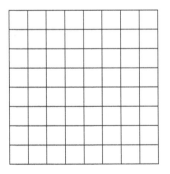

Plot 7–1

214

6. Compute X_{C1} for the 1.0 kHz frequency. Then, using this value and the measured resistance of R_1, find the total impedance, Z_T, of the circuit using the product-over-sum rule. The sense resistors can be ignored for this calculation.

$$X_{C1} = \underline{\hspace{3cm}} \qquad Z_T = \frac{R_1 X_C}{\sqrt{R_1^2 + X_C^2}} = \underline{\hspace{3cm}}$$

7. Using Z_T from step 6 and the applied voltage, V_S, compute the total current, I_T. The total current should basically agree with the value determined in step 4.

$$I_T = \underline{\hspace{3cm}}$$

8. Change the frequency of the generator to 2.0 kHz. Check that the generator voltage is still 3.0 V. Repeat steps 1–5 for the 2.0 kHz frequency. Enter the data in Table 7–2 and draw the current phasors on Plot 7–2.

Table 7–2 ($f = 2.0$ kHz)

	Listed Value	Measured Value	Voltage Drop	Computed Current
R_1	100 kΩ			
R_{S1}	1.0 kΩ			
R_{S2}	1.0 kΩ			
C_1	1000 pF			

Plot 7–2

CONCLUSION

EVALUATION AND REVIEW QUESTIONS

1. Explain how increasing the frequency affects:
   (a) the total impedance of the circuit

   (b) the phase angle between the generator voltage and the generator current

2. Assume the frequency had been set to 5.0 kHz in this experiment. Compute:

   (a)   the current in the resistor

   (b)   the current in the capacitor

   (c)   the total current

3. If a smaller capacitor had been substituted in the experiment, what would happen to the current phasor diagrams?

4. (a)   The high-frequency response of a transistor amplifier is limited by stray capacitance, as illustrated in Figure 7–3. The upper *cutoff* frequency is defined as the frequency at which the resistance R_{IN} is equal to the capacitive reactance X_C of the stray capacitance. An equivalent parallel RC circuit can simplify the problem. Compute the cutoff frequency for the circuit shown by setting $R_{IN} = X_C$ and solving for f_C.

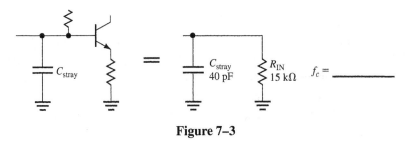

Figure 7–3

   (b)   How do the branch currents compare at the cutoff frequency?

   (c)   Explain what happens above this frequency to the current in the equivalent parallel RC circuit.

5. If the stray capacitance in Figure 7–3 is increased, what happens to the cutoff frequency?

FOR FURTHER INVESTIGATION

In a series *RC* circuit, the impedance phasor is the sum of the resistance and reactance phasors as shown in Experiment 6. In a parallel circuit, the admittance phasor is the sum of the conductance and the susceptance phasors. On Plot 7–3, draw the admittance, conductance, and susceptance phasors for the experiment at a frequency of 1.0 kHz. Hint: The admittance phasor diagram can be obtained directly from the current phasor diagram by dividing the current phasors by the applied voltage.

Plot 7–3

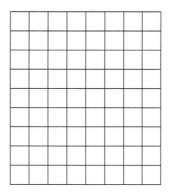

MULTISIM TROUBLESHOOTING

This experiment has four Multisim files on the website (www.prenhall.com/floyd). Three of the four files contain a simulated "fault"; one has "no fault". The file with no fault is named EXP21-2-nf. You may want to open this file to compare your results with the computer simulation. Then open each of the files with faults. Use the simulated instruments to investigate the circuit and determine the problem. The following are the filenames for circuits with troubleshooting problems for this experiment.

EXP21-2-f1

Fault: _____

EXP21-2-f2

Fault: _____

EXP21-2-f3

Fault: _____

Application Assignment 3

Name _____

Date _____

Class _____

REFERENCE

Floyd, Chapter 10, Application Assignment: Putting Your Knowledge to Work

Step 1 Evaluate the amplifier input circuit. Determine the equivalent resistance:
Equivalent resistance = _____

Step 2 Measure the response at frequency f_1. Sketch the waveform for channel 2 on Plot AA–3–1.

Step 3 Measure the response at frequency f_2. Sketch the waveform for channel 2 on Plot AA–3–2. Explain why the response is different than in step 2.

Step 4 Measure the response at frequency f_3. Sketch the waveform for channel 2 on Plot AA–3–3. Explain why the response is different from that in step 3.

Step 5 Plot a response curve for the amplifier input circuit on Plot AA–3–4.

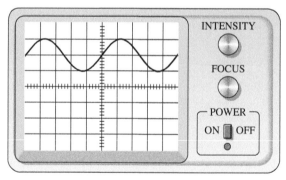

Plot AA–3–1

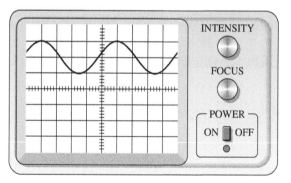

Plot AA–3–2

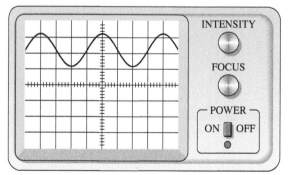

Plot AA–3–3

Plot AA–3–4

RELATED EXPERIMENT

MATERIALS NEEDED
One 100 kΩ resistor
One capacitor (value to be determined by student)

DISCUSSION
The application assignment requires you to consider the frequency response of a coupling capacitor. A circuit using a coupling capacitor was introduced in Application Assignment 2. The capacitor should look nearly like a short to the ac signal but appear open to the dc voltage. A simplified coupling circuit, with the dc portion removed, is illustrated in Figure AA–3–1. R_{input} represents the input resistance of an amplifier, and $C_{coupling}$ is the coupling capacitor.

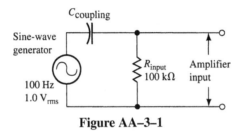

Figure AA–3–1

In this application, you need to find a capacitor that will allow a minimum of 90% of the generator signal to appear across R_{input} at a frequency of 100 Hz. Compute the value of a capacitor that will meet this requirement. Construct your circuit and test it by measuring the generator voltage, the voltage drop across the capacitor, and the voltage drop across the resistor using a 100 Hz signal from the generator. Summarize your calculations and measurements.

EXPERIMENTAL RESULTS

Checkup 3

REFERENCE

Floyd, Chap. 10, and Buchla, Experiments 20 and 21

1. If a sinusoidal voltage wave is applied to a capacitor, the current in the capacitor:
    (a) leads the voltage by 45°   (b) leads the voltage by 90°
    (c) lags the voltage by 45°   (d) lags the voltage by 90°

2. If a 0.1 μF capacitor is connected across a 50 V_{rms}, 1 kHz source, the current in the capacitor will be:
    (a) 2.00 nA   (b) 3.14 μA   (c) 0.795 mA   (d) 31.4 mA

3. In a series RC circuit in which $X_C = R$, the generator current:
    (a) leads the generator voltage by 45°   (b) leads the generator voltage by 90°
    (c) lags the generator voltage by 45°   (d) lags the generator voltage by 90°

4. In a parallel RC circuit in which $X_C = R$, the generator current:
    (a) leads the generator voltage by 45°   (b) leads the generator voltage by 90°
    (c) lags the generator voltage by 45°   (d) lags the generator voltage by 90°

5. If the frequency is raised in a series RC circuit and nothing else changes, the current in the circuit will:
    (a) increase   (b) stay the same   (c) decrease

6. If the frequency is raised in a parallel RC circuit and nothing else changes, the current in the circuit will:
    (a) increase   (b) stay the same   (c) decrease

7. The reciprocal of reactance is:
    (a) conductance   (b) susceptance   (c) admittance   (d) impedance

8. If the phase angle between the voltage and current in a series RC circuit is 30°, what is the power factor?
    (a) 0.5   (b) 0.707   (c) 0.866   (d) 1.0

9. In a purely capacitive circuit, the power factor is:
    (a) 0.0   (b) 0.5   (c) 0.707   (d) 1.0

10. To use a series RC circuit as a high-pass filter, the output should be taken from:
    (a) the resistor   (b) the capacitor   (c) the generator

11. In a series circuit, the generator current is frequently used as the reference (see Experiment 6), but in a parallel circuit, the generator voltage is almost always used as the reference (see Experiment 7). Explain why.

12. An *RC* circuit uses a 10 kΩ resistor in series with a 0.047 µF capacitor and is connected to a generator set to 10 V$_{rms}$.
    (a) Determine the frequency at which $X_C = R$.

    (b) At this frequency, what is the current in the circuit?

    (c) At this frequency, what is the voltage across the resistor?

13. In a certain parallel *RC* circuit, the generator current leads the generator voltage by 60°. Assume the generator is set to 10 V$_{rms}$ and the resistor has a value of 12.5 kΩ. Sketch the current phasor diagram on the Plot C–3–1. Label the values of currents on your diagram.

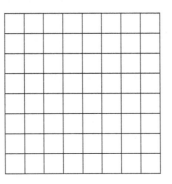

Plot C–3–1

14. In Experiment 7, two 1.0 kΩ sense resistors were used to determine quickly the total current and the current in the capacitor. Would it be reasonable to use these same sense resistors for the problem circuit described in Question 13? Justify your answer.

8 Inductors

Name _____
Date _____
Class _____

READING
Floyd, Sections 11–1 through 11–4

OBJECTIVES
After performing this experiment, you will be able to:
1.   Describe the effect of Lenz's law in a circuit.
2.   Measure the time constant of an *LR* circuit and test the effects of series and parallel inductances on the time constant.

MATERIALS NEEDED
Two 7 H inductors (approximate value) (The secondary of a low-voltage transformer will work.
        The second inductor may be shared from another experiment.)
One neon bulb (NE-2 or equivalent)
One 33 kΩ resistor
For Further Investigation:
    One unknown inductor

SUMMARY OF THEORY
When there is a current through a coil of wire, a magnetic field is created around the wire. This electromagnetic field accompanies any moving electric charge and is proportional to the magnitude of the current. If the current changes, the electromagnetic field causes a voltage to be induced across the coil, which opposes the change. This property, which causes a voltage to oppose a change in current, is called *inductance*.

Inductance is the electrical equivalent of inertia in a mechanical system. It opposes a change in *current* in a manner similar to the way capacitance opposed a change in *voltage*. This property of inductance is described by Lenz's law. According to Lenz's law, an inductor develops a voltage across it that counters the effect of a *change* in current in the circuit. The induced voltage is equal to the inductance times the rate of change of current. Inductance is measured in *henries. One henry is defined as the quantity of inductance present when one volt is generated as a result of a current changing at the rate of one ampere per second.* Coils that are made to provide a specific amount of inductance are called *inductors*.

When inductors are connected in series, the total inductance is the sum of the individual inductors. This is similar to resistors connected in series. Likewise, the formula for parallel inductors is similar to the formula for parallel resistors. Unlike resistors, an additional effect can appear in inductive circuits. This effect is called *mutual inductance* and is caused by the interaction of the magnetic fields. The total inductance can be either increased or decreased due to mutual inductance.

Inductive circuits have a time constant associated with them, just as capacitive circuits do, except the rising exponential curve is a picture of the *current* in the circuit rather than the *voltage* as in the case of the capacitive circuit. Unlike the capacitive circuit, if the resistance is greater, the time constant is shorter. The time constant is found from the equation

$$\tau = \frac{L}{R}$$

where τ represents the time constant in seconds when L is in henries and R is in ohms.

PROCEDURE

1. In this step, you can observe the effect of Lenz's law. Connect the circuit shown in Figure 8–1 with a neon bulb in parallel with a large inductor. As noted in the materials list, the secondary of a low-voltage transformer can be used. Power should NOT be applied to the primary. Neon bulbs contain two insulated electrodes in a glass envelope containing neon gas. The gas will not conduct unless the voltage reaches approximately 70 V. When the gas conducts, the bulb will glow. When the switch is closed, dc current in the inductor is determined by the inductor's winding resistance. Close and open S_1 several times and observe the results.

    Observations:

2. Find out if the neon bulb will fire if the voltage is lowered. How low can you reduce the voltage source and still observe the bulb to glow? _____

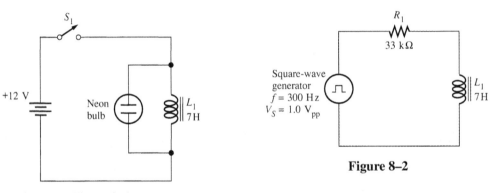

Figure 8–1   **Figure 8–2**

3. Connect the circuit shown in Figure 8–2. This circuit will be used to view the waveforms from a square wave generator. Set the generator, V_S, for a 1.0 V_{pp} square wave at a frequency of 300 Hz. This frequency is chosen to allow sufficient time to see the effects of the time constant. View the generator voltage on CH1 of a two-channel oscilloscope and the inductor waveform on CH2. If both channels are calibrated and have the VOLTS/DIV controls set to the same setting, you will be able to see the voltage across the resistor using the difference channel. Set the oscilloscope SEC/DIV control to 0.5 ms/div. Sketch the waveforms you see on Plot 8–1.

$V_S =$

$V_L =$

$V_R =$

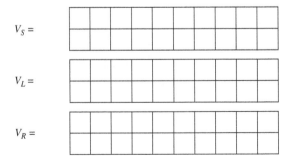

Plot 8–1

224

4.   Compute the time constant for the circuit. Enter the computed value in Table 8–1. Now measure the time constant by viewing the waveform across the resistor. The resistor voltage has the same shape as the current in the circuit, so you can measure the time constant by finding the time required for the resistor voltage to change from 0 to 63% of its final value. Stretch the waveform across the oscilloscope screen to make an accurate time measurement. Enter the measured time constant in Table 8–1.

Table 8–1

	Computed	Measured
Time constant, τ		

5.   When inductors are connected in series, the total inductance increases. When they are connected in parallel, the total inductance decreases. You can see the effect of decreasing the inductance by connecting a second 7 H inductor in parallel with the first. Note what happens to the voltage waveforms across the resistor and the inductor. Then connect the inductors in series and compare the effect on the waveforms. Describe your observations.

CONCLUSION

EVALUATION AND REVIEW QUESTIONS
1.   The ionizing voltage for a neon bulb is approximately 70 V. Explain how a 12 V source was able to cause the neon bulb to conduct.

2.   When a circuit containing an inductor is opened suddenly, an arc may occur across the switch. How does Lenz's law explain this?

3.   What is the total inductance when two 100 mH inductors are connected
      in series? _____   in parallel? _____

4.   What would happen to the time constant in Figure 8–2 if a 3.3 kΩ resistor were used instead of the 33 kΩ resistor?

5.   What effect does an increase in the frequency of the square wave generator have on the waveforms observed in Figure 8–2?

FOR FURTHER INVESTIGATION
Suggest a method in which you could use a square wave generator and a known resistor to determine the inductance of an unknown inductor. Then obtain an unknown inductor from your instructor and measure its inductance. Report on your method, results, and how your result compares to the accepted value for the inductor.

 **9** **Inductive Reactance**

Name _____

Date _____

Class _____

READING
Floyd, Sections 11–5 and 11–6

OBJECTIVES
After performing this experiment, you will be able to:
1. Measure the inductive reactance of an inductor at a specified frequency.
2. Compare the reactance of inductors connected in series and parallel.

MATERIALS NEEDED
Two 100 mH inductors
One 1.0 kΩ resistor
For Further Investigation:
   One 12.6 V center-tapped transformer

SUMMARY OF THEORY
When a sine wave is applied to an inductor, a voltage is induced across the inductor as given by Lenz's law. When the *change* in current is a maximum, the largest induced voltage appears across the inductor. This is illustrated in Figure 9–1. Notice that when the current is not changing (at the peaks), the induced voltage is zero. For this reason, the voltage that appears across an inductor leads the current in the inductor by 1/4 cycle.

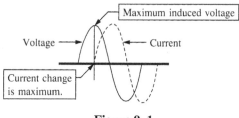

Figure 9–1

If we *raise* the frequency of the sine wave, the rate of change of current is increased and the value of the opposing voltage is increased. This results in a net *decrease* in the amount of current. Thus, the inductive reactance is increased by an increase in frequency. The inductive reactance is given by the equation

$$X_L = 2\pi f L$$

This equation reveals that a linear relationship exists between the inductance and the reactance at a constant frequency. Recall that in series, the total inductance is the sum of individual inductors (ignoring mutual inductance). The reactance of series inductors is, therefore, also the sum of the individual reactances. Likewise, in parallel, the reciprocal formula which applies to parallel resistors can be applied to both the inductance and the inductive reactance.

Ohm's law can be applied to inductive circuits. The reactance of an inductor can be found by dividing the voltage across the inductor by the current in it. That is,

$$X_L = \frac{V_L}{I_L}$$

PROCEDURE

1.   Measure the inductance of each of two 100 mH inductors and record their measured values in Table 9–1. Measure and record the value of a 1.0 kΩ resistor. Use the listed values if you cannot measure the inductors.

2.   Connect the circuit shown in Figure 9–2. Set the generator for a 1.0 kHz sine wave with a 1.0 V_{rms}. Measure the generator voltage with your DMM while it is connected to the circuit.[1] Check the frequency and voltage with the oscilloscope. Remember to convert the oscilloscope voltage reading to rms voltage to compare it to the DMM.

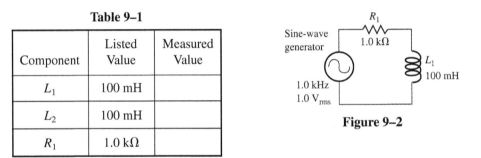

Table 9–1

Component	Listed Value	Measured Value
L_1	100 mH	
L_2	100 mH	
R_1	1.0 kΩ	

Figure 9–2

3.   The circuit is a series circuit, so the current in the resistor is the identical current that is through the inductor. First, find the voltage across the resistor with the DMM. Then apply Ohm's law to the resistor to find the current in the circuit. Record the measured voltage and the computed current in Table 9–2 in the column labeled Inductor L_1.

4.   Measure the voltage across the inductor with the DMM. Then find the inductive reactance by Ohm's law. Enter the values in Table 9–2.

5.   Now compute the inductance based on the equation

$$L = \frac{X_L}{2\pi f}$$

Enter the computed inductance in Table 9–2.

---

[1]DMMs have a relatively low bandwidth, although most can measure 1.0 kHz. Verify that the DMM you are using has at least a 1.0 kHz bandwidth; if it does not, use the oscilloscope for all voltage measurements.

Table 9–2

	Inductor L_1	Inductor L_2
Voltage across R_1, V_R		
Total current, I		
Voltage across L, V_L		
Inductive reactance, X_L		
Computed inductance, L		

6. Replace L_1 with L_2 and repeat steps 3, 4, and 5. Enter the data in Table 9–2 in the column labeled Inductor L_2.

7. Place L_2 in series with L_1. Then find the inductive reactance for the series combination of the inductors as if they were one inductor. Enter the data in Table 9–3 in the column labeled Series Inductors. The following steps will guide you:
    (a) Check that the generator is set to 1.0 V rms. Find the current in the circuit by measuring the voltage across the resistor as before and dividing by the resistance.
    (b) Measure the voltage across *both* inductors.
    (c) Use Ohm's law to find the inductive reactance of both inductors. Use the voltage measured in step (b) and the current found in step (a).
    (d) Compute the total inductance by using the equation

$$L = \frac{X_L}{2\pi f}$$

8. Connect the inductors in parallel and repeat step 7. Assume the parallel inductors are one equivalent inductor for the measurements. Enter the data in Table 9–3 in the column labeled Parallel Inductors.

Table 9–3

Step		Series Inductors	Parallel Inductors
(a)	Voltage across R_1, V_R		
	Total current, I		
(b)	Voltage across inductors, V_L		
(c)	Inductive reactance, X_L		
(d)	Computed inductance, L		

CONCLUSION

EVALUATION AND REVIEW QUESTIONS

1.   (a)   Using the data in Table 9–2, compute the sum of the inductive reactances of the two inductors:

$$X_{L1} + X_{L2} =$$

      (b)   Using the data in Table 9–2, compute the product-over-sum of the inductive reactances of the two inductors:

$$\frac{(X_{L1})(X_{L2})}{X_{L1} + X_{L2}} =$$

      (c)   Compare the results from (a) and (b) with the reactances for the series and parallel connections listed in Table 9–3. What conclusion can you draw from these data?

2.   Repeat Question 1 using the data for the inductance, L. Compare the inductance of series and parallel inductors.

3.   What effect would an error in the frequency of the generator have on the data for this experiment?

4.   How could you apply the method used in this experiment to find the value of an unknown inductor?

5.   Compute the inductive reactance of a 50 μH inductor at a frequency of 50 MHz.

FOR FURTHER INVESTIGATION

A transformer consists of two or more coils wound on a common iron core. Frequently, one or more windings has a *center tap,* which splits a winding into two equal inductors. Because the windings are on the same core, mutual inductance exists between the windings. Obtain a small power transformer that has a low-voltage center-tapped secondary winding. Determine the inductance of each half of the winding using the method in this experiment. Then investigate what happens if the windings are connected in series. Keep the output of the signal generator constant for the measurements. Summarize your results.

MULTISIM TROUBLESHOOTING

This experiment has four Multisim files on the website (www.prenhall.com/floyd). Three of the four files contain a simulated "fault"; one has "no fault". The file with no fault is named EXP23-2-nf. You may want to open this file to compare your results with the computer simulation. Then open each of the files with faults. Use the simulated instruments to investigate the circuit and determine the problem. The following are the filenames for circuits with troubleshooting problems for this experiment.

EXP23-2-f1
    Fault: _____

EXP23-2-f2
    Fault: _____

EXP23-2-f3
    Fault: _____

Application Assignment 4

Name _____
Date _____
Class _____

REFERENCE

Floyd, Chapter 11, Application Assignment: Putting Your Knowledge to Work

Step 1   Measure the coil resistance and select a series resistor.

Step 2   Determine the time constant and the approximate inductance of coil 1.

Step 3   Determine the time constant and the approximate inductance of coil 2.

Step 4   Discuss how you could find the approximate inductance of the coils using a sinusoidal input instead of a square wave.

RELATED EXPERIMENT

MATERIALS NEEDED

Two decade resistance boxes
One 0.1 μF capacitor (for a standard)
One 1.0 kΩ resistor
One 100 mH indicator (or other value from about 1 mH to 100 mH)

DISCUSSION

A Maxwell bridge is commonly used to measure inductors that do not have a very high Q. It employs a fixed capacitor and two resistors as standards. The circuit for a Maxwell bridge is shown in Figure AA–4–1. Construct the bridge using two decade resistance boxes for R_1 and R_2 and a measured capacitor of 0.1 μF for C_1. A 100 mH inductor from Experiment 9 (or any unknown inductor from about 1 mH to 100 mH) can be used for the unknown. R_3 is a fixed 1.0 kΩ resistor. Measure the output voltage between terminals **A** and **B** with your DMM. Adjust both decade resistance boxes for the minimum voltage observed on the DMM.

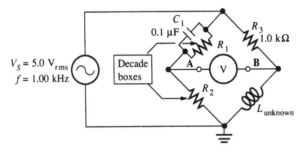

Figure AA–4–1

After you have adjusted the decade resistance boxes for minimum voltage across the **A** and **B** terminals, the circuit is a balanced ac bridge. The bridge is balanced when the product of the impedance of the diagonal elements is equal. The equations for the Maxwell bridge, given without proof, are

$$L_{\text{unknown}} = R_2 R_3 C_1$$

$$Q = 2\pi f C_1 R_1$$

Measure the unknown inductor with your Maxwell bridge. Compare your measurement with a laboratory bridge. What measurement errors account for the differences in the two measurements?

EXPERIMENTAL RESULTS

Checkup 4

REFERENCE

Floyd, Chap. 11, and Buchla, Experiments 22 and 23

1. The voltage induced across an inductor by a changing magnetic field tends to:
    (a) oppose the current in the inductor
    (b) oppose a change in the current
    (c) oppose the voltage across the inductor
    (d) oppose a change in the voltage

2. Assume a neon bulb is in parallel with a large inductor. When current is interrupted by opening a switch, the neon bulb glows for a short time. This is due to:
    (a) the rapid change in resistance
    (b) the time constant of the circuit
    (c) collapsing electric field
    (d) induced voltage across the inductor

3. The total inductance of parallel inductors is always:
    (a) less than the smallest inductor
    (b) less than the largest inductor
    (c) greater than the smallest inductor
    (d) greater than the largest inductor

4. Assume two inductors have the same physical size and core material but inductor A has twice the number of windings of inductor B. From this we can conclude that the:
    (a) inductance of A is one-fourth that of B
    (b) inductances are equal
    (c) inductance of A is twice that of B
    (d) inductance of A is four times that of B

5. The time constant for a series RL circuit consisting of a 10 kΩ resistor and a 30 mH inductor is:
    (a) 3 μs   (b) 15 μs   (c) 30 μs   (d) 300 μs

6. The instant after the switch is closed in a series RL circuit, the voltage across the inductor is:
    (a) zero
    (b) equal to the voltage across the resistor
    (c) 63% of the source voltage
    (d) equal and opposite to the source voltage

7. The instant after the switch is closed in a series RL circuit, the voltage across the resistor is:
    (a) zero
    (b) equal to the voltage across the inductor
    (c) 63% of the source voltage
    (d) equal and opposite to the source voltage

8. One time constant after a switch is closed in a series RL circuit, the current will be:
    (a) 37% of its final value
    (b) 50% of its final value
    (c) 63% of its final value
    (d) 100% of its final value

9. The unit of inductive reactance is the:
    (a) farad   (b) henry   (c) ohm   (d) second

10. An inductor is connected across a sinusoidal generator. If the generator frequency is increased, the inductance:

(a) decreases   (b) stays the same   (c) increases

11. Name four factors that affect the inductance of a coil.

12. In Experiment 8, a large (7 H) inductor was used to "fire" the neon bulb. Why do you think a large inductor was specified? Would a smaller one work as well?

13. For a sinusoidal input, compare the phase difference between voltage and current for an RC circuit with that of an RL circuit.

14. The total inductance of two series inductors is 900 μH.

(a)   If one of the inductors is 350 μH, what is the inductance of the other?

(b)   Assume a 10 V sinusoidal waveform is applied to the two series inductors. What is the voltage across the 350 μH inductor?

15. In Experiment 8 (Figure 8–2), the frequency of the generator was set to 300 Hz. Could a higher frequency have been specified for this experiment? Why or why not?

16. For the circuit in Figure C–4–1, assume the voltage across the resistor is 2.1 V, and the voltage across the inductor is 4.0 V. If the source frequency is 100 kHz, determine the inductive reactance and the inductance of the unknown.

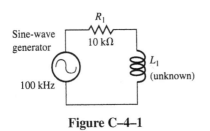

Figure C–4–1

10 Series *RL* Circuits

Name _____
Date _____
Class _____

READING
Floyd, Sections 12–1 through 12–3

OBJECTIVES
After performing this experiment, you will be able to:
1.   Compute the inductive reactance of an inductor from voltage measurements in a series *RL* circuit.
2.   Draw the impedance and voltage phasor diagram for the series *RL* circuit.
3.   Measure the phase angle in a series circuit using either of two methods.

MATERIALS NEEDED
One 10 kΩ resistor
One 100 mH inductor

SUMMARY OF THEORY
When a sine wave drives a linear series circuit, the phase relationships between the current and the voltage are determined by the components in the circuit. The current and voltage are always in phase across resistors. With capacitors, the current is always leading the voltage by 90°, but for inductors, the voltage always leads the current by 90°. (A simple memory aid for this is *ELI the ICE man,* where *E* stands for voltage, *I* for current, and *L* and *C* for inductance and capacitance.)

   Figure 10–1(a) illustrates a series *RL* circuit. The graphical representation of the phasors for this circuit is shown in Figure 10–1(b) and (c). As in the series *RC* circuit, the total impedance is obtained by adding the resistance and inductive reactance using the algebra for complex numbers. In this example, the current is 1.0 mA, and the total impedance is 5 kΩ. The current is the same in all components of a series circuit, so the current is drawn as a reference in the direction of the *x*-axis. If the current is multiplied by the impedance phasors, the voltage phasors are obtained as shown in Figure 10–1(c).

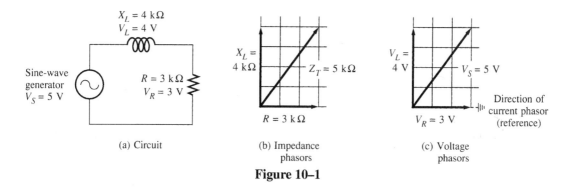

(a) Circuit   (b) Impedance   (c) Voltage
                    phasors   phasors

Figure 10–1

   In this experiment, you learn how to make measurements of the phase angle. Actual inductors may have enough resistance to affect the phase angle in the circuit. You will use a series resistor that is large compared to the inductor's resistance to avoid this error.

PROCEDURE

1. Measure the actual resistance of a 10 kΩ resistor and the inductance of a 100 mH inductor. If the inductor cannot be measured, record the listed value. Record the measured values in Table 10–1.

2. Connect the circuit shown in Figure 10–2. Set the generator voltage with the circuit connected to 3.0 V_{pp} at a frequency of 25 kHz. The generator should have no dc offset. Measure the generator voltage and frequency with the oscilloscope as many meters cannot respond to the 25 kHz frequency. Use peak-to-peak readings for all voltage and current measurements in this experiment.

Table 10–1

Component	Listed Value	Measured Value
L_1	100 mH	100 mH
R_1	10 kΩ	9.9

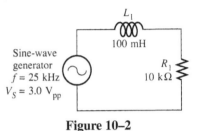

Figure 10–2

3. Using a two-channel oscilloscope, measure the peak-to-peak voltage across the resistor (V_R) and the peak-to-peak voltage across the inductor (V_L). (See Figure 10–3 for the setup.) Measure the voltage across the inductor using the difference technique described in Experiment 2. Record the voltage readings in Table 10–2.   16583

Table 10–2   (f = 25 kHz)

V_R	V_L	I	X_L	Z_T
.75	3	76μA	39.5	39.4k

4. Compute the peak-to-peak current in the circuit by applying Ohm's law to the resistor. That is,

    .75

    $$I = \frac{V_R}{R}$$

    Enter the computed current in Table 10–2.

5. Compute the inductive reactance, X_L, by applying Ohm's law to the inductor. The reactance is

    3
    76μA

    $$X_L = \frac{V_L}{I}$$

    Enter the computed reactance in Table 10–2.

6. Calculate the total impedance (Z_T) by applying Ohm's law to the entire circuit. Use the generator voltage set in step 2 (V_S), and the current determined in step 4. Enter the computed impedance in Table 10–2.

238

7. Using the values listed in Tables 10–1 and 10–2, draw the impedance phasors on Plot 10–1(a) and the voltage phasors on Plot 10–1(b) for the circuit at a frequency of 25 kHz.

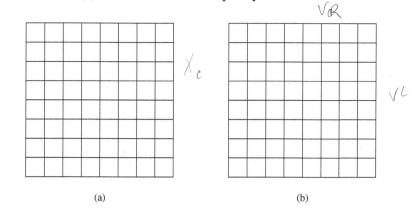

(a)   (b)

Plot 10–1

8. Compute the phase angle between V_R and V_S using the trigonometric relation

76.9

$$\theta = \tan^{-1}\left(\frac{V_L}{V_R}\right)$$

Enter the computed phase angle in Table 10–3.

9. Two methods for measuring phase angle will be explained. The first method can be used with any oscilloscope. The second can only be used with oscilloscopes that have a "fine" or variable SEC/DIV control. Measure the phase angle between V_R and V_S using one or both methods. The measured phase angle will be recorded in Table 10–3.

Phase Angle Measurement—Method 1
(a)   Connect the oscilloscope so that channel 1 is across the generator and channel 2 is across the resistor. (See Figure 10–3.) Obtain a stable display showing between one and two cycles while viewing channel 1 (V_S). The scope should be triggered from channel 1.
(b)   Measure the period, T, of the generator. Record it in Table 10–3. You will use this time in step (e).

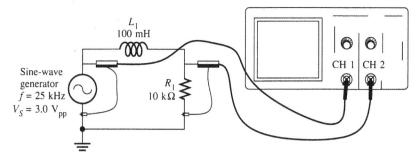

Figure 10–3

239

(c)   Set the oscilloscope to view both channels. (Do not have channel 2 inverted.) Adjust the amplitudes of the signals using the VOLTS/DIV, VERT POSITION, and the vernier controls until both channels *appear* to have the same amplitude as seen on the scope face.

(d)   Spread the signal horizontally using the SEC/DIV control until both signals are just visible across the screen. The SEC/DIV control must remain calibrated. Measure the time between the two signals, Δt, by counting the number of divisions along a horizontal graticule of the oscilloscope and multiplying by the SEC/DIV setting. (See Figure 10–4.) Record the measured Δt in Table 10–3.

(e)   The phase angle may now be computed from the equation

$$\theta = \left(\frac{\Delta t}{T}\right) \times 360°$$

Enter the measured phase angle in Table 10–3 under Phase Angle—Method 1.

Table 10–3

Computed Phase Angle θ	Measured Period T	Time Difference Δt	Phase Angle Method 1 θ	Phase Angle Method 2 θ
76	40ms	.35 ms		

$$\frac{.35\,ms}{40\,ms}$$

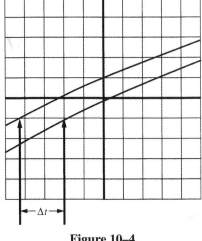

Figure 10–4

Phase Angle Measurement—Method 2

(a)   In this method the oscilloscope face will represent degrees, and the phase angle can be measured directly. The probes are connected as before. View channel 1 and obtain a stable display. Then adjust the SEC/DIV control and its vernier until you have exactly one cycle across the scope face. This is equivalent to 360° in 10 divisions, so each division is worth 36°.[1]

(b)   Now switch the scope to view both channels. As before, adjust the amplitudes of the signals using the VOLTS/DIV, VERT POSITION, and the vernier controls until both channels *appear* to have the same amplitude.

(c)   Measure the number of divisions between the signals and multiply by 36° per division. Record the measured phase angle in Table 10–3 under Phase Angle—Method 2.

---

[1]For even better resolution, you can set one-half cycle across the screen, making each division worth 18°. Care must be taken to center the waveform.

CONCLUSION

EVALUATION AND REVIEW QUESTIONS

1. (a) What will happen to the impedance in this experiment if the frequency increases?

    (b) What would happen to the impedance if the inductance were larger?

2. (a) What will happen to the phase angle in this experiment if the frequency increases?

    (b) What would happen to the phase angle if the inductance were larger?

3. Compute the percent difference between the computed phase angle and the method 1 phase angle measurement.

4. The critical frequency for an RL circuit occurs at the frequency at which the resistance is equal to the inductive reactance. That is, $R = X_L$. Since $X_L = 2\pi fL$ for an inductor, it can easily be shown that the circuit frequency for an RL circuit is

$$f_{crit} = \frac{R}{2\pi L}$$

Compute the critical frequency for this experiment. What is the phase angle between V_R and V_S at the critical frequency?

$f_{crit} =$ _____ $\theta =$ _____

5. A series *RL* circuit contains a 100 Ω resistor and a 1.0 H inductor and is operating at a frequency of 60 Hz. If 3.0 V are across the resistor, compute:

(a) the current in the inductor _____

(b) the inductive reactance, X_L _____

(c) the voltage across the inductor, V_L _____

(d) the source voltage, V_S _____

(e) the phase angle between V_R and V_S _____

FOR FURTHER INVESTIGATION

An older method for measuring phase angles involved interpreting Lissajous figures. A Lissajous figure is the pattern formed by the application of a sinusoidal waveform to both the *x*- and *y*-axes of an oscilloscope. Two signals of equal amplitude and exactly in phase will produce a 45° line on the scope face. If the signals are the same amplitude and exactly 90° apart, the waveform will appear as a circle. Other phase angles can be determined by applying the formula

$$\theta = \arcsin\frac{OA}{OB}$$

Figure 10–5 illustrates a Lissajous figure phase measurement. The measurements of *OA* and *OB* are along the *y*-axis. Try measuring the phase angle in this experiment using a Lissajous figure. You will have to have the signals the same amplitude and centered on the oscilloscope face. Then switch the time base of the oscilloscope to the **XY** mode.

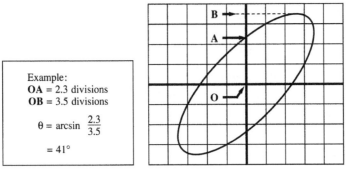

Example:
OA = 2.3 divisions
OB = 3.5 divisions

$\theta = \arcsin \frac{2.3}{3.5}$

$= 41°$

Figure 10–5

Parallel *RL* Circuits

Name _____
Date _____
Class _____

READING
Floyd, Sections 12–4 through 12–9

OBJECTIVES
After performing this experiment, you will be able to:
1. Determine the current phasor diagram for a parallel *RL* circuit.
2. Measure the phase angle between the current and voltage for a parallel *RL* circuit.
3. Explain how an actual circuit differs from the ideal model of a circuit.

MATERIALS NEEDED
Resistors:
    One 3.3 kΩ, two 47 Ω
One 100 mH inductor

SUMMARY OF THEORY
The parallel *RC* circuit was investigated in Experiment 7. Recall that the circuit phasor diagram was drawn with current phasors and the voltage phasor was used as a reference, since voltage is the same across parallel components. In a parallel *RL* circuit, the current phasors will again be drawn with reference to the voltage phasor. The direction of the current phasor in a resistor is always in the direction of the voltage. Since current lags the voltage in an inductor, the current phasor is drawn at an angle of $-90°$ from the voltage reference. A parallel *RL* circuit and the associated phasors are shown in Figure 11–1.

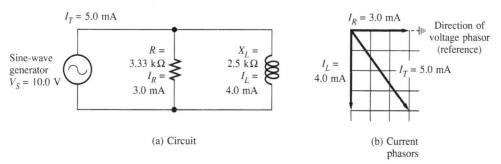

(a) Circuit   (b) Current
                         phasors

Figure 11–1

Practical inductors contain resistance that frequently is large enough to affect the purely reactive inductor phasor drawn in Figure 11–1. The resistance of an inductor can be thought of as a resistor in series with a pure inductor. The effect on the phasor diagram is to reduce an angle between I_L and I_R. In a practical circuit this angle will be slightly less than the $-90°$ shown in Figure 11–1. This experiment illustrates the difference between the approximations of circuit performance based on ideal components and the actual measured values.

Recall that in Experiment 10, the phase angle between the source voltage, V_S, and the resistor voltage, V_R, in a series circuit were measured. The oscilloscope is a voltage-sensitive device, so comparing these voltages is straightforward. In parallel circuits, the phase angle of interest is usually between the total current, I_T, and one of the branch currents. To use the oscilloscope to measure the phase angle in a parallel circuit, we must convert the current to a voltage. This was done by inserting a small resistor in the branch where the current is to be measured. The resistor must be small enough not to have a major effect on the circuit.

PROCEDURE

1.   Measure the actual resistance of a resistor with a color-code value of 3.3 kΩ and the resistance of two current-sensing resistors of 47 Ω each. Measure the inductance of a 100 mH inductor. Use the listed value if you cannot measure the inductor. Record the measured values in Table 11–1.

2.   Measure the winding resistance of the inductor, R_W, with an ohmmeter. Record the resistance in Table 11–1.

3.   Construct the circuit shown in Figure 11–2. Notice that the reference ground connection is at the low side of the generator. This connection will enable you to use a generator that does not have a "floating" common connection. Using your oscilloscope, set the generator to a voltage of 6.0 V_{pp} at 5.0 kHz. Check both the voltage and frequency with your oscilloscope. Record all voltages and currents in this experiment as peak-to-peak values.

Table 11–1

	Listed Value	Measured Value	Voltage Drop	Computed Current
R_1	3.3 kΩ			
R_{S1}	47 Ω			
R_{S2}	47 Ω			
L_1	100 mH			
$R_W (L_1$ resistance)				

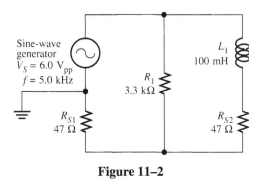

Figure 11–2

4.   Using the oscilloscope, measure the peak-to-peak voltages across R_1, R_{S1}, and R_{S2}. Use the two-channel difference method (described in Experiment 2) to measure the voltage across the two ungrounded resistors. Apply Ohm's law to compute the current in each branch. Record the measured voltage drops and the computed currents in Table 11–1. Since L_1 is in series with R_{S2}, enter the same current for both.

5.   The currents measured indirectly in step 4 are phasors because the current in the inductor is lagging the current in R_1 by 90°. The current in the inductor is the same as the current in R_{S2}, and the total current is through R_{S1}. Using the computed peak-to-peak currents from Table 11–1, draw the current phasors for the circuit on Plot 11–1. (Ignore the effects of the sense resistors.)

$I_R \longrightarrow$

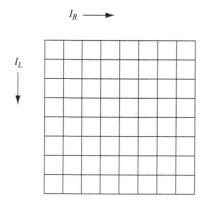

Plot 11–1

Table 11–2

Phase Angle Between:	Computed	Measured
I_T and I_R		
I_R and I_L	90°	
I_T and I_L		

6. The phasor diagram illustrates the relationship between the total current and the current in each branch. Using the measured currents, compute the phase angle between the total current (I_T) and the current in R_1 (I_R). Then compute the phase angle between the total current (I_T), and the current in L_1 (I_L). Enter the computed phase angles in Table 11–2. (Note that the computed angles should add up to 90°, the angle between I_R and I_L.)

7. In this step, you will measure the phase angle between the generator voltage and current. This angle is approximately equal to the angle between I_T and I_R as shown in Figure 11–1. (Why?) Connect the oscilloscope probes as shown in Figure 11–3. Measure the phase angle using one of the methods in Experiment 10. The signal amplitudes in each channel are quite different, so the vertical sensitivity controls should be adjusted to make each signal appear to have the same amplitude on the scope. Record the measured angle between I_T and I_R in Table 11–2.

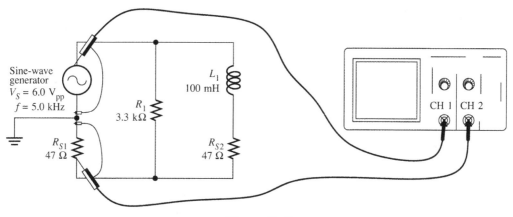

Figure 11–3

8. Replace R_{S1} with a jumper. This procedure enables you to reference the low side of R_1 and R_{S2}. Measure the angle between I_L and I_R by connecting the probes as shown in Figure 11–4. Ideally, this measurement should be 90°, but because of the coil resistance, you will likely find a smaller value. Adjust both channels for the same apparent amplitude on the scope face. Record your measured result in the second line in Table 11–2.

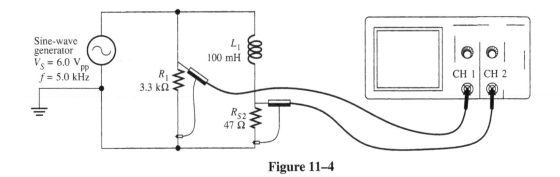

Figure 11–4

9. By subtracting the angle measured in step 7 from the angle measured step 8, you can find the phase angle between the I_T and I_L. Record this as the measured value on the third line of Table 11–2.

CONCLUSION

EVALUATION AND REVIEW QUESTIONS

1. If we assume that the currents determined in step 4 are 90° apart, the magnitude of the total current can be computed by applying the Pythagorean theorem to the current phasors. That is

$$I_T = \sqrt{I_{R1}^2 + I_{L1}^2}$$

(a) Compare the total current measured in R_{S1} (Table 11–1) with the current found by applying the Pythagorean theorem to the current phasors.

(b) What factors account for differences between the two currents?

2. How does the coil resistance measured in step 2 affect the angle between the current in the resistor and the current in the inductor?

3.   In Experiment 7, a 1.0 kΩ resistor was used as a current-sensing resistor. Why would this value be unsatisfactory in this experiment?

4.   If the inductor were open, what would happen to each?
      (a)   the total current in the circuit

      (b)   the phase angle between the generator voltage and current

      (c)   the generator voltage

5.   If the frequency were increased, what would happen to each?
      (a)   the total current in the circuit

      (b)   the phase angle between the generator voltage and current

      (c)   the generator voltage

FOR FURTHER INVESTIGATION

We could find the *magnitude* of the total current by observing the loading effect of the circuit on a signal generator. Consider the signal generator as a Thevenin circuit consisting of a zero impedance signal generator driving an internal series resistor consisting of the Thevenin source impedance. (See Figure 11–5.) When there is current to the external circuit, there is a voltage drop across the Thevenin resistance. The voltage drop across the Thevenin resistor, when divided by the Thevenin resistance, represents the total current in the circuit. To find the voltage drop across the Thevenin resistance, simply measure the difference in the generator voltage with the generator connected and disconnected from the circuit.

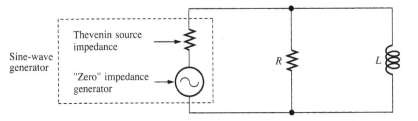

Figure 11–5

In addition to loading effects, the generator impedance also changes the phase angles in the circuit connected to it. If the impedance is smaller, the effect is greater. Investigate the loading effects for this experiment. Try finding the total current by the difference in loaded and unloaded voltage from the generator. What effect does the generator's impedance have on the phase angle?

Application Assignment 5

Name _____
Date _____
Class _____

REFERENCE
Floyd, Chapter 12, Application Assignment: Putting Your Knowledge to Work

Step 1   From the resistance measurements of module 1, determine the arrangement of the two components and the values of the resistor and the winding resistance. Show the arrangement in the space provided.

Step 2   From the ac measurements of module 1, determine the value of the inductor indicated by the oscilloscope readings. Show your calculation.

Step 3   From the resistance measurements of module 2, determine the arrangement of the two components and the values of the resistor and the winding resistance. Show the arrangement in the space provided.

Step 4   From the ac measurements of module 2, determine the value of the inductor indicated by the oscilloscope readings. Show your calculation.

RELATED EXPERIMENT

MATERIALS NEEDED
One variable capacitor 12–100 pF (Mouser # ME242-3610-100 or equivalent)
One 100 mH inductor
One 27 kΩ resistor

DISCUSSION

A circuit will transfer maximum power to a load when the power factor is equal to 1. Maximum power factor is useful in certain impedance matching networks.

You can easily detect when the power factor is not maximum by observing a Lissajous figure on an oscilloscope. (See Experiment 10—For Further Investigation.) The phase angle is zero (power factor of 1) when the Lissajous figure shows a straight line on the oscilloscope display.

Construct the circuit shown in Figure AA–5–1. The oscilloscope is connected as shown. Adjust the VOLTS/DIV, VERT POSITION, and the vernier controls until both channels *appear* to have the same amplitude. Then, switch the oscilloscope to the XY mode. Measure and record the phase shift using the Lissajous figure as described in Experiment 10.

The results of the preceding measurement clearly show that the power factor is not 1. Add a variable capacitor of approximately 12–100 pF in series with the inductor, as shown in Figure AA–5–2. Observe the Lissajous figure and adjust the capacitor until the power factor is 1. Then, remove the capacitor and measure its value. Compare the reactance of the capacitor with the reactance of the inductor when the power factor is 1. What conclusion can you draw from this?

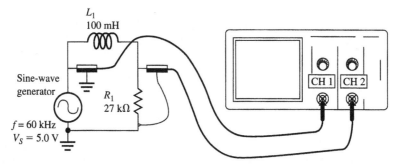

Figure AA–5–1

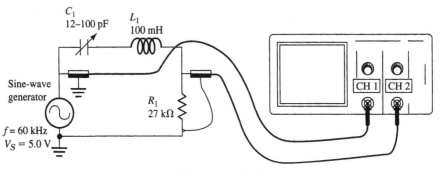

Figure AA–5–2

EXPERIMENTAL RESULTS

Checkup 5

REFERENCE
Floyd, Chap. 12, and Buchla, Experiments 24 and 25

1. If a sinusoidal voltage wave is applied to an inductor, the current in the inductor:
   - (a) leads the voltage by 45°
   - (b) leads the voltage by 90°
   - (c) lags the voltage by 45°
   - (d) lags the voltage by 90°

2. A 191 μH inductor is connected across a 20 V$_{rms}$, 50 MHz source. The current in the inductor will be approximately:
   - (a) 333 μA
   - (b) 3.3 mA
   - (c) 33 mA
   - (d) 333 mA

3. In a series *RL* circuit in which $X_L = R$, the generator current:
   - (a) leads the generator voltage by 45°
   - (b) leads the generator voltage by 90°
   - (c) lags the generator voltage by 45°
   - (d) lags the generator voltage by 90°

4. In a parallel *RL* circuit in which $X_L = R$, the generator current:
   - (a) leads the generator voltage by 45°
   - (b) leads the generator voltage by 90°
   - (c) lags the generator voltage by 45°
   - (d) lags the generator voltage by 90°

5. If the frequency is raised in a series *RL* circuit and nothing else changes, the current in the circuit:
   - (a) increases
   - (b) stays the same
   - (c) decreases

6. If the frequency is raised in a parallel *RL* circuit and nothing else changes, the current in the circuit:
   - (a) increases
   - (b) stays the same
   - (c) decreases

7. The admittance of a parallel *RL* circuit is 200 μS. If the total current is 400 μA, the applied voltage is:
   - (a) 0.5
   - (b) 2.0 V
   - (c) 6.0 V
   - (d) 8.0 V

8. A series *RL* circuit contains a 300 Ω resistor and an inductor with a reactance of 400 Ω. The total impedance of the circuit is:
   - (a) 171 Ω
   - (b) 350 Ω
   - (c) 500 Ω
   - (d) 700 Ω

9. A parallel *RL* circuit is connected to a 500 kHz voltage source of 16 V. The current in the inductor is 0.5 mA. The inductance is approximately:
   - (a) 64 μH
   - (b) 640 μH
   - (c) 1.0 mH
   - (d) 10 mH

10. In a certain series *RL* circuit, the phase angle is measured at 60° between the generator current and voltage. If the voltage across the inductor is 10 V, the voltage across the resistor is:
    - (a) 5 V
    - (b) 5.8 V
    - (c) 8.66 V
    - (d) 17.3 V

11. In Experiment 10 (step 9c), you were directed to make both signals appear to have the same amplitude on the scope face. Why is this best for minimizing measurement error?

12. In Experiment 11 (step 7), the statement is made that the phase angle between the generator voltage and current is approximately equal to the angle between I_T and I_R. Explain.

13. A parallel RL circuit is connected to a 10 V source. The current in the inductor has twice the magnitude of the current in the resistor. The total current is 7.0 mA.
    (a)   What is the phase angle between the generator current and voltage?

    (b)   Draw the current phasor diagram on Plot C–5–1.

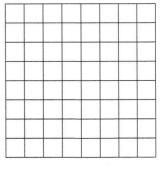

Plot C–5–1

14. For the circuit shown in Figure C–5–1, compute:
    (a)   the impedance seen by the generator _____
    (b)   total current from the generator _____
    (c)   voltage across L_1 _____
    (d)   phase angle between generator voltage and voltage across L_1 _____

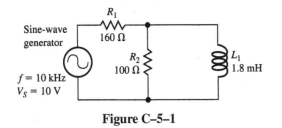

Figure C–5–1

252

12 Series Resonance

READING
Floyd, Sections 13–1 through 13–4

OBJECTIVES
After performing this experiment, you will be able to:
1. Compute the resonant frequency, Q, and bandwidth of a series resonant circuit.
2. Measure the parameters listed in objective 1.
3. Explain the factors affecting the selectivity of a series resonant circuit.

MATERIALS NEEDED
Resistors:
> One 100 Ω, one 47 Ω

One 0.01 µF capacitor
One 100 mH inductor

SUMMARY OF THEORY
The reactance of inductors increases with frequency according to the equation

$$X_L = 2\pi f L$$

On the other hand, the reactance of capacitors decreases with frequency according to the equation

$$X_C = \frac{1}{2\pi f C}$$

Consider the series LC circuit shown in Figure 12–1(a). In any LC circuit, there is a frequency at which the inductive reactance is equal to the capacitive reactance. The point at which there is equal and opposite reactance is called *resonance*. By setting $X_L = X_C$, substituting the relations given above, and solving for f, it is easy to show that the resonant frequency of an LC circuit is

$$f_r = \frac{1}{2\pi\sqrt{LC}}$$

where f_r is the resonant frequency. Recall that reactance phasors for inductors and capacitors are drawn in opposite directions because of the opposite phase shift that occurs between inductors and capacitors. At series resonance these two phasors are added and cancel each other. This is illustrated in Figure 12–1(b). The current in the circuit is limited only by the total resistance of the circuit. The current in this example is 5.0 mA. If each of the impedance phasors is multiplied by this current, the result is the voltage phasor diagram as shown in Figure 12–1(c). Notice that the voltage across the inductor and the capacitor can be *greater* than the applied voltage!

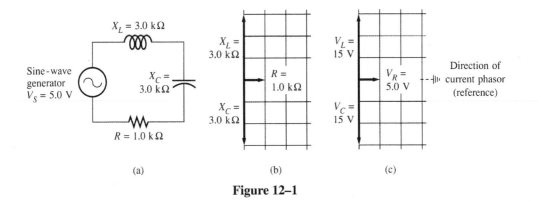

Figure 12–1

At the resonant frequency, the cancellation of the inductive and capacitive phasors leaves only the resistive phasor to limit the current in the circuit. Therefore, at resonance, the impedance of the circuit is a *minimum* and the current is a *maximum* and equal to V_S/R. The phase angle between the source voltage and current is zero. If the frequency is lowered, the inductive reactance will be smaller and the capacitive reactance will be larger. The circuit is said to be capacitive because the source current leads the source voltage. If the frequency is raised, the inductive reactance increases, and the capacitive reactance decreases. The circuit is said to be inductive.

The *selectivity* of a resonant circuit describes how the circuit responds to a group of frequencies. A highly selective circuit responds to a narrow group of frequencies and rejects other frequencies. The *bandwidth* of a resonant circuit is the frequency range at which the current is 70.7% of the maximum current. A highly selective circuit thus has a narrow bandwidth. The sharpness of the response to the frequencies is determined by the circuit Q. The Q for a series resonant circuit is the reactive power in either the coil or capacitor divided by the true power, which is dissipated in the total resistance of the circuit. The bandwidth and resonant frequency can be shown to be related to the circuit Q by the equation

$$Q = \frac{f_r}{BW}$$

Figure 12–2 illustrates how the bandwidth can change with Q. Responses 1 and 2 have the same resonant frequency but different bandwidths. The bandwidth for curve 1 is shown. Response curve 2 has a higher Q and a smaller *BW*. A useful equation that relates the circuit resistance, capacitance, and inductance to Q is

$$Q = \frac{1}{R}\sqrt{\frac{L}{C}}$$

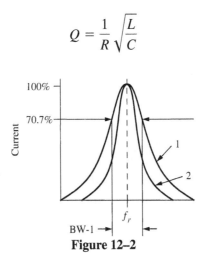

Figure 12–2

254

The value of R in this equation is the total equivalent series resistance in the circuit. Using this equation, the circuit response can be tailored to the application. For a highly selective circuit, the circuit resistance is held to a minimum and the L/C ratio is made high.

The Q of a resonant circuit can also be computed from the equation

$$Q = \frac{X_L}{R}$$

where X_L is the inductive reactance and R is again the total equivalent series resistance of the circuit. The result is the same if X_C is used in the equation, since the values are the same at resonance, but usually X_L is shown because the resistance of the inductor is frequently the dominant resistance of the circuit.

PROCEDURE

1. Measure the value of a 100 mH inductor, a 0.1 μF capacitor, a 100 Ω resistor, and a 47 Ω resistor. Enter the measured values in Table 12–1. If it is not possible to measure the inductor or capacitor, use the listed values.

2. Measure the winding resistance of the inductor, R_W. Enter the measured inductor resistance in Table 12–1.

Table 12–1

	Listed Value	Measured Value
L_1	100 mH	
C_1	0.01 μF	
R_1	100 Ω	
R_{S1}	47 Ω	
R_W (L_1 resistance)		

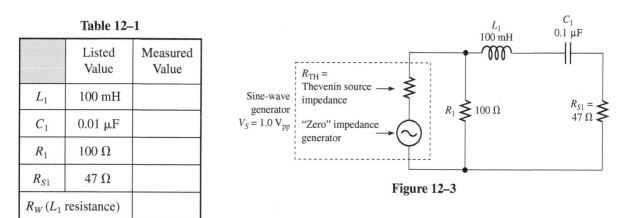

Figure 12–3

3. Construct the circuit shown in Figure 12–3. The purpose of the parallel 100 Ω resistor is to reduce the Thevenin driving impedance of the generator and, therefore, the total equivalent series resistance of the circuit.[1] Compute the total resistance of the equivalent series circuit. Note that looking back to the generator, R_{TH} is in parallel with R_1. In equation form, the equivalent series resistance, R_T, is

$$R_T = (R_{TH} \| R_1) + R_W + R_{S1}$$

Enter the computed total resistance in Table 12–2.

---

[1] Some high-quality generators have a Thevenin resistance of 50 Ω. If you are using a 50 Ω generator, it is not necessary to include R_1.

Table 12–2

	Computed	Measured
R_T		
f_r		
Q		
V_{RS1}		
f_2		
f_1		
BW		

4. Using the measured values from Table 12–1, compute the resonant frequency of the circuit from the equation:

$$f_r = \frac{1}{2\pi\sqrt{LC}}$$

Record the computed resonant frequency in Table 12–2.

5. Use the total resistance computed in step 3 and the measured values of L and C to compute the approximate Q of the circuit from the equation:

$$Q = \frac{1}{R_T}\sqrt{\frac{L}{C}}$$

Enter the computed Q in Table 12–2.

6. Compute the bandwidth from the equation:

$$BW = \frac{f_r}{Q}$$

Enter this as the computed BW in Table 12–2.

7. Using your oscilloscope, tune for resonance by observing the voltage across the sense resistor, R_{S1}. As explained in Floyd's text, the current in the circuit rises to a maximum at resonance. The sense resistor will have the highest voltage across it at resonance. Measure the resonant frequency with the oscilloscope. Record the measured resonant frequency in Table 12–2.

8. Check that the voltage across R_1 is 1.0 V_{pp}. Measure the peak-to-peak voltage across the sense resistor at resonance. The voltage across R_{S1} is directly proportional to the current in the series LC branch, so it is not necessary to compute the current. Record in Table 12–2 the measured peak-to-peak voltage across R_{S1} (V_{RS1}).

9. Raise the frequency of the generator until the voltage across R_{S1} falls to 70.7% of the value read in step 7. Do not readjust the generator's amplitude in this step; this means that the Thevenin resistance of the generator is included in the measurement of the bandwidth. Measure and record this frequency as f_2 in Table 12–2.

10. Lower the frequency to below resonance until the voltage across R_{S1} falls to 70.7% of the value read in step 8. Again, do not adjust the generator amplitude. Measure and record this frequency as f_1 in Table 12–2.

11. Compute the bandwidth by subtracting f_1 from f_2. Enter this result in Table 12–2 as the measured bandwidth.

12. At resonance, the current in the circuit, the voltage across the capacitor, and the voltage across the inductor are all at a maximum value. Tune across resonance by observing the voltage across the capacitor, then try it on the inductor. Use the oscilloscope difference function technique described in Experiment 2. What is the maximum voltage observed on the capacitor? Is it the same or different than the maximum voltage across the inductor?

V_C (max) = _____ V_L (max) = _____

CONCLUSION

EVALUATION AND REVIEW QUESTIONS
1. (a) Compute the percent difference between the computed and measured bandwidth.

    (b) What factors account for the difference between the computed and measured values?

2. (a) What is the total impedance of the experimental circuit at resonance?_____

    (b) What is the phase shift between the total current and voltage?_____

3. (a) In step 12, you measured the maximum voltage across the capacitor and the inductor. The maximum voltage across either one should have been larger than the source voltage. How do you account for this?

    (b) Is this a valid technique for finding the resonant frequency? _____

4. (a) What happens to the resonant frequency, if the inductor is twice as large and the capacitor is half as large? _____

   (b) What happens to the bandwidth? _____

5. (a) Compute the resonant frequency for a circuit consisting of a 50 μH inductor in series with a 1000 pF capacitor. f_r = _____

   (b) If the total resistance of the above circuit is 10 Ω, what are Q and the bandwidth?
      Q = _____ BW = _____

FOR FURTHER INVESTIGATION

In this experiment, you measured three points on the response curve similar to Figure 12–1. Using the technique of measuring the voltage across R_{S1}, find several more points on the response curve. Graph your results on Plot 12–1.

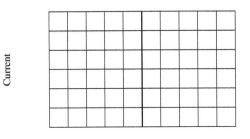

f_r
Frequency

Plot 12–1

MULTISIM TROUBLESHOOTING

This experiment has four Multisim files on the website (www.prenhall.com/floyd). Three of the four files contain a simulated "fault"; one has "no fault". The file with no fault is named EXP26-3-nf. You may want to open this file to compare your results with the computer simulation. Then open each of the files with faults. Use the simulated instruments to investigate the circuit and determine the problem. The following are the filenames for circuits with troubleshooting problems for this experiment.

EXP26-3-f1
   Fault: _____

EXP26-3-f2
   Fault: _____

EXP26-3-f3
   Fault: _____

13 Parallel Resonance

Name _____
Date _____
Class _____

READING
Floyd, Sections 13–5 through 13–8

OBJECTIVES
After performing this experiment, you will be able to:
1.   Compute the resonant frequency, Q, and bandwidth of a parallel resonant circuit.
2.   Measure the frequency response of a parallel resonant circuit.
3.   Use the frequency response to determine the bandwidth of a parallel resonant circuit.

MATERIALS NEEDED
One 100 mH inductor
One 0.047 µF capacitor
One 1.0 kΩ resistor

SUMMARY OF THEORY
In an RLC parallel circuit, the current in each branch is determined by the applied voltage and the impedance of that branch. For an "ideal" inductor (no resistance), the branch impedance is X_L, and for a capacitor the branch impedance is X_C. Since X_L and X_C are functions of frequency, it is apparent that the currents in each branch are also dependent on the frequency. For any given L and C, there is a frequency at which the currents in each are equal and of opposite phase. This frequency is the resonant frequency and is found using the same equation as was used for series resonance:

$$f_r = \frac{1}{2\pi\sqrt{LC}}$$

The circuit and phasor diagram for an ideal parallel RLC circuit at resonance is illustrated in Figure 13–1. Some interesting points to observe are: The total source current at resonance is equal to the current in the resistor. The total current is actually less than the current in either the inductor or the capacitor. This is because of the opposite phase shift which occurs between inductors and capacitors, causing the addition of the currents to cancel. Also, the impedance of the circuit is solely determined by

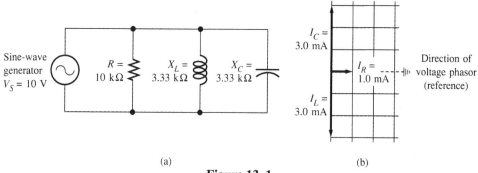

(a)   (b)

Figure 13–1

R, as the inductor and capacitor appear to be open. In a two-branch circuit consisting of only L and C, the source current would be zero, causing the impedance to be infinite! Of course, this does not happen with actual components that do have resistance and other effects.

In a practical two-branch parallel circuit consisting of an inductor and a capacitor, the only significant resistance is the winding resistance of the inductor. Figure 13–2(a) illustrates a practical parallel LC circuit containing winding resistance. By network theorems, the practical LC circuit can be converted to an equivalent parallel RLC circuit, as shown in Figure 13–2(b). The equivalent circuit is easier to analyze. The phasor diagram for the ideal parallel RLC circuit can then be applied to the equivalent circuit as was illustrated in Figure 13–1. The equations to convert the inductance and its winding resistance to an equivalent parallel circuit are

$$ L_{eq} = L \left(\frac{Q^2 + 1}{Q^2} \right) \qquad\qquad R_{p(eq)} = R_W (Q^2 + 1) $$

where $R_{p(eq)}$ represents the parallel equivalent resistance, and R_W represents the winding resistance of the inductor. The Q used in the conversion equation is the Q for the inductor:

$$ Q = \frac{X_L}{R_W} $$

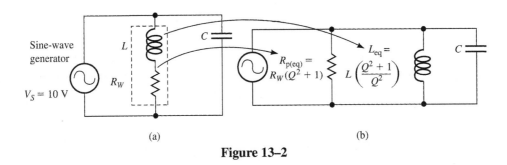

(a)   (b)

Figure 13–2

The *selectivity* of series circuits was discussed in Experiment 12. Parallel resonant circuits also respond to a group of frequencies. In parallel resonant circuits, the impedance as a function of frequency has the same shape as the current versus frequency curve for series resonant circuits. The *bandwidth* of a parallel resonant circuit is the frequency range at which the circuit impedance is 70.7% of the maximum impedance. The sharpness of the response to frequencies is again measured by the circuit Q. The circuit Q will be different from the Q of the inductor if there is additional resistance in the circuit. If there is no additional resistance in parallel with L and C, then the Q for a parallel resonant circuit is equal to the Q of the inductor.

PROCEDURE

1. Measure the value of a 100 mH inductor, a 0.047 μF capacitor, and a 1.0 kΩ resistor. Enter the measured values in Table 13–1. If it is not possible to measure the inductor or capacitor, use the listed values.

2. Measure the resistance of the inductor. Enter the measured inductor resistance in Table 13–1.

	Table 13–1	
	Listed Value	Measured Value
L_1	100 mH	
C_1	0.047 μF	
R_{S1}	1.0 kΩ	
R_W (L_1 resistance)		

	Table 13–2	
	Computed	Measured
f_r		
Q		
BW		
$f_i = \dfrac{BW}{4}$		

3. Construct the circuit shown in Figure 13–3. The purpose of R_{S1} is to develop a voltage that can be used to sense the total current in the circuit. Compute the resonant frequency of the circuit using the equation

$$f_r = \frac{1}{2\pi\sqrt{LC}}$$

Enter the computed resonant frequency in Table 13–2. Set the generator to the f_r at 1.0 V_{pp} output, as measured with your oscilloscope. Use peak-to-peak values for all voltage measurements in this experiment.

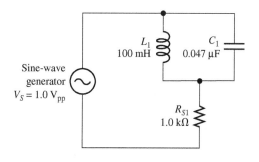

Sine-wave generator
$V_S = 1.0$ V_{pp}

L_1 100 mH C_1 0.047 μF
R_{S1} 1.0 kΩ

Figure 13–3

4. The Q of a parallel LC circuit with no resistance other than the inductor winding resistance is equal to the Q of the inductor. Compute the approximate Q of the parallel LC circuit from

$$Q = \frac{X_L}{R_W}$$

Enter the computed Q in Table 13–2.

5. Compute the bandwidth from the equation

$$BW = \frac{f_r}{Q}$$

Enter this as the computed BW in Table 13–2.

261

6. Connect your oscilloscope across R_{S1} and tune for resonance by observing the voltage across the sense resistor, R_{S1}. Resonance occurs when the voltage across R_{S1} is a minimum, since the impedance of the parallel LC circuit is highest. Measure the resonant frequency (f_r) and record the measured result in Table 13–2.

7. Compute a frequency increment (f_i) by dividing the computed bandwidth by 4. That is,

$$f_i = \frac{BW}{4}$$

Enter the computed f_i in Table 13–2.

8. Use the measured resonant frequency (f_r) and the frequency increment (f_i) from Table 13–2 to compute 11 frequencies according to the Computed Frequency column of Table 13–3. Enter the 11 frequencies in column 1 of Table 13–3.

Table 13–3

Computed Frequency	V_{RS1}	I	Z
$f_r - 5f_i =$			
$f_r - 4f_i =$			
$f_r - 3f_i =$			
$f_r - 2f_i =$			
$f_r - 1f_i =$			
$f_r =$			
$f_r + 1f_i =$			
$f_r + 2f_i =$			
$f_r + 3f_i =$			
$f_r + 4f_i =$			
$f_r + 5f_i =$			

9. Tune the generator to each of the computed frequencies listed in Table 13–3. At each frequency, check that the generator voltage is still at 1.0 V_{pp}; then measure the peak-to-peak voltage across R_{S1}. Record the voltage in column 2 of Table 13–3.

10. Compute the total peak-to-peak current, I, at each frequency by applying Ohm's law to the sense resistor R_{S1}. (That is, $I = V_{RS1}/R_{S1}$.) Record the current in column 3 of Table 13–3.

11. Use Ohm's law with the measured source voltage (1.0 V_{pp}) and source current at each frequency to compute the impedance at each frequency. Complete Table 13–3 by listing the computed impedances.

12.   On Plot 13–1, draw the impedance versus frequency curve. From your curve determine the bandwidth. Complete Table 13–2 with the measured bandwidth.

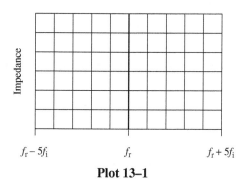

Plot 13–1

CONCLUSION

EVALUATION AND REVIEW QUESTIONS
1.   (a)   Compare the impedance as a function of frequency for series and parallel resonance.

       (b)   Compare the current as a function of frequency for series and parallel resonance.

2.   What was the phase shift between the total current and voltage at resonance?

3.   At resonance the total current was a minimum, but the branch currents were not. How could you find the value of the current in each branch?

4.   What factors affect the Q of a parallel resonant circuit?

5.   In the circuit of Figure 13–2(a), assume the inductor is 100 mH with 120 Ω of winding resistance
        and the capacitor is 0.01 μF. Compute:
        (a)   the resonant frequency _____

        (b)   the reactance, X_L, of the inductor at resonance _____

        (c)   the Q of the circuit _____

        (d)   the bandwidth, BW _____

FOR FURTHER INVESTIGATION

The oscilloscope can be used to display the resonant dip in current by connecting a sweep generator to the
circuit. This converts the time base on the oscilloscope to a frequency base. The sweep generator produces
an FM (frequency modulated) signal, which is connected in place of the signal generator. In addition, the
sweep generator has a synchronous sweep output that should be connected to the oscilloscope on the X
channel input. The Y channel input is connected across the 1.0 kΩ sense resistor. The oscilloscope is
placed in the XY mode. A diagram of the setup is shown in Figure 13–4. Build the circuit shown,
determine a method to calibrate the frequency base, and summarize your procedure in a report.

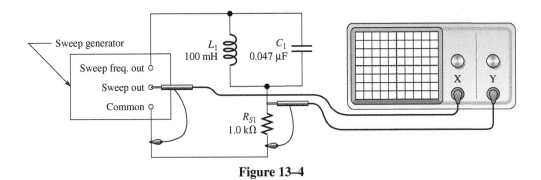

Figure 13–4

MULTISIM TROUBLESHOOTING

This experiment has four Multisim files on the website (www.prenhall.com/floyd). Three of the four files contain a simulated "fault"; one has "no fault". The file with no fault is named EXP27-3-nf. You may want to open this file to compare your results with the computer simulation. Then open each of the files with faults. Use the simulated instruments to investigate the circuit and determine the problem. The following are the filenames for circuits with troubleshooting problems for this experiment.

EXP27-3-f1

Fault: _____

EXP27-3-f2

Fault: _____

EXP27-3-f3

Fault: _____

14 Passive Filters

Name _____
Date _____
Class _____

READING
Floyd, Sections 13–4 through 13–7

OBJECTIVES
After performing this experiment, you will be able to:
1. Compare the characteristics and responses of low-pass, high-pass, bandpass, and notch filters.
2. Construct a T filter, a pi filter, and a resonant filter circuit and measure their frequency responses.

MATERIALS NEEDED
Resistors:
    One 680 Ω, one 1.6 kΩ
Capacitors:
    One 0.033 μF, two 0.1 μF
One 100 mH inductor

SUMMARY OF THEORY
In many circuits, different frequencies are present. If some frequencies are not desired, they can be rejected with special circuits called *filters*. Filters can be designed to pass either low or high frequencies. For example, in communication circuits, an audio frequency (AF) signal may be present with a radio frequency (RF) signal. The AF signal could be retained and the RF signal rejected with a *low-pass* filter. A *high-pass* filter will do the opposite: it will pass the RF signal and reject the AF signal. Sometimes the frequencies of interest are between other frequencies that are not desired. This is the case for a radio or television receiver, for example. The desired frequencies are present along with many other frequencies coming into the receiver. A resonant circuit is used to select the desired frequencies from the band of frequencies present. A circuit that passes only selected frequencies from a band is called a *bandpass* filter. The opposite of a bandpass filter is a *band reject* or *notch* filter. A typical application of a notch filter is to eliminate a specific interfering frequency from a band of desired frequencies. Figure 14–1 illustrates representative circuits and the frequency responses of various types of filters.

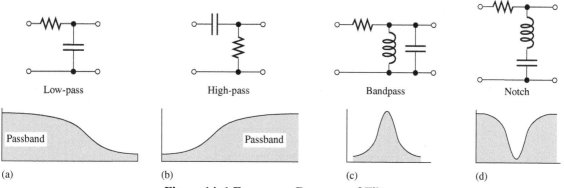

Figure 14–1 Frequency Response of Filters

The simplest filters are *RC* and *RL* series circuits studied in Experiments 6 and 10. These circuits can be used as either high-pass or low-pass filters, depending on where the input and output voltages are applied and removed. A problem with simple *RC* and *RL* filters is that they change gradually from the passband to the stop band. You illustrated this characteristic on Plot 6–3 of Experiment 6.

Improved filter characteristics can be obtained by combining several filter sections. Unfortunately, you cannot simply stack identical sections together to improve the response as there are loading effects that must be taken into account. Two common improved filters are the *T* and the *pi* filters, so named because of the placement of the components in the circuit. Examples of T and pi filters are shown in Figure 14–2. Notice that the low-pass filters have inductors in series with the load and capacitors in parallel with the load. The high-pass filter is the opposite.

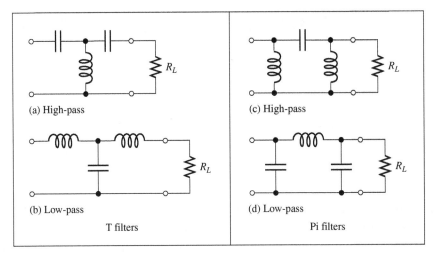

(a) High-pass   (c) High-pass

(b) Low-pass   (d) Low-pass

T filters   Pi filters

Figure 14–2

The choice of using a T or pi filter is determined by the load resistor and source impedance. If the load resistor is much larger than the source impedance, then the T-type filter is best. If the load resistor is much lower than the source impedance, then the pi filter is best.

PROCEDURE

1. Obtain the components listed in Table 14–1. For this experiment, it is important to have values that are close to the listed ones. Measure all components and record the measured values in Table 14–1. Use listed values for those components that you cannot measure.

Table 14–1

	Listed Value	Measured Value
L_1	100 mH	
C_1	0.1 μF	
C_2	0.1 μF	
C_3	0.033 μF	
R_{L1}	680 Ω	
R_{L2}	1.6 kΩ	

2. Construct the pi filter circuit illustrated in Figure 14–3. Set the signal generator for a 500 Hz sine wave at 3.0 V$_{rms}$. The voltage should be measured at the generator with the circuit connected. Set the voltage with a voltmeter and check both voltage and frequency with the oscilloscope.

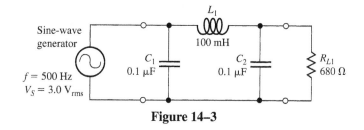

Figure 14–3

3. Measure and record the rms voltage across the load resistor (V_{RL1}) at 500 Hz. Record the measured voltage in Table 14–2.

4. Change the frequencies of the generator to 1000 Hz. Readjust the generator's amplitude to 3.0 V$_{rms}$. Measure V_{RL1}, and enter the data in Table 14–2. Continue in this manner for each frequency listed in Table 14–2. (Note: You may be unable to obtain 3.0 V from the generator at 8.0 kHz.)

5. Graph the voltage across the load resistor (V_{RL1}) as a function of frequency on Plot 14–1.

Table 14–2

Frequency	V_{RL1}
500 Hz	
1000 Hz	
1500 Hz	
2000 Hz	
3000 Hz	
4000 Hz	
8000 Hz	

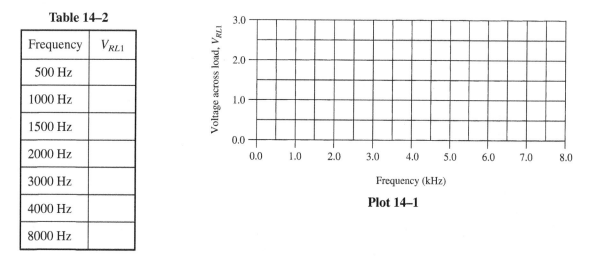

Plot 14–1

6. Construct the T filter circuit illustrated in Figure 14–4. Set the signal generator for a 500 Hz sine wave at 3.0 V$_{rms}$. The voltage should be measured with the circuit connected. Set the voltage with a voltmeter and check both voltage and frequency with the oscilloscope as before.

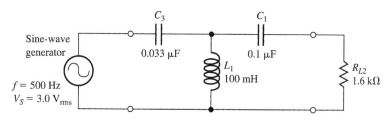

Figure 14–4

269

7. Measure and record the voltage across the load resistor (V_{RL2}) for each frequency listed in Table 14–3. Keep the generator voltage at 3.0 V$_{rms}$. Graph the voltage across the load resistor (V_{RL2}) as a function of frequency on Plot 14–2.

Table 14–3

Frequency	V_{RL2}
500 Hz	
1000 Hz	
1500 Hz	
2000 Hz	
3000 Hz	
4000 Hz	
8000 Hz	

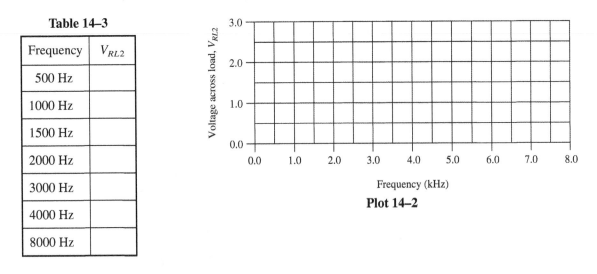

Plot 14–2

8. Construct the series resonant filter circuit illustrated in Figure 14–5. Set the generator for 3.0 V$_{rms}$ at 500 Hz.

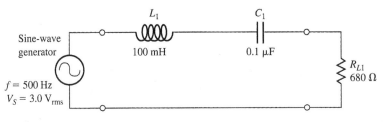

Figure 14–5

9. Measure and record the voltage across the load resistor (V_{RL1}) for each frequency listed in Table 14–4. Graph the voltage across the load resistor as a function of frequency on Plot 14–3.

Table 14–4

Frequency	V_{RL1}
500 Hz	
1000 Hz	
1500 Hz	
2000 Hz	
3000 Hz	
4000 Hz	
8000 Hz	

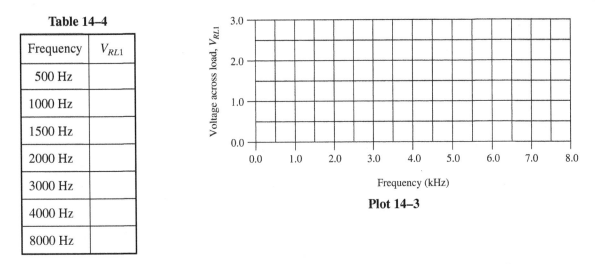

Plot 14–3

270

CONCLUSION

EVALUATION AND REVIEW QUESTIONS

1. The cutoff frequency for each filter in this experiment is that frequency at which the output is 70.7% of its maximum value. From the frequency response curves in Plots 14–1 and 14–2, estimate the cutoff frequency for the high- and low-pass filters.

   Pi filter cutoff frequency = _____

   T filter cutoff frequency = _____

2. Compare the response curve of the high and low filters in this experiment with the response curve from the simple *RC* filter in Experiment 6.

3. For each filter constructed in this experiment, identify it as a low-pass, high-pass, bandpass, or notch filter:

   (a) Plot 14–1 (pi filter): _____

   (b) Plot 14–2 (T filter): _____

   (c) Plot 14–3 (resonant filter): _____

4. Explain what would happen to the response curve from the series resonant filter if the output were taken across the inductor and capacitor instead of the load resistor.

5. (a) Sketch the circuit for a parallel resonant filter used as a bandpass filter.

   (b) Sketch the circuit for a parallel resonant filter used as a notch filter.

FOR FURTHER INVESTIGATION

Using the components from this experiment, construct a parallel resonant notch filter. Measure the frequency response with a sufficient number of points to determine the bandwidth accurately. The bandwidth (*BW*) of a resonant filter is the difference in the two frequencies at which the response is 70.7% of the maximum output. From your data, determine the *BW* of the parallel notch resonant filter. Complete Table 14–5 and plot the data in Plot 14–4 for your notch filter. Write a conclusion.

Table 14–5

Frequency	V_{RL1}
500 Hz	
1000 Hz	
1500 Hz	
2000 Hz	
3000 Hz	
4000 Hz	
8000 Hz	

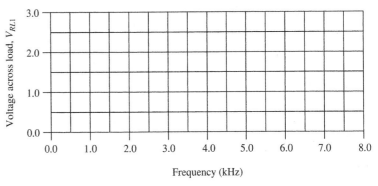

Plot 14–4

MULTISIM TROUBLESHOOTING

This experiment has four Multisim files on the website (www.prenhall.com/floyd). Three of the four files contain a simulated "fault"; one has "no fault". The file with no fault is named EXP28-3-nf. You may want to open this file to compare your results with the computer simulation. Then open each of the files with faults. Use the simulated instruments to investigate the circuit and determine the problem. The following are the filenames for circuits with troubleshooting problems for this experiment.

EXP28-3-f1

    Fault: _____

EXP28-3-f2

    Fault: _____

EXP28-3-f3

    Fault: _____

Application Assignment 6

Name _____
Date _____
Class _____

REFERENCE
Floyd, Chapter 13, Application Assignment: Putting Your Knowledge to Work

Step 1   From the oscilloscope displays shown in Floyd's text, plot the frequency response of the filter.

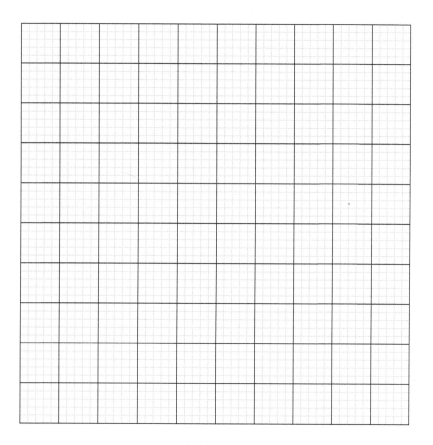

Plot AA–6–1

Step 2   Specify the type of filter and determine the resonant frequency and the bandwidth.

Type of filter is _____

Resonant frequency = _____   Bandwidth = _____

RELATED EXPERIMENT

MATERIALS NEEDED
Resistors:
   Two 10 kΩ, one 5.1 kΩ
Four 1000 pF capacitors

DISCUSSION
A bandstop, or notch, filter, as described in the text, is capable of removing certain undesired frequencies from a signal. Another application of a notch filter is the twin-T oscillator shown in Figure AA–6–1(a). It oscillates at the notch frequency, which is given by the equation

$$f_r = \frac{1}{2\pi RC}$$

     Test the filter portion of the oscillator by constructing the circuit shown in Figure AA–6–1(b). Use two 1000 pF capacitors in parallel for $2C$. Connect a signal generator to the input and set it for a sine wave at 3.0 V$_{pp}$ near the computed notch frequency. Vary the frequency of the generator and observe the output. Graph the response by plotting the voltage out as a function of the frequency for several points around the notch frequency.

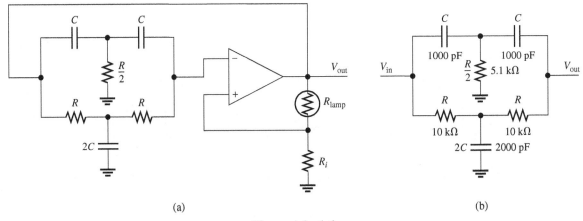

(a)   (b)

Figure AA–6–1

EXPERIMENTAL RESULTS

Checkup 6

REFERENCE

Floyd, Chap. 13, and Buchla, Experiments 26, 27, and 28

1. In a series resonant circuit at resonance:
   (a) current is a maximum
   (b) total impedance is zero
   (c) inductive reactance is larger than capacitive reactance
   (d) capacitive reactance is larger than inductive reactance

2. In a series RLC circuit, the phase angle between the capacitor voltage and inductor voltage is:
   (a) 0° (b) 90° (c) 180° (d) dependent on the frequency

3. In a resonant circuit, if L is halved and C is doubled, the resonant frequency will:
   (a) remain the same (b) double (c) quadruple (d) be halved

4. In a resonant circuit, if L is halved and C is doubled, Q will:
   (a) remain the same (b) double (c) be halved (d) be one-fourth

5. In a parallel resonant circuit, if the frequency is higher than resonance, the circuit is said to be:
   (a) purely resistive (b) inductive (c) capacitive (d) cutoff

6. At the cutoff frequency of a filter, the output voltage is approximately:
   (a) 10% of the input voltage   (b) 50% of the input voltage
   (c) 71% of the input voltage   (d) 100% of the input voltage

7. A bandstop filter can be made with a series resonant circuit and a resistor. The output is taken across:
   (a) the capacitor and the inductor   (b) the capacitor and resistor
   (c) the inductor and resistor   (d) the resistor

8. If the inductor in a resonant circuit is replaced with an identical inductor but the replacement inductor has higher coil resistance, the new bandwidth will be:
   (a) unchanged (b) larger (c) smaller

9. If a load is connected to a parallel resonant circuit, the selectivity will:
   (a) decrease (b) remain the same (c) increase

10. Assume a series RLC circuit is connected across a dc source. The dc voltage will be across:
    (a) the inductor (b) the capacitor (c) the resistor

11. A series *RLC* circuit has a 200 pF capacitor and a 100 μH inductor. If the inductor has a winding resistance of 20 Ω, calculate:
    (a) the resonant frequency

    (b) the impedance of the circuit at resonance

    (c) the *Q* of the coil

12. The series resonant circuit in Experiment 12 used a 100 Ω resistor in parallel with the source. Explain how this resistor affected the *Q* of the circuit.

13. A tank circuit is constructed using a 200 μH inductor and a variable capacitor. The circuit is required to tune the frequency range from 535 to 1605 kHz (AM radio band).
    (a) Compute the range of capacitance required to cause resonance over the range of frequencies.

    (b) Assuming the inductor has a resistance of 10 Ω, compute the *Q* of the circuit at each end of the tuning range.

    (c) Using the *Q* value found in (b), determine the bandwidth at each end of the tuning range.

14. Observe the parallel resonant circuit shown in Figure C–6–1. Assume the inductor has a winding resistance of 25 Ω. At resonance, calculate:
    (a) the inductive reactance

    (b) the *Q* of the coil

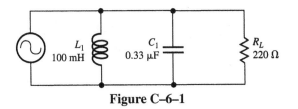

Figure C–6–1

276

READING
Floyd, Sections 14–1 through 14–9

OBJECTIVES
After performing this experiment, you will be able to:
1.   Determine the turns ratio for a transformer.
2.   Show the phase relationships between the primary and secondary of a center-tapped transformer.
3.   Compute the turns ratio required for matching a signal generator to a speaker.
4.   Demonstrate how an impedance-matching transformer can increase the power transferred to a load.

MATERIALS NEEDED
One 12.6 V center-tapped transformer
One small impedance-matching transformer (approximately 600 Ω to 800 Ω)
One small speaker (4 or 8 Ω)
For Further Investigation
    One 100 Ω resistor

SUMMARY OF THEORY
A transformer consists of two (or more) closely coupled coils that share a common magnetic field. When an ac voltage is applied to the first coil, called the *primary,* a voltage is induced in the second coil, called the *secondary.* The voltage that appears across the secondary is proportional to the transformer turns ratio. The turns ratio is found by dividing the number of turns in the secondary winding by the number of turns in the primary winding. The turns ratio, *n,* is directly proportional to the primary and secondary voltages. That is,

$$n = \frac{N_S}{N_P} = \frac{V_S}{V_P}$$

For most work, we can assume that a transformer has no internal power dissipation and that all the magnetic flux lines in the primary also cut through the secondary—that is, we can assume the transformer is *ideal.* The ideal transformer delivers to the load 100% of the applied power. Actual transformers have losses due to magnetizing current, eddy currents, coil resistance, and so forth. In typical power applications, transformers are used to change the ac line voltage from one voltage to another or to isolate ac grounds. For the ideal transformer, the secondary voltage is found by multiplying the turns ratio by the applied primary voltage. That is,

$$V_S = nV_P$$

Since the ideal transformer has no internal losses, we can equate the power delivered to the primary to the power delivered by the secondary. Since $P = IV$, we can write:

$$\text{Power} = I_P V_P = I_S V_S$$

This equation shows that if the transformer causes the secondary voltage to be higher than the primary voltage, the secondary current must be less than the primary current. Also, if the transformer has no load, then there will be no primary or secondary current in the ideal transformer.

In addition to their ability to change voltages and isolate grounds, transformers are useful to change the resistance (or *impedance*) of a load as viewed from the primary side. (Impedance is a more generalized word meaning opposition to ac current.) The load resistance appears to increase by the turns ratio squared (n^2) when viewed from the primary side. Transformers used to change impedance are designed differently from power transformers. They need to transform voltages over a band of frequencies with low distortion. Special transformers called *audio*, or *wideband*, transformers are designed for this. To find the correct turns ratio needed to match a load impedance to a source impedance, use the following equation:

$$ n = \sqrt{\frac{R_{load}}{R_{source}}} $$

In this experiment, you will examine both a power transformer and an impedance-matching transformer and calculate parameters for each.

PROCEDURE

1. Obtain a low-voltage power transformer with a center-tapped secondary (12.6 V secondary). Using an ohmmeter, measure the primary and secondary resistance. Record in Table 15–1.

2. Compute the turns ratio based on the normal line voltage (V_P) of 115 V and the specified secondary voltage of 12.6 V. Record this as the computed turns ratio, n, in Table 15–1.

3. For safety, we will use an audio generator in place of ac line voltages. Connect the circuit illustrated in Figure 15–1. Power transformers are designed to operate at a specific frequency (generally 60 Hz). Set the generator to a 60 Hz sine wave at 5.0 V_{rms} on the primary. Measure the secondary voltage. From the measured voltages, compute the turns ratio for the transformer. Enter this value as the measured turns ratio in Table 15–1.

4. Compute the percent difference between the computed and measured turns ratio and enter the result in Table 15–1. The percent difference is found from the equation:

$$ \%diff = \frac{n(meas.) - n(comp.)}{n(comp.)} \times 100\% $$

Table 15–1

Primary winding resistance, R_P	
Secondary winding resistance, R_S	
Turns ratio, n (computed)	
Turns ratio, n (measured)	
% difference	

Transformer

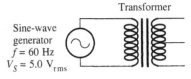

Sine-wave generator
$f = 60$ Hz
$V_S = 5.0$ V_{rms}

Figure 15–1

5. Connect a two-channel oscilloscope to the secondary, as illustrated in Figure 15–2(a). Trigger the oscilloscope from channel 1. Compare the phase of the primary side viewed on channel 1 with the phase of the secondary side viewed on channel 2. Then reverse the leads on the secondary side. Describe your observations.

6. Connect the oscilloscope ground to the center tap of the transformer and view the signals on each side at the center tap at the same time as illustrated in Figure 15–2(b). Sketch the waveforms beside the figures showing measured voltages.

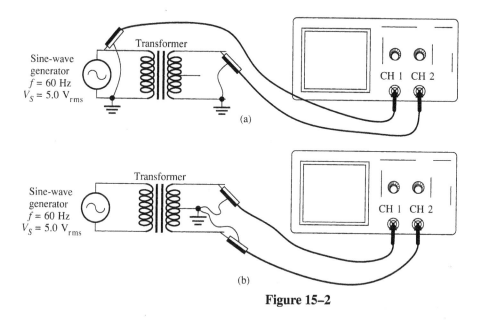

Figure 15–2

7. In this step, a transformer will be used to match a source impedance to a load impedance. A small speaker represents a low impedance (typically 4 or 8 Ω), whereas a signal generator is typically 600 Ω of Thevenin impedance. An impedance-matching transformer can make the load appear to have the same impedance as the source. This allows maximum power to be transferred to the load. Connect a small speaker directly to your signal generator and set the frequency to approximately 2 kHz. Note the volume of the sound from the speaker. Measure the voltage across the speaker.

    $V_{SPKR} =$ _____

8. Using the specified Thevenin impedance of the generator and the specified speaker impedance, compute the turns ratio required to match the speaker with your signal generator.

    $n =$ _____

9. Connect a small impedance-matching transformer into the circuit. It is not necessary to obtain the precise turns ratio required to note the improvement in the power delivered to the speaker. You can find the correct leads to the primary and secondary of the impedance-matching transformer using an ohmmeter. Since the required transformer is a step down type, the primary resistance will be higher than the secondary resistance. Often, the primary winding will have a center tap for push-pull amplifiers. Again measure the voltage across the speaker.

V_{SPKR} = _____

CONCLUSION

EVALUATION AND REVIEW QUESTIONS

1. (a) Using the data from step 1, compute a resistance ratio between the secondary and primary coils by dividing the measured secondary resistance by the measured primary resistance.

Resistance ratio = _____

(b) What factors could cause the computed resistance ratio to differ from the turns ratio?

2. What factors might cause a difference between the measured and computed turns ratio in steps 2 and 3?

3. Compare the voltage across the speaker as measured in step 7 and in step 9. Explain why there is a difference.

4. The power supplied to an ideal transformer should be zero if there is no load. Why?

5. (a) If an ideal transformer has 115 V across the primary and draws 200 mA of current, what power is dissipated in the load?

    (b) If the secondary voltage in the transformer of part (a) is 24 V, what is the secondary current?

    (c) What is the turns ratio?

FOR FURTHER INVESTIGATION

The ideal transformer model neglects a small current that is in the primary independent of secondary load current. This current, called the *magnetizing* current, is required to produce the magnetic flux and is added to the current that is present due to the load. The magnetizing current appears to be through an equivalent inductor parallel to the ideal transformer. Investigate this current by connecting the circuit in Figure 15–3 using the impedance-matching transformer. Calculate the magnetizing current, I_M, in the primary by measuring the voltage across a series resistor with no load and applying Ohm's law:

$$I_M = \frac{V_R}{R}$$

Find out if the magnetizing current changes as frequency is changed. Be sure to keep the generator at a constant 5.0 V$_{rms}$.

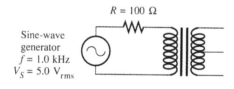

$R = 100\ \Omega$

Sine-wave generator
$f = 1.0$ kHz
$V_S = 5.0$ V$_{rms}$

Figure 15–3

Application Assignment 7

REFERENCE

Floyd, Chapter 14, Application Assignment: Putting Your Knowledge to Work

Step 1   Familiarization with the power supply.

Step 2   Measure voltages on power supply board 1. Determine from the readings whether or not the board is working properly. If not, isolate the problem to one of the items in Table AA–7–1.

Table AA–7–1

Board 1 is:
A. working properly
B. has the following problem:
(a)   rectifier, filter, or regulator
(b)   transformer
(c)   fuse
(d)   power source

Step 3   Measure voltages on power supply boards 2, 3, 4. Determine from the readings whether or not the board is working properly. If not, isolate the problem to one of the items in Table AA–7–2.

Table AA–7–2

Board 2 is:	Board 3 is:	Board 4 is:
A. working properly	A. working properly	A. working properly
B. has the following problem:	B. has the following problem:	B. has the following problem:
(a) rectifier, filter, or regulator	(a) rectifier, filter, or regulator	(a) rectifier, filter, or regulator
(b) transformer	(b) transformer	(b) transformer
(c) fuse	(c) fuse	(c) fuse
(d) power source	(d) power source	(d) power source

RELATED EXPERIMENT

MATERIALS NEEDED

One small speaker (4 or 8 Ω)

One 20 Ω variable resistor (approximate value)

DISCUSSION

To match the impedance of a speaker to an amplifier, you need to know the impedance of the speaker. You can measure the impedance of a speaker by the circuit shown in Figure AA–7–1. Set the scope controls as follows: CH 1, 0.1 V/div; CH 2, 50 mV/div (this is a 2:1 ratio); and SEC/DIV, 0.5 ms/div. The variable controls should be in the calibrated position. Adjust the peak-to-peak amplitude of the function generator to about 300 mV$_{pp}$ (actual value is not critical) and center both traces. Then adjust the potentiometer until the two signals appear as one—they should appear superimposed on each other. At this point, the impedance of the speaker is the same as the impedance of the potentiometer. (Why?) Remove the potentiometer and measure its resistance.

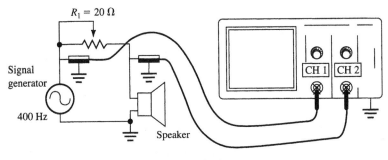

$R_1 = 20\ \Omega$

Signal generator

400 Hz

Speaker

CH 1 CH 2

Figure AA–7–1

A variation of the method is to observe the waveform using the XY mode. Switch to XY mode but do not change the vertical sensitivity of the channels. At 400 Hz, the speaker impedance is primarily resistive, and a straight line at a 45° slope should be observed. Note how changing the potentiometer affects the line. Now try raising the frequency. Does the impedance of the speaker change? Try 20 kHz and see what happens. Summarize your findings.

EXPERIMENTAL RESULTS

Checkup 7

REFERENCE

Floyd, Chap. 14, and Buchla, Experiment 29

1.   Transformers work by the principle of:
      (a) self-inductance   (b) mutual inductance
      (c) hysteresis   (d) coupled electric fields

2.   The efficiency of an ideal transformer is:
      (a) 90%   (b) 95%   (c) 100%   (d) dependent on the transformer

3.   Air core transformers are primarily used for:
      (a) impedance matching   (b) isolation
      (c) power   (d) radio frequencies

4.   The impedance seen on the primary side of an impedance-matching transformer is called:
      (a) load resistance   (b) primary resistance
      (c) reflected resistance   (d) winding resistance

5.   A transformer with a single winding that can be adjusted with a sliding mechanism is known as a(n):
      (a) variac   (b) rheostat   (c) isolation transformer   (d) tapped transformer

6.   If a transformer has a much lower secondary voltage than primary voltage, which of the following is true?
      (a) $P_S > P_P$ (b) $N_S > N_P$ (c) $I_S > I_P$ (d) efficiency is very poor

7.   A transformer with a turns ratio of 2 has a primary voltage of 110 V. The secondary voltage is:
      (a) 55 V   (b) 110 V   (c) 220 V   (d) 440 V

8.   An ideal transformer with a turns ratio of 5 has a primary voltage of 110 V and a secondary load consisting of a 100 Ω resistor. The primary current is:
      (a) 0.22 A   (b) 1.1 A   (c) 5.5 A   (d) 27.5 A

9.   An impedance-matching transformer is needed to match an 8 Ω load to a 600 Ω source. The ideal reflected resistance is:
      (a) 8 Ω (b) 16 Ω (c) 600 Ω (d) 1200 Ω

10.   The turns ratio for the transformer in Question 9 is:
      (a) 0.0133   (b) 0.115   (c) 8.66   (d) 75

11.   In Experiment 15, you tested an impedance-matching transformer and a power transformer. Which transformer do you think is closest to the ideal transformer? Why?

12.   A power transformer with a primary voltage of 110 V has a secondary voltage of 28 V connected to a 47 Ω load resistor. If the primary power is 18 W, calculate:
       (a)   the efficiency

       (b)   the primary current

       (c)   the turns ratio

13.   Explain the difference between a tapped transformer and a multiple-winding transformer.

14.   What is the purpose of an isolation transformer?

15.   Assume you need to replace a missing fuse that is in series with the primary winding of a power transformer. The primary is designed for a 120 V, and the secondary is rated for 12.6 V at 1.0 A. What size fuse should you use? Justify your answer.

16.   An amplifier with a 50 Ω Thevenin impedance is used to drive a speaker with an 8 Ω impedance. Assume the amplifier has an unloaded output voltage of 10 V_{rms}.
       (a)   Compute the power delivered to the speaker with no impedance-matching transformer.

       (b)   Calculate the turns ratio of the impedance-matching transformer needed to maximize the power transfer.

16

Integrating and Differentiating Circuits

Name _____
Date _____
Class _____

READING
Floyd, Sections 15–1 through 15–9

OBJECTIVES
After performing this experiment, you will be able to:
1.   Explain how an *RC* or *RL* series circuit can integrate or differentiate a signal.
2.   Compare the waveforms for *RC* and *RL* circuits driven by a square wave generator.
3.   Determine the effect of a frequency change for pulsed *RC* and *RL* circuits.

MATERIALS NEEDED
One 10 kΩ resistor
Capacitors:
   One 0.01 μF, one 1000 pF
One 100 mH inductor

SUMMARY OF THEORY
In mathematics, the word *integrate* means to sum. If we kept a running sum of the area under a horizontal straight line, the area would increase linearly. An example is the speed of a car. Let's say the car is traveling a constant 40 miles per hour. In 1/2 hour the car has traveled 20 miles. In 1 hour the car has traveled 40 miles, and so forth. The car's rate is illustrated in Figure 16–1(a). Each of the three areas shown under the rate curve represents 20 miles. The area increases linearly with time and is shown in Figure 16–1(b). This graph represents the integral of the rate curve.

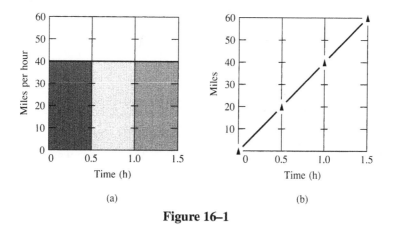

(a)   (b)

Figure 16–1

     A similar situation exists when a capacitor starts to charge. If the applied voltage is a constant, the voltage on the capacitor rises exponentially. However, if we examine the beginning of this exponential rise, it appears to rise in a linear fashion. As long as the voltage change across the capacitor is small compared to the final voltage, the output will represent integration. An *integrator* is any circuit in which the output is proportional to the integral of the input signal. *If the RC time constant of the circuit is long compared to the period of the input waveform, then the waveform across the capacitor is integrated.*

The opposite of integration is *differentiation*. Differentiation means rate of change. *If the RC time constant of the circuit is short compared to the period of the input waveform, then the waveform across the resistor is differentiated.* A pulse waveform that is differentiated produces spikes at the leading and trailing edge as shown in Figure 16–2. Differentiator circuits can be used to detect the leading or trailing edge of a pulse. Diodes can be used to remove either the positive or negative spike.

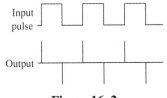

Figure 16–2

An *RL* circuit can also be used as an integrator or differentiator. As in the *RC* circuit, the time constant for the *RL* integrating circuit must be long compared to the period of the input waveform, and the time constant for the differentiator circuit must be short compared to the input waveform. The *RL* circuit will have similar waveforms to the *RC* circuit except that the output signal is taken across the inductor for the differentiating circuit and across the resistor for the integrating circuit.

PROCEDURE
1. Measure the value of a 100 mH inductor, a 0.01 μF and a 1000 pF capacitor, and a 10 kΩ resistor. Record their values in Table 16–1. If it is not possible to measure the inductor or capacitors, use the listed values.

Table 16–1

	Listed Value	Measured Value
L_1	100 mH	
C_1	0.01 μF	
C_2	1000 pF	
R_1	10 kΩ	

2. Construct the circuit shown in Figure 16–3. The 10 kΩ resistor is large compared to the Thevenin impedance of the generator. Set the generator for a 1.0 V_{pp} square wave with no load at a frequency of 1.0 kHz. You should observe that the capacitor fully charges and discharges at this frequency because the *RC* time constant is short compared to the period. On Plot 16–1, sketch the waveforms for the generator, the capacitor, and the resistor. Label voltage and time on your sketch. To look at the voltage across the resistor, use the difference function technique described in Experiment 2. The scope should be dc coupled for those measurements.

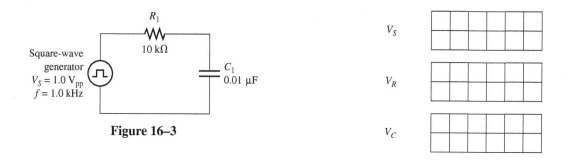

Figure 16–3

V_S

V_R

V_C

Plot 16–1

3. Compute the *RC* time constant for the circuit. Include the generator's Thevenin impedance as part of the resistance in the computation. Enter the computed time constant in Table 16–2.

Table 16–2

	Computed	Measured
RC time constant		

4. Measure the *RC* time constant using the following procedure:
   (a) With the generator disconnected from the circuit, set the output square wave on the oscilloscope to cover 5 vertical divisions (0 to 100%).
   (b) Connect the generator to the circuit. Adjust the SEC/DIV and trigger controls to stretch the capacitor-charging waveform across the scope face to obtain best resolution.
   (c) Count the number of horizontal divisions from the start of the rise to the point where the waveform crosses 3.15 *vertical* divisions (63% of the final level). Multiply the number of *horizontal* divisions that you counted by the setting of the SEC/DIV control. Alternatively, if you have cursor measurements on your oscilloscope, you may find they allow you to make a more precise measurement. Enter the measured *RC* time constant in Table 16–2.

5. Observe the capacitor waveform while you increase the generator frequency to 10 kHz. On Plot 16–2, sketch the waveforms for the generator, the capacitor, and the resistor at 10 kHz. Label the voltage and time on your sketch.

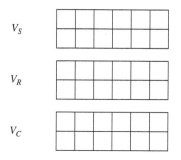

V_S

V_R

V_C

Plot 16–2

6. Temporarily, change the generator from a square wave to a triangle waveform. Describe the waveform across the capacitor.

7. Change back to a square wave at 10 kHz. Replace the capacitor with a 1000 pF capacitor. Using the difference channel, observe the waveform across the resistor. If the output were taken across the resistor, what would this circuit be called? _____

8. Replace the 1000 pF capacitor with a 100 mH inductor. Using the 10 kHz square wave, look at the signal across the generator, the inductor, and the resistor. On Plot 16–3, sketch the waveforms for each. Label the voltage and time on your sketch.

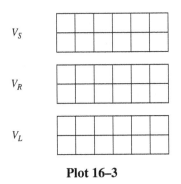

V_S

V_R

V_L

Plot 16–3

CONCLUSION

EVALUATION AND REVIEW QUESTIONS

1. (a) Explain why the Thevenin impedance of the generator was included in the calculated RC time constant measurement in step 3.

   (b) Suggest how you might find the value of an unknown capacitor using the RC time constant.

2.	(a)	Compute the percent difference between the measured and computed RC time constant.

	(b)	List some factors that affect the accuracy of the measured result.

3.	What accounts for the change in the capacitor voltage waveform as the frequency was raised in step 5?

4.	(a)	Draw an RC integrating circuit and an RC differentiating circuit.

	(b)	Draw an RL integrating circuit and an RL differentiating circuit.

5.	Assume you had connected a square wave to an oscilloscope but saw a signal that was differentiated as illustrated in Figure 16–2. What could account for this effect?

FOR FURTHER INVESTIGATION

The rate at which a capacitor charges is determined by the RC time constant of the equivalent series resistance and capacitance. The RC time constant for the circuit illustrated in Figure 16–4 can be determined by applying Thevenin's theorem to the left of points **A–A.** The Thevenin resistance of the generator is part of the charging path and *should* be included. The capacitor is not charging to the generator voltage but to a voltage determined by the voltage divider consisting of R_1 and R_2. Predict the time constant and the waveforms across each resistor. Investigate carefully the waveforms across each of the components.

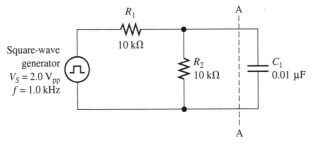

Figure 16–4

MULTISIM TROUBLESHOOTING

This experiment has four Multisim files on the website (www.prenhall.com/floyd). Three of the four files contain a simulated "fault"; one has "no fault". The file with no fault is named EXP30-3-nf. You may want to open this file to compare your results with the computer simulation. Then open each of the files with faults. Use the simulated instruments to investigate the circuit and determine the problem. The following are the filenames for circuits with troubleshooting problems for this experiment.

EXP30-3-f1

      Fault: _____

EXP30-3-f2

      Fault: _____

EXP30-3-f3

      Fault: _____

Application Assignment 8

REFERENCE

Floyd, Chapter 15, Application Assignment: Putting Your Knowledge to Work

Step 1   From the list of standard capacitors, specify the five capacitors for the integrator delay circuit.

$C_1 =$ _____ $C_2 =$ _____ $C_3 =$ _____
$C_4 =$ _____ $C_5 =$ _____

Step 2   Complete the wire list for the breadboard using the circled numbers. The first one has been completed as an example.

From	To	From	To	From	To
1	5				

Step 3   Specify the amplitude, frequency, and duty cycle settings for the function generator in order to test the delay times.

Amplitude = _____
Frequencies for each delay time:
$f_1 =$ _____ $f_2 =$ _____
$f_3 =$ _____ $f_4 =$ _____ $f_5 =$ _____
Develop a test procedure.

Step 4   Explain how you will verify that each switch setting produces the proper output delay time.

RELATED EXPERIMENT

MATERIALS NEEDED
One 7414 hex inverter (Schmitt trigger)
One 10 kΩ potentiometer
One 0.01 μF capacitor

DISCUSSION
An interesting variation of the application assignment uses a Schmitt trigger as a switching device. A Schmitt trigger is a circuit with two thresholds for change. The switching level is dependent on whether the input signal is rising or falling. Consider the circuit shown in Figure AA–8–1. The charging and discharging of the capacitor is determined by the switching points of the Schmitt trigger. The input voltage is initially low and the output voltage is high (near 5.0 V). The capacitor begins to charge toward the higher output voltage. As the capacitor charges, the input voltage passes a trip point, causing the input voltage to go high and the output voltage to go low. The capacitor begins to discharge toward the lower voltage until it passes the lower trip point causing the process to repeat.

Construct the circuit and measure the output waveform and the waveform across the capacitor. Try varying R as you observe the capacitor voltage. What is the output waveshape and frequency? Can you determine the threshold voltages of the Schmitt trigger by observing the output?

EXPERIMENTAL RESULTS

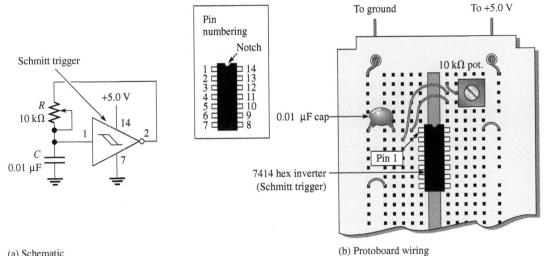

(a) Schematic

(b) Protoboard wiring

Figure AA–8–1

Checkup 8

REFERENCE
Floyd, Chap. 15, and Buchla, Experiment 30

1. A circuit that can be used to change a square wave into a triangle wave is:
   (a) a tuned circuit   (b) a ladder circuit   (c) an integrator   (d) a differentiator

2. For an RC circuit driven by a pulse, the capacitor will fully charge in:
   (a) one time constant   (b) 1 s
   (c) five time constants   (d) a time depending on the amplitude of the pulse

3. An RC integrator circuit is driven by a square wave that goes from 0 V to 10 V. The time constant is very short compared to the input square wave. The output will be:
   (a) a 5 V dc level   (b) a triangle waveform
   (c) an exponentially rising and falling waveform   (d) a series of positive and negative spikes

4. Assume an RC differentiator circuit is driven by a square wave. The output is a square wave with a slight droop and overshoot. The time constant of the circuit (τ) is:
   (a) much longer than the pulse width   (b) much shorter than the pulse width
   (c) equal to the pulse width

5. A 4.7 kΩ resistor is connected in series with a 0.1 μF capacitor. The time constant is:
   (a) 0.47 μs   (b) 0.47 ms   (c) 21.3 ns   (d) 21.3 μs

6. A 4.7 kΩ resistor is connected in series with a 10 mH inductor. The time constant is:
   (a) 0.47 μs   (b) 47 ms   (c) 4.7 s   (d) 2.13 μs

7. Assume that a switch is closed in a series RC circuit that has a time constant of 10 ms. The current in the circuit will be 37% of its initial value in:
   (a) 1.0 ms   (b) 3.7 ms   (c) 6.3 ms   (d) 10 ms

8. When a single pulse is applied to a series RL circuit, the greatest *change* in current occurs:
   (a) at the beginning   (b) at the 50% point
   (c) after one time constant   (d) at the end

9. A 1.0 kHz square wave is applied to an RL differentiator circuit. The current in the circuit will reach steady-state conditions if the time constant is equal to:
   (a) 100 μs   (b) 1.0 ms   (c) 6.3 ms   (d) 10 ms

10. If you need to couple a square wave into a circuit through a capacitor, for best fidelity you should have an RC time constant that is:
    (a) very short
    (b) equal to the rise time of the square wave
    (c) equal to the pulse width of the square wave
    (d) very long

11. Explain how you could use a known resistor, a square wave generator, and an oscilloscope to find the value of an unknown inductor.

12. Assume you wanted to lengthen the time constant for the circuit in Figure 16–3 to 330 μs.
    (a)   What change would you make to the circuit?

    (b)   Draw an RL integrator with a 10 kΩ resistor and a 330 μs time constant.

13. (a)   Compute the time constant for the circuit shown in Figure C–8–1.

    (b)   What is the maximum frequency for the pulse generator in order to allow the capacitor time to charge and discharge fully?

    (c)   Assume the generator is set to the frequency determined in (b); sketch the waveform across the capacitor. Show the voltage and time on your sketch.

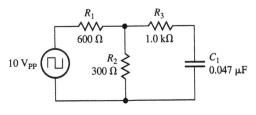

Figure C–8–1

Appendix A: Manufacturers' Data Sheets

National Semiconductor

Operational Amplifiers/Buffers

LM741/LM741A/LM741C/LM741E Operational Amplifier

General Description

The LM741 series are general purpose operational amplifiers which feature improved performance over industry standards like the LM709. They are direct, plug-in replacements for the 709C, LM201, MC1439 and 748 in most applications.

The amplifiers offer many features which make their application nearly foolproof: overload pro-

tection on the input and output, no latch-up when the common mode range is exceeded, as well as freedom from oscillations.

The LM741C/LM741E are identical to the LM741/LM741A except that the LM741C/ LM741E have their performance guaranteed over a 0°C to +70°C temperature range, instead of −55°C to +125°C.

Absolute Maximum Ratings

	LM741A	LM741E	LM741	LM741C
Supply Voltage	±22V	±22V	±22V	±18V
Power Dissipation (Note 1)	500 mW	500 mW	500 mW	500 mW
Differential Input Voltage	±30V	±30V	±30V	±30V
Input Voltage (Note 2)	±15V	±15V	±15V	±15V
Output Short Circuit Duration	Indefinite	Indefinite	Indefinite	Indefinite
Operating Temperature Range	−55°C to +125°C	0°C to +70°C	−55°C to +125°C	0°C to +70°C
Storage Temperature Range	−65°C to +150°C	−65°C to +150°C	−65°C to +150°C	−65°C to +150°C
Lead Temperature (Soldering, 10 seconds)	300°C	300°C	300°C	300°C

Electrical Characteristics (Note 3)

PARAMETER	CONDITIONS	LM741A/LM741E MIN	TYP	MAX	LM741 MIN	TYP	MAX	LM741C MIN	TYP	MAX	UNITS
Input Offset Voltage	$T_A = 25°C$, $R_S \leq 10\,k\Omega$		0.8	3.0		1.0	5.0		2.0	6.0	mV
	$R_S \leq 50\,\Omega$										mV
	$T_{AMIN} \leq T_A \leq T_{AMAX}$										mV
	$R_S \leq 50\,\Omega$			4.0							mV
	$R_S \leq 10\,k\Omega$						6.0			7.5	mV
Average Input Offset Voltage Drift				15							μV/°C
Input Offset Voltage Adjustment Range	$T_A = 25°C$, $V_S = \pm 20V$	10				±15			±15		mV
Input Offset Current	$T_A = 25°C$		3.0	30		20	200		20	200	nA
	$T_{AMIN} \leq T_A \leq T_{AMAX}$			70		85	500			300	nA
Average Input Offset Current Drift				0.5							nA/°C
Input Bias Current	$T_A = 25°C$		30	80		80	500		80	500	nA
	$T_{AMIN} \leq T_A \leq T_{AMAX}$		6.0	0.210		2.0	1.5		2.0	0.8	μA
Input Resistance	$T_A = 25°C$, $V_S = \pm 20V$	1.0	6.0		0.3	2.0		0.3	2.0		MΩ
	$T_{AMIN} \leq T_A \leq T_{AMAX}$, $V_S = \pm 20V$	0.5									MΩ
Input Voltage Range	$T_A = 25°C$				±12	±13		±12	±13		V
	$T_{AMIN} \leq T_A \leq T_{AMAX}$	50			50			20			V
Large Signal Voltage Gain	$T_A = 25°C$, $R_L \geq 2\,k\Omega$										V/mV
	$V_S = \pm 20V$, $V_O = \pm 15V$										V/mV
	$V_S = \pm 15V$, $V_O = \pm 10V$										V/mV
	$T_{AMIN} \leq T_A \leq T_{AMAX}$	32			25			15			V/mV
	$R_L \geq 2\,k\Omega$										
	$V_S = \pm 20V$, $V_O = \pm 15V$										V/mV
	$V_S = \pm 15V$, $V_O = \pm 10V$	10									V/mV
	$V_S = \pm 5V$, $V_O = \pm 2V$										V/mV
Output Voltage Swing	$V_S = \pm 20V$										
	$R_L \geq 10\,k\Omega$	±16									V
	$R_L \geq 2\,k\Omega$	±15									V
	$V_S = \pm 15V$				±12	±14		±12	±14		V
	$R_L \geq 10\,k\Omega$				±10	±13		±10	±13		V
	$R_L \geq 2\,k\Omega$										V
Output Short Circuit Current	$T_A = 25°C$	10	25	35		25			25		mA
	$T_{AMIN} \leq T_A \leq T_{AMAX}$	10		40							mA
Common-Mode Rejection Ratio	$T_{AMIN} \leq T_A \leq T_{AMAX}$										
	$R_S \leq 10\,k\Omega$, $V_{CM} = \pm 12V$	80	95		70	90		70	90		dB
	$R_S \leq 50\,k\Omega$, $V_{CM} = \pm 12V$										dB

Schematic and Connection Diagrams (Top Views)

Metal Can Package

Order Number LM741H, LM741AH, LM741CH or LM741EH
See NS Package H08C

Dual-In-Line Package

Order Number LM741CN or LM741EN
See NS Package N08B
Order Number LM741CJ
See NS Package J08A

Dual-In-Line Package

Order Number LM741CN-14
See NS Package N14A
Order Number LM741-14, LM741AJ-14,
or LM741CJ-14
See NS Package J14A

(Reprinted with permission of National Semiconductor Corp.)

298

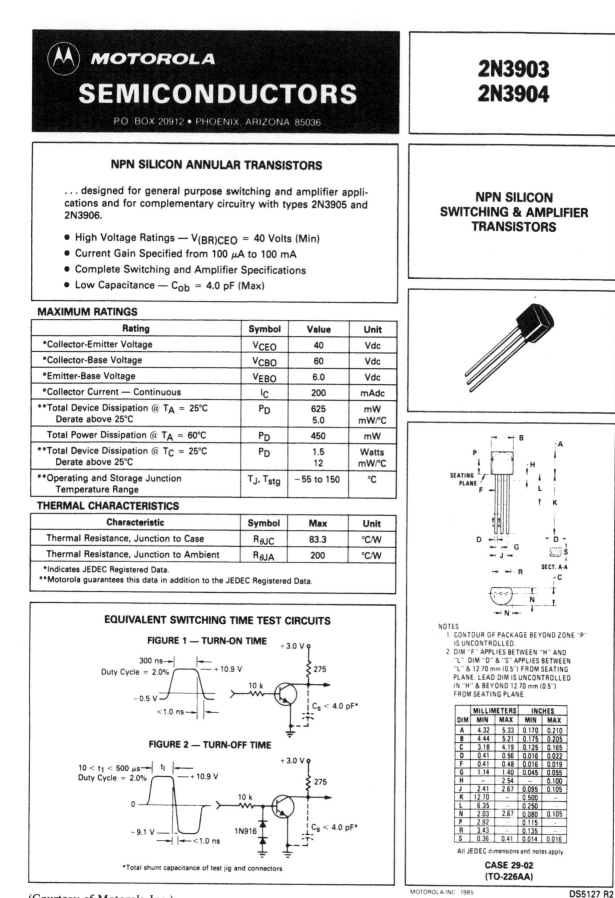

NPN SILICON ANNULAR TRANSISTORS

. . . designed for general purpose switching and amplifier applications and for complementary circuitry with types 2N3905 and 2N3906.

- High Voltage Ratings — $V_{(BR)CEO}$ = 40 Volts (Min)
- Current Gain Specified from 100 μA to 100 mA
- Complete Switching and Amplifier Specifications
- Low Capacitance — C_{ob} = 4.0 pF (Max)

NPN SILICON SWITCHING & AMPLIFIER TRANSISTORS

MAXIMUM RATINGS

Rating	Symbol	Value	Unit
*Collector-Emitter Voltage	V_{CEO}	40	Vdc
*Collector-Base Voltage	V_{CBO}	60	Vdc
*Emitter-Base Voltage	V_{EBO}	6.0	Vdc
*Collector Current — Continuous	I_C	200	mAdc
**Total Device Dissipation @ T_A = 25°C Derate above 25°C	P_D	625 5.0	mW mW/°C
Total Power Dissipation @ T_A = 60°C	P_D	450	mW
**Total Device Dissipation @ T_C = 25°C Derate above 25°C	P_D	1.5 12	Watts mW/°C
**Operating and Storage Junction Temperature Range	T_J, T_{stg}	−55 to 150	°C

THERMAL CHARACTERISTICS

Characteristic	Symbol	Max	Unit
Thermal Resistance, Junction to Case	$R_{\theta JC}$	83.3	°C/W
Thermal Resistance, Junction to Ambient	$R_{\theta JA}$	200	°C/W

*Indicates JEDEC Registered Data.
**Motorola guarantees this data in addition to the JEDEC Registered Data.

EQUIVALENT SWITCHING TIME TEST CIRCUITS

FIGURE 1 — TURN-ON TIME

300 ns
Duty Cycle = 2.0%
+ 10.9 V
− 0.5 V
<1.0 ns
10 k
+3.0 V
275
C_S < 4.0 pF*

FIGURE 2 — TURN-OFF TIME

10 < t_1 < 500 μs
Duty Cycle = 2.0%
+ 10.9 V
0
− 9.1 V
<1.0 ns
10 k
1N916
+3.0 V
275
C_S < 4.0 pF*

*Total shunt capacitance of test jig and connectors

NOTES:
1. CONTOUR OF PACKAGE BEYOND ZONE "P" IS UNCONTROLLED.
2. DIM "F" APPLIES BETWEEN "H" AND "L". DIM "D" & "S" APPLIES BETWEEN "L" & 12.70 mm (0.5") FROM SEATING PLANE. LEAD DIM IS UNCONTROLLED IN "H" & BEYOND 12.70 mm (0.5") FROM SEATING PLANE.

DIM	MILLIMETERS		INCHES	
	MIN	MAX	MIN	MAX
A	4.32	5.33	0.170	0.210
B	4.44	5.21	0.175	0.205
C	3.18	4.19	0.125	0.165
D	0.41	0.56	0.016	0.022
F	0.41	0.48	0.016	0.019
G	1.14	1.40	0.045	0.055
H	–	2.54	–	0.100
J	2.41	2.67	0.095	0.105
K	12.70	–	0.500	–
L	6.35	-	0.250	–
N	2.03	2.67	0.080	0.105
P	2.92	-	0.115	–
R	3.43	-	0.135	–
S	0.36	0.41	0.014	0.016

All JEDEC dimensions and notes apply.

CASE 29-02
(TO-226AA)

(Courtesy of Motorola Inc.)

MOTOROLA INC. 1985

DS5127 R2

2N5457
2N5458
2N5459

CASE 29-04, STYLE 5
TO-92 (TO-226AA)

2 Source
3 Gate
1 Drain

JFET
GENERAL PURPOSE

N-CHANNEL — DEPLETION

Refer to 2N4220 for graphs.

MAXIMUM RATINGS

Rating	Symbol	Value	Unit
Drain-Source Voltage	V_{DS}	25	Vdc
Drain-Gate Voltage	V_{DG}	25	Vdc
Reverse Gate-Source Voltage	V_{GSR}	−25	Vdc
Gate Current	I_G	10	mAdc
Total Device Dissipation @ T_A = 25°C Derate above 25°C	P_D	310 2.82	mW mW/°C
Junction Temperature Range	T_J	125	°C
Storage Channel Temperature Range	T_{stg}	−65 to +150	°C

ELECTRICAL CHARACTERISTICS (T_A = 25°C unless otherwise noted.)

Characteristic		Symbol	Min	Typ	Max	Unit
OFF CHARACTERISTICS						
Gate-Source Breakdown Voltage (I_G = −10 μAdc, V_{DS} = 0)		$V_{(BR)GSS}$	−25	—	—	Vdc
Gate Reverse Current (V_{GS} = −15 Vdc, V_{DS} = 0) (V_{GS} = −15 Vdc, V_{DS} = 0, T_A = 100°C)		I_{GSS}	 — —	 — —	 −1.0 −200	nAdc
Gate Source Cutoff Voltage (V_{DS} = 15 Vdc, I_D = 10 nAdc)	2N5457 2N5458 2N5459	$V_{GS(off)}$	−0.5 −1.0 −2.0	— — —	−6.0 −7.0 −8.0	Vdc
Gate Source Voltage (V_{DS} = 15 Vdc, I_D = 100 μAdc) (V_{DS} = 15 Vdc, I_D = 200 μAdc) (V_{DS} = 15 Vdc, I_D = 400 μAdc)	2N5457 2N5458 2N5459	V_{GS}	— — —	−2.5 −3.5 −4.5	— — —	Vdc
ON CHARACTERISTICS						
Zero-Gate-Voltage Drain Current* (V_{DS} = 15 Vdc, V_{GS} = 0)	2N5457 2N5458 2N5459	I_{DSS}	1.0 2.0 4.0	3.0 6.0 9.0	5.0 9.0 16	mAdc
SMALL-SIGNAL CHARACTERISTICS						
Forward Transfer Admittance Common Source* (V_{DS} = 15 Vdc, V_{GS} = 0, f = 1.0 kHz)	2N5457 2N5458 2N5459	$\|y_{fs}\|$	1000 1500 2000	— — —	5000 5500 6000	μmhos
Output Admittance Common Source* (V_{DS} = 15 Vdc, V_{GS} = 0, f = 1.0 kHz)		$\|y_{os}\|$	—	10	50	μmhos
Input Capacitance (V_{DS} = 15 Vdc, V_{GS} = 0, f = 1.0 MHz)		C_{iss}	—	4.5	7.0	pF
Reverse Transfer Capacitance (V_{DS} = 15 Vdc, V_{GS} = 0, f = 1.0 MHz)		C_{rss}	—	1.5	3.0	pF

*Pulse Test: Pulse Width ≤ 630 ms; Duty Cycle ≤ 10%.

6